Preacher
of the
People

Preacher of the People

A Biography of S. G. Shetler (1871-1942)
Bishop, Evangelist, Pastor, Teacher

Sanford G. Shetler

Introduction by J. C. Wenger

HERALD PRESS
Scottdale, Pennsylvania
Kitchener, Ontario
1982

Library of Congress Cataloging in Publication Data

Shetler, Sanford Grant, 1912-
   Preacher of the people.

   Bibliography: p.
   1. Shetler, S. G. (Samuel Grant), 1871-1942.
   2. Mennonites—Bishops—Biography. 3. Bishops—United
States—Biography. I. Title.
BX8143.S53S53   289.7'3 [B]   81-13387
ISBN 0-8361-1247-4   AACR2
ISBN 0-8361-1248-2 (pbk.)

To my companion who
labored faithfully with me for many years,
and who, like my father, exhibited a deep
loyalty to the Mennonite Church, and
to my family which, likewise,
has always been very
supportive of my own ministry.

Contents

Introduction

Sanford G. Shetler has given us all a great gift in the definitive biography of his father which he has completed after many years of research and writing. The first I heard of "S. G." was when I was still a lad, and my father told me of a great preacher who could quote Scripture in a remarkable manner. Later, in the 1920s, I heard him myself, and was impressed with his learning. He spoke, for example, of the petals and *sepals* of a rose! S. G. Shetler lived 1871-1942.

The author writes in an unhurried manner. In a vivid chapter he takes us back to Waldeck, Germany, introducing us to the origins of his family. In fact, regardless of what topic he is treating, he takes time to portray patiently the historical background in a most illuminating way. He did his research well. And he included his remarkable mother.

S. G. Shetler was indeed a "Preacher of the People," lively in the classroom, vigorous in the pulpit, loyal to the Word, a great lover of people. Elected as the first principal of what is now Eastern Mennonite College, he refused the office, for he felt called to hold Bible conferences, teach in winter Bible schools, serve in Young People's Institutes, and preach all over North America. Although faced with such threats as tar and feathers, he never flinched in his conviction that war was wrong. This book illuminates the era, 1890 to 1940, and has much to teach the Mennonite Church about that period.

J. C. Wenger
Goshen, Indiana

Author's Preface

SAMUEL GRANT SHETLER, best known to his many friends and co-workers as "S. G. Shetler" or, simply, "S. G.," was my father, and I have profoundly delighted in telling this story of his life, in the process reliving the many happy years that we spent together as a family and the decade that the two of us served together in the ministry of our home congregation.

The idea of writing his biography first came to my mind shortly after my father's death. Almost immediately I began to gather materials for a book. Many other tasks intervened, however, chief among them the writing of my book on the history of the Mennonites of western Pennsylvania, *Two Centuries of Struggle and Growth*, published in 1963.

The 38 years since my father's passing have cast a revealing perspective on his life and allowed me to gain a measure of objectivity on his person and contribution. To write about a man, especially one's own father, too soon after his death can easily result in a distorted perspective and an exaggerated image of his real impact. However, the unsolicited testimonies that I continue to hear in my travels throughout the brotherhood repeatedly confirm my judgment that his contribution was large and authentic. Many are still living who can recall vividly the early days of his

11

evangelistic and Bible conference ministry at the turn of the century—or his years as a teacher and schoolmaster. An even greater number of middle-aged persons remember him almost larger than life, which indicates that he still was leaving his dynamic imprint on the lives of many throughout the Mennonite Church near the end of his own life.

To tell the story of a man's life in the pages of a book is always an impossible task. So much fascinating and no doubt enlightening detail must be omitted. Every person would tell the story differently, and I make no apology for telling it my way, as a devoted son and Christian co-worker, although I have tried scrupulously not to be self-serving or cheaply sentimental.

This is more than the story of a man; it is a chapter from Mennonite history in North America. The period of his lifetime was a notable one in the Mennonite brotherhood of this continent. The simple genius of Anabaptism as it came to be practiced in the New World still persisted and flourished, and S. G. Shetler played a significant role in perpetuating this uncomplicated message without elaborate theological introspection, premise, or prediction. Convinced that the Bible is the message for all time and that the Anabaptists occupied a unique place in history, the spiritual leaders of his period marched forward as pioneers. They believed they had a manifest destiny to see that all men hear and heed the simple Mennonite message. The church leaders of his day seemed concerned primarily about their place in God's kingdom. "Existentialism," "situation ethics," and "the new theology" had not yet become part of the Mennonite lexicon.

The European background to which I have devoted considerable space does not relate directly to my father's life, but I have brought together some unpublished notes of mine to paint this historical vignette for the light that it sheds on the routine life in the province of Waldeck, Germany, because Waldeck was the womb of many of our Mennonite ancestors. Admittedly, this section in my book will be of greater interest to those who bear the Shetler name.

Samuel G. Shetler was born on January 13, 1871, 111 years

ago, and this biography, though originally planned for publication in 1971 at the hundredth anniversary of his birth, is now offered as a belated tribute. By design, it is a first-person narrative account rather than a heavily documented, impersonal treatise. The reader has been deliberately spared of the extensive documentation that pleases scholars, so that the book above all will be readable and, I trust, enjoyable. I have tried, nevertheless, to make use of all readily available sources accurately and objectively, crediting them where necessary or appropriate while at the same time trying to avoid documenting the obvious or presenting documentation for its own sake.

For their generous assistance, I am grateful to many colleagues and friends; to the members of my family, particularly my eldest son Stanwyn Gerald Shetler who bears the name "S. G. Shetler" to the third generation and who has read large parts of the manuscript and offered suggestions; to my sisters Luella Shetler Miller, Goldie Shetler Sala, now deceased, and Margaret Shetler Kaufman, who also have read parts of the manuscript and offered many helpful remembrances and suggestions. Above all, I'm thankful to my wife, Florence, also deceased, who shared many of the experiences related here, encouraged me throughout the preparation of this biography, and suggested the title for the book. I also wish to recognize the help of the late Grant M. Stoltzfus of Eastern Mennonite College for permitting me to use certain important materials and for reading the first part of my manuscript.

I submit this biography in the hope that all those who read it will in some measure be strengthened spiritually and given a new vision for the work ahead through reflections on the life and times of S. G. Shetler.

Sanford G. Shetler
Johnstown, Pennsylvania

Preacher of the People

The old spring house at the home in Somerset County where
S. G. Shetler lived as a youth (ink drawing by Lloy A. Kniss).

1

"Mr. Mennonite"

The story of S. G. Shetler is in part the story of American Mennonites, for he was one of the outspoken and well-recognized Mennonite leaders of his time. He was the product of the awakening in the late 1800s and early 1900s that was molding the Mennonite Church into a thriving evangelistic and mission-minded brotherhood. If he was a product of this awakening, the church was, in turn, also a product in part of his moving spirit and the moving spirit of the likeminded leaders of his time.

Through effective revival meetings, Bible conferences, summer and winter Bible schools, and Bible-centered preaching, S. G. Shetler exercised a strong influence on the thinking of the church for many years. Generations of younger men and women were trained through his many educational efforts, and they continue to extend his influence from the pulpit as well as the pew in the church even today. An educator by training and experience and a teacher by instinct, he, perhaps more than any other leader of his time, blended the work of preaching and teaching to promote the Church's ministry. One can never divorce the image of S. G. Shetler the teacher and educator from S. G. Shetler the preacher and church leader.

The strong motive of service tied together his whole life. He was fond of quoting the Scripture: "For David, after he had served his own generation by the will of God, fell on sleep, and was laid unto his fathers . . ." (Acts 13:36). Truly S. G. Shetler served his generation. He labored faithfully "in the vineyard of the Lord," as he liked to express it, and, recognizing his own heritage, thought of himself as having entered into the labors of those who had gone before and having initiated those who would enter into his labors after him.

"S. G.," as many preferred to call him, was a uniquely dominant figure on the American Mennonite scene. His personality and work virtually epitomized the Mennonite Church in numerous quarters during his active years. He was an authentic church-wide personality in America for several decades, and it is not presumptuous to say that to many of his admirers he was *Mr. Mennonite*. To them, S. G. spoke for the church; and what he thought, the church thought! He enjoyed this standing among his contemporaries in the ministry as well as among the laity, and he enjoyed it to an even greater degree among the many non-Mennonites ("outsiders") with whom he came into contact in daily life, even among many casual acquaintances made in the course of his numerous travels. This point was underscored by the large, cosmopolitan audience who attended his funeral to pay final tribute. Bishop John L. Horst, in his brief eulogy, seemed to sum up the singular feeling of that mass audience in the simple statement, "There will never be another S. G."

In fairness, it should be added, however, that S. G. Shetler never was without his detractors especially among the small but influential theologically educated elite of the church. They regarded him as a folksy preacher of limited credentials and vision either as an Anabaptist or an ecumenical church leader. His popular appeal, in their view, may have been more that of a folk hero who articulates the simple views of the masses, exploiting their limited understanding and playing on their emotions and prejudices to bring about desired ends. To be sure, his message was always the practical message of salvation, and he had little patience with those who insisted on dissecting the Bible in endless intellectual discourse or who preached ecumenicity at the expense of obedience and discipleship.

S. G. Shetler was a Mennonite's Mennonite. His love for the Mennonite Church was secondary only to his love for the Bible and its gospel. This was evident in all facets of his life, public and private. Although he certainly believed in the salvation of persons in various denominations and never was one to be intolerant of other Christian views or to create the impression that only a Mennonite could be a Christian, he was a Mennonite in every fiber of his body. He worked incessantly to enlighten others on what he believed to be the biblical purity of the views of his church. While he believed in the larger invisible church of Christ, the concrete church for which he worked during this lifetime was the one he believed to be true to Christ's message, the Mennonite Church. I cannot let this matter drop without saying that I find his single-minded dedication to his church the sincerest and surest form of dedication to the building of the church in the most general, ecumenical sense. If a man does not build on a visible foundation, how can he stand a chance of having built also on the invisible foundation?

Without being disrespectful of the views of others, S. G. could hold an uncompromising belief in the doctrines of the Mennonite Church. He was not quick to endorse, not to mention promote, interdenominational fellowships, particularly where organic connections were required or seemed likely to evolve. The church, he felt, had much to lose in such alliances and little if anything to gain. In his revival meetings he always was deeply concerned that those led to Christ also should become members of the Mennonite Church, and his record of success in bringing this about with his converts was high. His evangelistic sermons frequently were prefaced with talks on the doctrines of the church, a practice that later evangelists began to disparage. To present the gospel as merely an ecstatic experience not requiring obedience and discipleship was, in his view, to preach a partial gospel and a false hope. He did not like the term "Mennonite doctrines," because, as he often stated, the church should not be adhering to any doctrines that could not be defended as biblical doctrines. What Mennonites observed, therefore, were to his mind the doctrines that all people must keep. This simple biblicism had characterized his Anabaptist forefathers, and he made no apology for his theologically uncomplicated view of the Mennonite Church, its doctrine, and mission. Through his particular ministry many persons who otherwise would never have been reached were brought into the church with a deep conviction for the observance of Bible teaching.

Despite my father's Mennonite-centric life and work and despite his living in an era when non-Mennonites were often spoken of as "outsiders" with a tinge of prejudice in tone, he himself was not religiously intolerant or prejudiced. In fact, he always enjoyed very good relationships with community leaders and ministers and church workers in other denominations, who respected him for his strong Mennonite identification and made positive use of it. He had numerous lifelong friends in other denominations and was a frequent speaker before community groups, teachers' institutes, and other churches. When, for example, the new local area high school held its first baccalaureate service in 1939, he was the natural choice for speaker because he was recognized throughout the area as the unofficial dean of educators and ministers in Conemaugh Township, Somerset County, Pennsylvania.

It was not uncommon for Christians of other faiths to be touched by his ministry, even through basically secular forums in the community, to the point of affiliating with the Mennonites because they saw in this fellowship through his preaching a more perfect obedience to the gospel. My father tried to live and to minister so that his life and work would enhance the Mennonite image among those outside his own church, and there can be no doubt that he succeeded. The church members who made him the most sad were those professed Mennonites who were not Mennonites at heart. Why, if they wanted to belong, did they not want to be authentic models? Why should anyone who had voluntarily elected to be a Mennonite apologize by word or deed for being identified as one? To him, the only true Mennonite was the one who exemplified this faith in his daily life and Christian practice.

S. G. Shetler served the church of his generation with all of his mind and energy and in this service no doubt realized the zenith of his potential as a Christian and as a human being. For him church work never was a marginal thing, nor was he tempted to follow other pursuits that could have been far more remunerative. He had native abilities and a good education for his time that could have brought him success in any number of careers, but he chose instead to "serve the Master" and never to be deflected from his vows. More church leaders would do well to heed this record today.

He was active until the end of his life. He became ill on the afternoon of July 11, 1942, shortly before he was to preach the evening sermon at the then-new Meadow Mountain Church, a rural Mennonite mission near Grantsville, Maryland. He did not recover from this attack and died exactly one month later on August 11.

2

Arolsen in Waldeck

Nestled among the rolling hills of west-central Germany, in the historical province of Waldeck, lies the small thriving town of Arolsen. The name of the town is not German, betraying the historical fact that in post-medieval times a Swedish king had attempted to establish colonies in Germany. The town today is very German.

In September 1964, a dream of many years was fulfilled when my wife and I, accompanied by our youngest daughter and her fiancé (now husband), drove west from the city of Kassel some 40 kilometers to visit the birthplace of my great-grandfather. It was one of those unforgettable autumn days that the Germans sometimes call a *herrlicher Tag*. The countryside in Waldeck is picturesque. The region is promoted in the travel brochures as *Ferienland Waldeck* ("Vacationland Waldeck")—and the town of Arolsen as *Die Stadt im Wald* ("The Town in the Forest"). Waldeck offers "water, sun, and woodlands" and can be appreciated only by living there, the tourist is told.

On the way to Arolsen we stopped to chat in our broken German with two farmers who were harvesting potatoes by hand. In the distance we could see a small town with its quaint European-style houses under their red-tiled roofs. At one point along the highway the road was lined on each side by a row of trees, reminding one of Hobbema's famous painting, "Avenue of Trees." At another point we encountered a farmer on a wagon being pulled by a team of oxen, something I had never seen before in my life.

At the entrance to Arolsen there was a charming new restaurant where we stopped for lunch. The host informed us that we were close to *Hünighausen*, the estate within the limits of Arolsen that was to mark for us the birthplace of Christian Schöttler. The landmark *Gut Hünighausen*, a quadrangle of historic buildings, was on the western edge of the town near the hospital.

Emotions are hard to describe and particularly this one. Here I was seeing for the first time the home of my father's paternal ancestors. After 130 years, we could say in the sentiment of General Pershing in 1917 when he had arrived at the grave of the French officer who had aided the colonial army in the Revolutionary War, "Lafayette (Christian), we are here." For a sentimental moment I wished my ancestors could be there: Great-grandfather Johannes Schöttler, his wife, Mary, and son Christian. But they were lying in their graves in America. In their day, a *Gut* or "Domaine" was a landed estate under the ownership and proprietorship of the *Fürstel* or earl of the province, who operated the farm in feudal style. *Gut Hünighausen*, a large dairy farm once comprising several hundred acres, was worked by tenant farmers who leased the land from the earl and who in turn employed numerous farmhands known as *Knechten* or *Arbeiter*. Until as recently as World War I there were up to 30 hands working at *Hünighausen* at any one time.

The fields surrounding the *Gut* once extended far beyond the present (1964) farm site, and the *Gut* formed the chief industry of the town, employing tanners, shoemakers, toolmakers, blacksmiths, coopers, and weavers. From the *Gut* itself and extending to the east side of town ran the *Grosse Allee* (Main Street) on which parades were held on national holidays and other special occasions. It led to the *Schloss*, the elaborate baroque castle of the earl which had been built as a small replica of the

Palace of Versailles in the period of the early eighteenth century. In its time the *Schloss* was an ornate showplace and still is, though now as a museum.

Today the *Gross Allee* is a beautiful treelined parkway, and the original main street is now a walkway. The *Gut*, much of which has since been torn down, consisted of a huge quadrangle, with shops and dwellings built along three sides and a long barn down the fourth. The oldest and quaintest building of the *Gut*, the proprietor of the farm, Rudolph Thomas, informed us, probably is the one in which *Knecht* Johannes Schöttler lived and in which his son Christian was born. The civil records state that "on the evening of July 17, 1804, at eleven o'clock, a baby boy was born." This building would be a fascinating landmark in any town, old or new, but it was being used as a granary in 1964. In one corner of the first floor stood an old ceramic stove, reminding one of *Hirschvogel* in the old story, "The Nürnburg Stove." Upstairs in one of the cobwebby rooms stood a huge crib where Christian may once have slept! Realizing the deep sentiment I felt for the place, Mr. Thomas kindly presented me with some keepsakes—one of the old-fashioned, hand-lever door latches and a piece of the antique ceramic stove. It seemed a shame to deface the stove, but everything was destined to be razed in any event, he said.

We walked around in the huge barn facing the *Hof* on one side and the fields on the other. It had huge wooden doors set in arched doorways and, inside, reminded me of the Pennsylvania barns with their overhead bays for hay and straw. Obviously our German ancestors had brought their farm-building architecture with them when they settled in Pennsylvania. As we surveyed the fields and pastures for several miles around, we surmised that the landscapes had changed little since 1830, except for the nearby service station.

The history surrounding the estate is interesting. In the 16th, 17th, and 18th centuries when Mennonites gradually had migrated northward through the Palatinate to flee persecution in Switzerland, many Mennonite farmers became the operators of the various *Güter*, the farms of the landed ruling class. It was David Möllinger, for example, a thrifty and enterprising Mennonite, who first introduced the system of crop rotation to Europe at a time when the three-field system was still in general use.[1] In this system one out of every three fields was allowed to lie fallow each year as a means of giving the land a chance to recover from the steady depletion of its mineral nutrients year after year. Pressed by necessity the Mennonites who were driven into the back parts of the countryside had to improvise ways of making the land produce *every* year.

The late Melvin Gingerich, well-known Mennonite historian of Goshen, Indiana, whose ancestor Peter Güngerich was leasing the *Hüninghausen* estate at the time when Johannes Schöttler was working there, discovered some interesting facts about the estate. According to the Waldeck archives (*State Archives at Marburg*, p. 447), as the records state, the estate was leased again to "*Schweitzer* [Swiss] Christian Güngerich." Further information states that in February, 1792, Prince Frederick of Waldeck decreed: "Inasmuch as Conductor Güngerich improved the dairy farms of *Hünighausen* to the best and inasmuch as my heart desires that a numerous and industrious family be maintained in the land, therefore upon Güngerich's request the lease is extended for 18 years."[2] According to the historian Ernst Correll, who copied the decree, Peter Güngerich, son of Christian, acquired the lease of the *Hünighausen* estate in 1792. Peter was the ancestor of many of the Gingeriches/Guengeriches in the state of Iowa.

In 1967, on my second visit to *Hünighausen*, the new proprietor, Rudolph Koch, showed me the interior of the other large house standing on the west side of the gateway. I had not been in this house on my earlier visit. In the basement of the building, where the fruit, potatoes, and roots were once stored, the walls and ceiling were constructed of huge cut stones, the ceiling being formed of a number of large arches. It seemed substantial enough to serve as a modern-day bomb shelter! In the apex of the central arch was inscribed "Roier, 1822," presumably the name of the stone mason and probably another Mennonite. The quadrangle no longer was complete; some of the buildings already had been razed. The barn, which we had seen in its entirety in 1964, now was partially dismantled. Other buildings were also in the process of being razed to make room for "progress." What was a quiet little town until the mid-1960s was rapidly becoming urbanized. The *Gut* itself had been farmed vigorously until World War II, when, because of the rising standard of living in Europe, farm owners no longer could compete with industry in providing adequate income, and the *Arbeiter* left the farm for more remunerative jobs.

Arolsen today is a bustling town with numerous small businesses—no major industry—and one gets the feeling that urbanization at last has reached even this "wooded corner" *(Wald-eck)* of the world. The land is well situated for urban development, and for the owners of *Hünighausen*, the Kochs, there is more opportunity to regain their investment in this way than through farming. In one of the buildings of the dairy building complex a small factory now manufactures light steel products.

In the town itself, a number of buildings predate my great-grandfather's time by many years. The picturesque *Rathaus* (city hall) still stands, for example, and many old stores and hotels are scattered about the town. In the center of Arolsen is the historic Evangelical (Protestant) Church, and at the east end of town is the palatial *Schloss* already mentioned with its well-landscaped gardens. The town is highly modernized, however, and has beautiful new shops. A pleasant and lively metropolis of 7,000 inhabitants, Arolsen is connected by good highways and good train service with the larger cities of Europe. At the same time it retains a great vacationland allure.

Less than a mile northeast of Arolsen is the village of Helsen, once the headquarters of the Arolsen-Helsen Earldom of Waldeck, where, according to the records, Christian Schöttler worked for a time as a youth. It, too, is a fascinating town, having houses that date back centuries. Three kilometers southwest of Arolsen is still another town of medieval origin—Mengeringhausen, where Peter Güngerich once lived and where, in a beautiful and well-kept cemetery, he is buried. Here, too, lived the Swartzentrubers, who once operated Galgenmühle ("Gallows Mill")—a flour and feed mill—and who later migrated to Garrett County, Maryland, where they also operated a similar mill. From the Waldeck area came also the Brennemans, Benders, Roths, and others.

The history of the Johannes Schöttler family never has been recorded, but from original documents in my possession I have been able to reconstruct the story in part. These papers also shed some light on the life and times in their day.

Johannes, great-grandfather of S. G. Shetler, was born in 1776 in the town of Gifflitz, located 32 kilometers (ca. 20 miles) southeast of Arolsen. He married Mary Joder (Yoder) in his early or mid-twenties. We do not know when he took the job of *Knecht* at *Hünighausen*, but we do know that Christian was born there in 1804. According to church records at Helsen, Johannes and Mary had no other children while at Hünighausen. However, at least one other child, Mary, had been born to them previously, perhaps at Gifflitz, and another child was born later, in 1818. Whether the family included more than these three children, we do not know from present records.

In 1808, Johannes visited his brothers at Erichsberg in Westphalia in the month of February. According to the brief record, the purpose was "to develop professionally." The meaning of this is unclear, but at that time a passport of sorts was required in order to travel from one place to another, and on it the reason for the trip had to be given.

Late in 1818 or early in 1819, the Schöttler family left *Hünighausen* after having lived there for at least 14 or 15 years. They moved to the village of Betzigerode, 44 kilometers to the southeast. Apparently Johannes worked in the woods. Betzigerode was only 12 kilometers from his birthplace at Gifflitz. He worked at Betzigerode for more than seven years, according to the "Recommendation," dated 1826, from the "Conductor" at this town, which probably was used to secure his next job at *Bad Wildungen*, where he worked until he migrated to America. *Bad*

Wildungen, a place noted for its "healing springs," was located five miles northwest of Betzigerode in the direction of Arolsen.

During the part of his lifetime spent in Europe, Johannes had lived in at least four places, all within a radius of 32 to 40 kilometers of Arolsen. The whole region of Waldeck, an area of approximately 1,024 square kilometers, was inhabited by many of his religious faith. The 1826 "Recommendation" furnishes some insights on the qualities of Johannes and his wife. Translated, it reads as follows:

> Mr. John Schöttler has been in my service for more than seven years. During this time he was faithful and industrious, and is to be especially recommended and at the same time it should be noted that also his wife was living here. Also in regard to her nothing can be said to disqualify her. I attest here that which is my duty. Betzigerode, July 15, 1826
>
> *Klüppel*
> Conductor

Little is recorded of Christian Schöttler's years in Waldeck. The story has passed down through the family that as a boy he once beat back a ferocious dog with his Bible on his way home from school. Bibles were used then as textbooks. As a youth, he was once sent on a mission to visit the various Mennonite settlements in Waldeck. The purpose of his tour is not clear from the records, but it has been suggested that he may have been sent to inform the scattered members of an upcoming communion service.[3] The list of 15 places visited gives an indication of how widely the Mennonites were spread across the province.

In 1967 I had the privilege of visiting the widow of Helmut Weber in Arolsen, who I was told had been the last Mennonite of Waldeck. *Frau* Weber was then in her 80s. Among the various other residents of Arolsen whom I interviewed was *Herr Rektor* Robert Wetekam, who until recently had been principal of the town's school system. Wetekam, a scholarly person who is much interested in Waldeckian history, had in his files a folder on Christian Schöttler, as well as folders of other early Mennonite families in the province. I visited, also, *Probst* Schüttler, pastor of the present-day Evangelical Church of Arolsen. The Schüttlers and the Schöttlers do not seem to be connected genealogically, as I had first thought, although in German the names are very close.

As far as I know, there are no Mennonites living in Waldeck today, a province that once abounded in Mennonite inhabitants. Many emigrated over a period of more than 100 years. The largest migrations took place between 1830 and 1850.

3
Waldeck to Somerset

With evidence of increasing military pressure in Europe in the early 1800s many Mennonites migrated to America to escape conscription. The economic factor was also important, however. Here there was opportunity for every man to own his own farm and to improve his lot in life. So Johannes and his family decided to move northward from Wildungen in 1831 to the seaport of Bremen where they might be able to secure some employment to help pay for their passage, and where, at their earliest they might be able to embark. On the passport, issued April 5, 1831, at Wildungen to ensure "free and unhindered" transit to Bremen via Kassel and Minden, it states that Johannes was "seeking" employment as a wine distiller, a seemingly strange job for a Mennonite. A Dr. Kampfmeyer, head city planner, whom I had occasion to consult and who had helped me in the translation of some of my papers, speculated that John may have listed this information on the passport to better enable him to secure a job. Actually he may have had no previous experience in brewing. It was interesting to observe Kampfmeyer's reaction to this bit of information. Although he apparently knew very little of Mennonite practices, he seemed to sense with some amusement that this was not altogether appropriate employment for these people![4]

The passport also contains an interesting description of Johannes' physical features, the nearest approach we have to a photograph. We give the German description with the English equivalents:

Beschreibung:	Description: (Translation)
Alter - 55 Jahr	Age - 55 years
Grösse - 5 Fuss 2½ Zoll	Height - 5 ft. 2½ inches
Harre - schwarz	Hair - black
Stern - gewölbt	Forehead - rounded
Augenbraunen - schwarz	Eyebrows - black
Augen - braun	Eyes - brown
Nase - gewöhnlich	Nose - normal
Mund - klein	Mouth - small
Bart - schwarz durchstochen	Beard - black with gray interspersed
Gesichtsform - oval	Facial shape - oval
Gesichtsfarbe - gesund	Facial color - robust and healthy

Just exactly who all comprised the party that sailed from Bremen in June 1831 is not known. The passport listed only John, his wife, and a "child of 13," not stating whether this was a son or daughter. And we know that Christian was in the group, although no passport (*Reisepasse)* of his is in my possession. Further research may reveal more of these details. Mary, sister of Christian, had arrived in America two years earlier to become the bride of Jacob Otto in the Casselman River region of Maryland. Mary, incidentally, became the great-grandmother of Roy and Walter Otto, bishop and minister respectively of the Springs (Pa.) Mennonite Church.

A whole new world lay ahead for young Christian when his party landed at the port of Baltimore in 1831. And as a part of this new world, dreams of a new home, all his own, a wife, perhaps, and a family. He certainly could not foresee himself at this time as someday becoming the grandfather of a little boy, who like the biblical patriarch, would be called Samuel—"child of God."

One tries to imagine how Christian Schöttler and his group felt as they began to work their way westward from Baltimore to Fredericktown (Frederick) and thence onward to Cumberland along the old Braddock Road. The cost of the trip by hired wagon at that time, according to the records of that period, was $90. While information is lacking, it is most likely that they stayed for a while with his sister Mary (the Jacob Ottos) who lived in the vicinity of the "River Congregation" near the present Grantsville, Maryland.

The trip northward from the Casselman region into Somerset County, Pennsylvania, took the group of immigrants through the famous "glades," the lush, grassy meadowlands of the Berlin area, where there was at the time a thriving Amish settlement. Here lived some of their acquaintances who had migrated earlier, and it is altogether possible that they stayed with them for a time before moving on.

The danger of Indians was no longer imminent, as most of them had moved westward. But the country itself was still wild, abounding in wild life. There were squirrels—reds, grays, and blacks—wild turkeys, deer, and bobcats. Occasional bears and cougars stalked the woods. Overhead were flocks of wild geese and ducks, and the streams, unpolluted in those days by mines and industry, abounded in slim speckled trout, white suckers, and bass. The woods were copious with wild grapes, chestnuts, and acorns.

It was summer, and Somerset County woodlands were in their full glory. About fifteen miles north of the Berlin settlement the party crossed the old Forbes Trail (now U.S. Route 30) as they followed a winding trail over somewhat rugged terrain toward the northern end of the county. To the west they saw the purple rim of the Laurel Hills and to the east, the Alleghenies. Somerset County, they learned, lay in a wide basin between the two mountain ranges, although the basin itself was made up of a series of hills and valleys.

The long trip, finally ended, saw the weary and eager travelers arriving in the vicinity of their new home. For better or for worse, life had begun for them in the New World! Although there is no record of their immediate residence or where they stayed in the months ahead, it is quite likely that they were pro-

vided for one way or another by preacher Christian Nisly who had
come to America already in 1804 and with whom they had
probably made some contact through letters prior to their arrival.
This is a reasonable assumption, since the farm the Schöttlers later
acquired was just nearby, and it was Nisly's daughter who later
became Christian's bride. Fortunately for them, the farm which
they came to possess was one of the best in the region. It remained
a well-known landmark through the years. It was well-situated,
about eight miles south of the young town of Johnstown and only
a few miles from Davidsville, then a thriving little farming village.
The village was named for a David Stutzman who lived in the
growing Amish settlement in this area. He had moved there from
what is now Westmont, a suburb of Johnstown, which was then
known as *Der Amish Hivel* (The Amish Hill) because of the many
of that faith who lived there at that time.

The connection between the Berlin area—the area through
which the settlers had passed on their way to the new location—
and the Johnstown area should be noted. In the Berlin area Christian Blauch and Joseph Schantz, ancestors to long lines of worthy
descendants, had settled around 1767. Christian's brother, Jacob,
had become the first Mennonite minister of northern Somerset
County, and Jacob's son, Jacob, Jr., had also become a minister,
and later bishop, in the same area. Schantz (Johns) had moved out
of the area in 1803 to the confluence of the Stony Creek and
Conemaugh River in southern Cambria County, just across the
line from the northern Somerset County Amish settlement, where
he had laid out plans for the city that was to bear his name. Later,
however, he moved out of town to the vicinity of Davidsville,
where he lived until his death in 1810. His namesake of the fourth
generation, who passed away in 1972, and Joseph Johns V, resided
on this same farm for years and both were interviewed for this
book. An imposing statue of the founder of the city occupies a
central spot in Johnstown's beautiful Central Park, honoring
probably one of the very few, if not the only, Amishman ever
honored for founding a city.

Just how many years Johannes Schöttler and his wife lived

after their coming to America is not known, but probably not more than fifteen or so. There is no inscription on the plain stone slabs which mark their graves in the family cemetery on the edge of the farm. We do know, however, that the first two graves from the west side of the cemetery are those of Johannes and Mary. This was pointed out by a relative from Ohio, Andy Shetler, to Abraham, one of Christian's sons in December of 1929.[5]

After living in the New World for six years Christian took out naturalization papers and two years later (1839), in line with the naturalization laws, he became an American citizen. These papers, also in the writer's possession, were issued at Somerset, the county seat of Somerset County, and were witnessed to by "Rich Isaac" Kaufman.

Just nearby, on what was in later years the Noah Kaufman farm, and what is presently (1980) the John M. Dovey farm, lived Preacher Nisly, mentioned earlier. Nisly was married to Sarah Miller, daughter of Abraham Miller, also an Amish minister, who lived in the Berlin area. His daughter, Veronica, also known as Frany, as stated, became the wife of Christian sometime prior to 1840. The exact date of this marriage is not known, but we do know that Nisly moved with his family to Baltic, Ohio, in 1840, leaving behind only his daughter, who was then already married. Descendants of Nisly (also spelled Nissley) are found today in Ohio, Indiana, Iowa, and in some other states. Among them, incidentally, are many ordained men.

Christian soon adapted himself to the routine of the new land to which he had come, and followed the type of diversified farming typical of that day. The county seemed particularly suited to the growing of grains, hay, and potatoes, very similar, in fact, to the province of Waldeck. Truck farming and fruit-growing became a specialty with many farmers, and huckster routes were maintained in nearby Johnstown. The typical little spring wagon loaded with homegrown vegetables, apples, other fruit, milk, butter, eggs, dressed and live poultry, and other farm products, was a beautiful and familiar sight.

Because of the limited room for expansion and the rugged

terrain, many Amish families migrated westward to Ohio and to other states to provide land for oncoming sons or to secure better farming land. Many of these settled in Holmes County, the eastern Ohio area where Preacher Nisly had gone. In the course of time Christian Shetler sold his farm and bought another farm near Baltic, Ohio, perhaps to be near his father-in-law. This would presumably have been after the decease of his aged parents. However, as it happened, when the time came to move, his buyer backed out on the deal, and Christian could not see his way clear to move without selling his farm here. Nevertheless he kept the Ohio farm and in time two of his sons, Moses and John, moved on it. This accounts for the sizable number of Christian Shetler's posterity living in that part of Ohio today.

Christian and Frany (Veronica) had eleven children, one of whom was Jacob, father of Samuel. Jacob was born in 1848. The others of the family were Mary, John, Moses, Christian, Lewis, and Abraham. Samuel, David, William, and Tobias had died in infancy. Lewis became the father of Jacob (Jake), Daniel, Mary, and William, the latter two of whom, with their father and mother, lived most of their lives in Atglen, Pennsylvania. Daniel's son, Clayton, became a minister, and also his grandson Dean and his great-grandson David. Christian became the father of Noah, Amanda, and Mary. Amanda married Deacon John Harshberger, and Mary became the wife of David Stull. Both of these lived the latter part of their lives in Scottdale, Pennsylvania. Abraham (Abe) had a son, David, who farmed the home place for many years. Three of David's sons also became ministers, Harry Y., Charles, and Ammon.

My grandfather Jacob used to tell many stories of those years when their family was growing up, but unfortunately these were never recorded in family records. As a result, much of this rich family lore has been lost. I do recall his telling of an encounter in his youth with a large "cat," presumably a cougar. Some of the details of this story have been added by my cousin, Paul Shetler, who also remembers his grandfather Abe's version of the event.

Christian and his sons were working in the "back fields" one day when their two dogs chased an animal into the nearby woods, and tangled with it. Young Jacob went to the house for a gun and ran to the scene. This was at a place called "The Rocks," just above Paint Creek in the vicinity of present Carpenter Park, near the spot where the huge bridge now spans the river on Route 219. Grandfather emptied three bullets into the animal but did not kill it. At wit's end he took his knife and finished it off. When his father and brothers saw him coming over the hill, he was dragging the large cat by the paws slung over his shoulder, the cat's tail dragging on the ground. This was said to be one of the last cougars shot in this area.

At the sale of the old Shetler homestead in the fall of 1970, Paul, mentioned above, who is also a great-grandson of Christian of Waldeck, bought the old gun with the initials "C. S." and the date "1804" inscribed on the stock. The price was $490. The same day on the sale grounds he had the opportunity of reselling it for $1,000, but he did not accept the offer. This type of gun, now a rare collector's item, was one of a number of firearms made by a Bedford, Pennsylvania, gunsmith in the early 1800s and is a prized possession of the present owner (1980).

My grandfather used to enjoy hunting—something which incidentally my father never pursued. The only shooting my father did was at butchering time when he killed the hogs with his "32." Interestingly, he shot lefthanded, although in everything else he was righthanded. I have in my possession my grandfather's old muzzle loader and the old powder horn. I remember being with him a few times when he hunted with this gun, and was greatly intrigued with the unique and slow method of loading it. First, powder had to be poured into the muzzle. This was followed with tamping in a wad of paper—a kind specially made for this purpose—with the "ramrod." The shot or bullet— depending on the type of game—was added. This was followed by tamping in another wad. The ramrod was fastened to the bottom of the barrel when not being used. The final act in loading was to place a tiny firing cap on a special place mounted at the top of the rear end of the barrel at a location right in front of the hammer. When the trigger was pulled the released hammer would strike the cap, igniting the powder through a tiny hole in the barrel, and the gun would discharge. The harder the load was tamped the greater would be the impact of the shot.

Our family lore has numerous tales. There was the time, for example, when Veronica, then up in years, retired for the night and found their pet coon in her upstairs bedroom. She took him down and put him outside, closed the door and returned to her room. But when she came into the room there was the coon again! In her slow way of closing the outside door the wily animal had slipped back in, and by the time she had made her way upstairs, he was already there ahead of her!

My father's maternal grandparents also lived in the area and were well-known residents. Their ancestry had come to America from Switzerland in much earlier times than the Shetlers, and hence much less is known of their place of origin. I have visited the beautiful countryside near Berne, where the Kaufmans had originated but have been unable to pinpoint the location of their original homes. Great-grandfather Sem Kaufman was a very interesting man and lived to a ripe old age. His wife, Great-grandmother Elizabeth, died, however, relatively young at 43. My father's mother, Amelia, was only three years old at the time of her mother's passing (1853) and the only real recollection Amelia had of her was the day of the funeral when the body was lying in the casket at the house. Her father was sitting there toddling her and her brother, Kore, on his knees, tears streaming down his cheeks, while he was also at the same time rocking with his foot the cradle in which little infant Jonas was lying. Her father, Sem, later remarried and his second wife, Anna, passed away in 1889, just a few months after Great-grandmother Veronica Shetler died.

My oldest sister, Luella, of Goshen, Indiana, remembered Great-grandfather Kaufman in his last years. She was four years old when he died in 1896. She remembered the plain Amish house with its bare floors—the wide boards with the large cracks between. On one occasion when she was there visiting, she was wearing a tiny string of beads as little girls frequently do in play.

Considering this inappropriate for the daughter of plain people he tugged at them a bit, making some unfavorable remark about this being *Hochmut* (pride). In the process he tore the string, scattering the tiny beads in the cracks of the floor. To make up for the loss, he presented her with a small homemade wooden tub, used in those days as a receptacle for pins and buttons, a relic which she greatly treasured all her life.

4
Mennonites and Amish

The story of the Mennonites, as indicated earlier, began in Europe as a part of the Protestant Reformation. In Zurich, Switzerland, Conrad Grebel and others organized a group of "Brethren" in 1525 on the same principles that still identify the Mennonite faith: (1) believer's baptism upon confession of faith as opposed to infant baptism; (2) a simple, nonconformed life with an emphasis on piety; (3) separation of church and state; (4) refusal to take part in the destruction of human life; (5) a strong brotherhood of believers, with mutual sharing in time of need; (6) radical discipleship—that is, following Christ, whatever the cost; (7) making the Word of God central in their lives. Some of their distinctive practices have included simple modes of apparel, the ritual of washing the saints' feet in connection with the communion ceremony, and the use of the women's veiling (1 Corinthians 11:1-16).

Out of the stream of immigrants who fled northward through the Palatinate were the original settlers of the province of Waldeck in Western Germany. Others migrated directly to America, and the Waldeckians in time also migrated to America.

Eleven years after the founding of the Swiss Brethren, Menno Simons, a priest at Witmarsum, Netherlands, broke away from Catholicism and joined a new movement with principles almost identical to those of the Swiss Brethren. From these two streams of Swiss and Dutch Anabaptists present-day Mennonitism has emerged. Like the Swiss Brethren, Dutch Anabaptists also encountered severe persecution. Menno Simons himself suffered persecution over a period of 25 years. He died a natural death, however, near the picturesque and historical city of Lübeck in Germany, where he spent the last years of his life and where many of his writings were published.

Because of the severe persecution by both intolerant rulers and church leaders who frequently collaborated with the authorities, Mennonites, along with some other religious groups, sought freedom in the New World. At the personal invitation of William Penn, founder of the "holy experiment" in the colony later named for him, a group of Mennonite colonists settled with the Quakers near Philadelphia in the late seventeenth century. From this meager beginning and from subsequent migrations from Germany and Switzerland came the early settlers who were to make up the Mennonite and Amish population of Pennsylvania, and eventually, of America. The later migrations at the beginning of the nineteenth century resulted from the pressures of military conscription brought on by the Napoleonic wars.

To meet the challenge of Napoleon's aggression the surrounding European nations began to arm themselves and to conscript soldiers. An interesting story told by my grandfather shows the extent of Napoleon's conquest and how the resulting pressures affected neighboring provinces. When his father Christian was quite small, some of Napoleon's soldiers were in the area of Waldeck doing some plundering. They needed horses and picked up little Christian, setting him on one of their own. They asked him where the horses were kept. Apparently the men were in the fields or hiding. Not able to understand French, and going only by their gestures, the lad led them to a stable where some donkeys were kept. Amused they let him go and moved on.

The economic factor as a cause for migration has always been underplayed a bit. No doubt many were also seeking better ways to make a living and a means of possessing land of their own. This was virtually impossible in Europe because of the system of landed estates and *Arbeiter*. There was certainly nothing wrong about this motive for migrating, but it should be clear that it was not all for the sake of religious liberty that Mennonites and other religious groups came to America. The spirit of adventure, too, was certainly not absent.

Whatever the exact purpose, during this particular period of migration Christian Schöttler and his parents sailed to America. Many of the Waldeckian Mennonites, as noted before, settled in Somerset County, Pennsylvania.

Mennonites, unlike common notions, are not a progressive offshoot of the Amish. The Mennonite Church began in 1525, but it was not until 1693 that an Amish church emerged. This came about through a schism of two prominent Mennonite leaders, Hans Reist and Jacob Ammann, on the matter of what to do with those who were excommunicated for violation of the church's rules. Ammann insisted they should be "shunned," basing his views on an interpretation of First Corinthians 5:11b, which says, "With such an one no not to eat." He applied this to the daily routine of meals rather than to the communion table. To this day the "ban," as it is also called, is often observed by the Amish against those who for some reason or other leave the church, either by excommunication or by withdrawal.

On nearly every point of doctrine, however, Reist and Ammann agreed. In practice the Amish tended toward a more conservative view in terms of outward forms, carrying down through the years some of the old customs and traditions and ways of dressing. The Amish who came to America were not however the "Old Order Amish" or horse-and-buggy Amish as we know them today. That label was not applied until the middle of the nineteenth century when a group of Amish, who resisted all efforts toward merging with other (more progressive) Amish groups in the long series of "General Conferences" held between 1862 and 1878, finally withdrew from these fellowships and started their own conservative group. Many of the European Amish, on the other hand, did merge with the Mennonites, closing a gap of several centuries' standing. Those who refused to move from their old positions and who rejected the use of modern conveniences like the car and the telephone, and who continued to worship in homes, are known today as the Old Order Amish.

The group of Amish who migrated to Somerset County, Pennsylvania—which included the Kaufmans and Schöttlers—were European Amish. They were never called Old Order Amish. They did, however, worship in homes and maintained simple dress and conservative practices. It must be remembered, further, that in this same area, as in many other areas of the country, there had also been Mennonite migrations as early as 1790. Yet, the differences that had existed in Europe were in many cases forgotten in the rigors of trying to establish new homes in the wilderness. In time, many of the Amish joined Mennonites near them. That is exactly what happened when Jacob Shetler, the father of S. G. Shetler, in the declining years of his own church, united with the Mennonites.

During the heyday of the Amish settlement in this area there came to be two sizable groups, one located in Conemaugh Township, Somerset County, and the other in Richland Township in Cambria County, just ten miles to the north. It is estimated that at one time about 200 members were in the combined groups, making up what was known in Amish circles as the "Conemaugh Congregation." Life in the Conemaugh congregation flourished for a period of more than 100 years after which a decline began to set in, which resulted in its eventual disintegration.

The story of this decline forms an interesting chapter in Amish history. There were a number of reasons for this, one of which was the migration of many families to better farming areas of the Midwest. But one main reason was the absorption of the Amish by other religious groups, chiefly the Mennonites. This defection was due largely to the strict adherence of the Amish Church to the German language in their church services. At that time other churches had begun to adapt themselves to the American culture and were changing to English. A third major reason was the lack of younger men to fill the ranks of the ministry. The younger men who would have had the qualifications for *Prediger* and *Diener* (preacher and deacon) had already united with the Mennonites and other groups. In the late 1800s when the older ministers were looking about for young men to ordain there were only a few left, and these refused to be considered either because they felt unqualified or for personal reasons. My grandfather, Jacob, had been one of these. By 1915 the Kaufman Amish Church, where he had attended for many years, was forced to close. Soon after, he transferred his membership to the Stahl Mennonite Church where his son, Samuel, was minister.

The story is told of one ordination service close to the end of the church's existence when the "lot" fell on a young man with little ability. The method of drawing lots was the church's method of selecting "God's man" from the list of candidates previously nominated by the congregation. When the truth of the situation seemed to dawn on the young man, he jumped up in a frenzy and headed for the door. Several men pursued him, one grabbing him while he clung to the door, kicking at his pursuers. He would not submit to ordination!

As a gesture toward saving the church in its years of decline, two meetinghouses had been erected, which was a strange departure from Amish practices. To continue to hold services in the homes had become difficult in later years because of the few families left to serve as host. Their turns came too often, and the task of setting up chairs or benches and entertaining the group for the Sunday meal was no small burden.

The first of the church buildings was built in the summer of 1875 on the Isaac Kaufman farm near the village of Davidsville. A few years later a second one was built on the Moses B. Miller farm in Cambria County inside the present limits of Geistown borough. The two meetinghouses were referred to simply as the Kaufman and Miller Amish churches. In childhood my father attended first the Miller Church and later, when they moved back to Somerset County, the Kaufman Church. After he became a minister in the Mennonite Church, he preached frequently in both, since the

Amish Church cooperated rather closely at this time with the Mennonite churches of the area.

In 1899 a Sunday school was organized in the Kaufman Amish Church which was also attended by Mennonites, Lutherans, Dunkards, and others. The school was conducted in the summer months only as was the custom then, until the summer of 1908, when it was continued in the new Kaufman Mennonite Meetinghouse built that same year just nearby. During the last years of the Miller and Kaufman Amish churches, these congregations shared with the Mennonite churches in holding district events. After the deaths of Bishop Moses B. Miller and Preacher Jonathan Hershberger (1902), ministerial help was supplied from the churches of Mifflin County for more than ten years. When the churches finally closed, services were held for a few years at the new Kaufman Mennonite Church. At the special invitation of the ministerial body of the Mennonite churches of the district, the 18 remaining members either united with the Mennonite Church or worshiped with them. But a number of the group retained their membership with the Amish. These traveled back and forth several times a year for communion services to the Amish settlement in Mifflin County ninety miles to the east. They were: Abraham Shetler, his wife, and Melinda Kaufman, wife of Noah Kaufman, who passed away in 1941.

I lived through the last years of the Amish Church there and recall with pleasure many visits made to the homes of those named. Hospitality reigned there. Both were comfortably situated and prosperous. Abe lived on the original Shetler homestead which his son David was then farming. This same farm remained in Shetler hands for a period of 139 years, up until the tragic death of David's son Ammon, who was its last owner. He was killed on the highway during the haying season, 1969, when he was thrown from a hay wagon pulled by a tractor. The following year the farm was sold. A part of the original farm, the section once owned by Lewis and later by his son Daniel, is still in possession of a Shetler descendant, however. The wife of the present owner, Carl Holsopple, is a sister to Ammon.

Reared as an Amish boy, my father naturally maintained a deep respect for these venerable people and, as stated before, frequently preached for them locally and in other areas of the church. He had the ability to preach fluently in German. He was always an ardent admirer of Bishop Moses B. Miller, whom he had known from boyhood days. Miller, a capable leader, teacher, and public speaker, had already been preaching four years, in fact, when my grandfather, Jacob, was born in 1848. He was held in high esteem among those inside and outside the faith and was widely used throughout the Amish Church. The very substantial home he had built around the turn of the century in what is now Geistown is still standing and is used as a dwelling. The barn has been torn down in recent years. Bishop Miller was well-versed in the Scriptures, a quality which my father emulated. A grandson of his, Algie E. Lehman, was for many years a missionary to China under what was then called the Evangelical Church, and a great-granddaughter, Elizabeth Luther Kniss (wife of Lloy A. Kniss) was a missionary to India under the auspices of the Mennonite Church. Preacher Jonathan Hershberger, referred to earlier, was also an esteemed leader and left a large group of descendants who have served the church. One of these, Ruth Hershberger, a great-granddaughter of Jonathan, is married to Marvin Kaufman, a grandson of S. G. Shetler, and a minister in the Mennonite Church.

A word of tribute to the Amish ancestry of S. G. Shetler is in order. Ammon Kaufman, a son of Noah, wrote one time: "It can be truthfully said of the people of the Amish Church that they were noted for their hospitality, conservative methods of life, general foresightedness, and ability to make progress in the affairs of life. . . . They were also pioneers in the making of a new nation, for it was they who entered into forests, building their own roads, cutting down mighty giants of the woods, and hewing the logs into the proper shape for building cabins which were to serve as homes. Here in these primitive homes were born to them children who were brought up in the nurture and admonition of the Lord. Their hospitality was of a kind that would cause them to entertain their friends, as well as the stranger or wayfaring man. Many of them started life in this country without any capital, excepting strong bodies and minds to work, but with their general foresightedness have been able to rise from the ranks of poverty to a position of wealth."[6]

It would be unfair, however, to paint a totally idealistic picture of these people. Obviously they also had their faults.

Interestingly, many people of that time were quite superstitious. Ghost and hex stories were a part of the Pennsylvania German tradition, and it would be an interesting study to see how far back this could be traced in their European traditions. Weird stories of "tokens" or signs of unusual events—of coming deaths and weddings—were commonly believed and told. Singing teakettles, strange footfalls at night, strange lights, handclasps in a window, were among the special tokens or omens that older folks talked about in a sort of reverent tone. Many believed religiously in the signs of the zodiac. Judge Wilson's description of the Mennonites of the Old Harmony colony north of Pittsburgh would characterize very well also the Amish and Mennonites of Somerset County. He wrote: "They plowed, planted, harvested, built fences, and shingled their roofs in accordance with the signs of the zodiac and the signs of the moon. They also believed in powwowing. Often when a cow was sick her illness would be diagnosed as hollow horn and a gimlet hole was bored in the horn to let in the air, or she had wolf in her tail for which the remedy was to split the skin in the tail near the base and rub in salt." Sties on the eyelid would be cured by powwowing and the "fire" could be taken out of a burn, warts could be removed, and bleeding stopped, all by saying certain words and incantations. Certain persons in the area were known to be good in the curing of particular maladies, such as "opnemida" (malnutrition) or for bleeding.[7]

Yet, at the same time there were many who were skeptical of these methods, more so as the churches began teaching against powwowing and superstitious beliefs. It is very difficult to describe totally their actual views on superstition for they were made up of both faith and doubt. My grandfather Shetler told of an incident where neighbors were reporting strange lights in a cemetery on several occasions as they passed back and forth nightly on their way to "sit up" with a sick person in the community. When it was my grandmother's turn to attend to the sick person, grandfather decided to accompany her and check on the strange episode. As they walked down the road, both straining to see the lights, their heads turned in the direction of the cemetery, grandfather in the darkness stumbled headlong over a cow that was lying directly in his path. Startled, he began to think for a moment that the ghost had really overtaken him! This was told as an amusing tale, however, and their views of the strange lights remained in the realm of the doubtful.

Frugality and industry were the prime virtues of the Amish and Mennonites, almost equated at some points with their faith. No higher tribute could be paid a man for example than to say that he was a *Schäffer* (worker), or, contrariwise, no greater stigma could be placed on a person than to say that the individual was *faul* (lazy). The very inflection in their voice when they applied these terms would tell what they thought of an individual. The idea of work was so ingrained in the Pennsylvania Dutch culture that even when a person sat down to relax he was made to feel guilty. I can hear some of these people say, "Oh, here I am again, sitting down and doing nothing!" This was long before the day of coffee breaks, and planned relaxation periods. "Vacation" also was not a word in their vocabulary. Yet, they did take their days off, actually, and had many good times. It certainly was not all work and no play.

As one travels through the former Amish area in Cambria County, the area lying between the villages of Geistown and Elton, one cannot escape a certain nostalgia, wondering just what this community might be like today had these people remained. Particularly does one think of this when he considers the many flourishing homesteads which clearly bear the marks of Amish vintage. Traveling through this region several times in recent years I could not help entertaining the wish that at least a sizable portion of the community had remained in Amish or Mennonite hands. One of the outstanding farms of the area, modernized in recent years, is the one that formerly belonged to Christian Shetler, son of the original Christian of Waldeck. The name is still remembered well enough that the residents of the area, after these many years, quickly point out the Shetler farm, a beautiful landmark of the area.

But signs of material progress have changed much of the original beauty of this lovely rural countryside. A four-lane highway cuts directly through the center of both the Cambria and Somerset areas, and midway between are several large shopping centers and the beautiful new campus of the University of Pittsburgh at Johnstown (UPJ). Also close by is the modern municipal airport. Amish life today might not blend too well with this kind of landscape.

5
Boyhood Years to Young Manhood
(1871-1887)

On January 13, 1871, a son was born to two members of the Conemaugh Amish congregation, Jacob and Amelia Kaufman Shetler. The birthplace was the old Shetler homestead in Conemaugh Township, Somerset County, where the new child's grandfather, Christian, had settled forty years earlier. The original log house was still standing though it was no longer being used as a dwelling.

One can imagine it was a typical cold, blustery January day. But with the coal kitchen range and the potbelly stove in the *Hukstub* (living room) going at full blast, the house was kept comfortably warm. A neighbor lady had served as midwife, and the little boy with the high forehead, destined to become a preacher, was in good hands.

The routine of the young parents changed rapidly after his arrival, and the need for expanded quarters became apparent. Eager to live alone with his family and to own his own farm, Jacob scouted around for a suitable place to live. He was able to locate a farm available in the Amish settlement in Richland Township, Cambria County, close to his brother Christian's farm. As we have already noted, this was actually not far from the northern Somerset County settlement. The old deed in possession of the owner interviewed at the time of this writing indicated that in April 1871, four months after the birth of Samuel, the transfer of titles was made, and probably they moved at this time. The two-story frame house in Richland was located in a beautiful corner of the farm, the rear of the house facing a low range of mountains in the distance. Surrounded by trees, it stood in a picturesque setting. A spring, walled in on three sides and covered with an arched stone top, in the typical style of the day, was located just a few feet from the front porch. The township road passed in front of the house just beyond the spring.

A springhouse, also used as a butcher house, stood on the west side of the house. On the opposite side of the house, about a hundred yards away was a red barn with its characteristic Swiss (sloped) bank leading to the upper floor, and the usual forebay.

A few stories survive these Richland years, but only one of Samuel's infancy. My oldest sister, Luella, remembered one incident as told her by our grandfather. When Samuel was a baby his parents rode horseback to the Berlin settlement to visit some relatives. At one point along the route the young father, Jacob, on his own horse with the baby in his arms, attempted to hand him across to the baby's mother, when the horse lurched suddenly to the side, leaving mother and infant to land in a heap on the ground. Amelia sat there laughing and unhurt.

It was a time of great economic uncertainty which eventually erupted into the Panic of 1873. President Grant was then in office. Near poverty faced the Shetler home for a time. I often heard my father refer to those lean years when lard was used on bread instead of butter and table fare was very simple. Store products were a rarity. Homemade garments were common then, which included the little woolen suits Samuel wore with their narrow trouser legs and tiny jackets. One of these he preserved for many years. The little leather boots made by a nearby shoemaker were from their own tanned cowhide.

On January 11, 1874, a sister was born, the only other child the Shetlers were to have. She was named Louisa. The two children apparently experienced a normal childhood, and they always maintained a warm relationship, living for most of their lives in the same community not too many miles apart. Louisa in maturity married a local resident, Joe Hostetler, who became a prosperous farmer. They had three children: Effie, Norman, and Edna, Effie passing away in 1915 while still in her teens. Visits to the Hostetlers in our childhood years was always a delight. We enjoyed our cousins. Aunt Louisa's Pennsylvania Dutch dinners were a treat and so was listening to their "talking machine," a luxury we were not allowed at the time because "papa was a preacher."

In spite of some poverty in those early days in Richland in the Shetler home—they lived here until 1877—there was also much fun. When quite small Samuel one day penned the family cat in the oven, and when his mother built fire in the range in preparation for a meal, the little boy jumped around in childish glee, saying in his fine voice, in Pennsylvania Dutch, "Now the cat will dance." Had he not spoken, the tragic plight of the cat might not have been discovered and there would have been not only a dancing cat but a baked cat. As a small child he slept in a trundle bed and one night he was afraid. He heard something "marching under his bed."

Physically, Samuel had his share of physical problems, being afflicted for a time with epileptic seizures. During one such fit it is said he bit through a tin cup. He also had some leg weakness which needed attention. There was no lengthy diagnosis and treatment by a bone specialist, but instead his parents took him to a blacksmith to have him fitted with a brace which he wore for some time.

In later years you would never have guessed that he had ever been a sickly child. In fact, he frequently boasted of his good health and of his teaching record of not having missed a day of school for many years on account of sickness. He often referred to his "iron stomach" which allowed him to eat anything. In stature, Samuel was of medium height, about five feet, five and a half inches tall, yet he was built strong enough to enable him to take his share of the work in his lifetime. During the years he carried on his summer truck farming he often worked long hours, and not infrequently capped the day with some kind of church service or committee meeting.

As a youth, however, he was considered frail. For that reason his father, fearing he would not be able to take hard work, decided he should prepare himself for teaching by attending summer teachers' normals, which were then considered "higher education." It is obvious, however, that his father saw something in his son which pointed in the direction of following intellectual pursuits for a future professional career.

Not too much is known of his grade school years, but when he had become old enough to write his own name, he decided to add his own middle name. Amish parents did not provide a child with a middle name. With the common people of the country President Grant was considered a great figure, and young Samuel decided that his middle name should be Grant. Looking back now it seems amusingly ironic that the young man who would one day as a Mennonite bishop represent his denomination in behalf of conscientious objectors before the United States Secretary of War, would choose for his middle name that of a great American general!

Most of his elementary education was obtained in the nearby Miller school in Conemaugh Township, although he may have started to school already while the family was still in the Richland area. It is lamentable that so little is known of his school days. Elizabeth Livingstone (later Mrs. Josiah Gindlesperger), a schoolmate, remembered one interesting sidelight of his school experience. She recalled how young Samuel used to get up on a stump during a recess or noon intermission periods and preach "funeral sermons."[8] This now seems rather prophetic considering how many funeral sermons he came to preach during the years of his ministry.

As a boy he also attended a Sunday school, presumably too in the Richland area. In an article written by request for the *Gospel Herald* on Sunday schools at the time of the 100th anniversary of Mennonite Sunday Schools (1940), he recalled this early Sunday school experience and paid high tribute to his teacher. In it he said, "As a boy less than six years of age I recall a Sunday school teacher in another denomination who exerted an influence on my life and instilled a Sunday school spirit within me."[9]

This added training also seems significant now when one considers that the Amish did not sponsor Sunday schools and even Mennonites did not have any in this area at this time. It certainly indicated that his parents were concerned to make provision for this added advantage in Bible training.

There is one other glimpse, this one in Samuel's teen years. He wrote a letter for "Our Letter Box" of the *Words of Cheer*, a former youth paper of the Mennonite Church, dated October 1888. He was then already a youth of 17. The letter, written in the style of the day, ran as follows:

> Dear Friend:
>   I take pleasure this rainy evening to let you know that I am well, hoping the many readers of the little "Cheer" are the same. My paper comes regularly. I received the cards, thanks for them. I take pleasure in reading the letters and seeing the many different names of the readers of this religious instructor and I think it is a wise plan to follow this Christian guide whereby we may avoid everlasting destruction and inherit the kingdom of God; and although we are strangers yet I feel almost acquainted with them, and hope we may once meet where we shall know as we are known.
>
> Your friend,
S. G. Shetler
Davidsville, Pa.

As the years passed the economic security of the family improved. Part of Jacob's income was derived from a thriving butchering business carried on in partnership with a neighbor. Together they would kill and quarter the livestock on their farms weekly and go to their butchershop in Cambria City, then a small village adjoining Johnstown. Here the meat was cut up and marketed. They also sold some produce from this store. This was while they were still living in the Richland area.

In 1877 Jacob and Amelia moved back to Somerset County,

after locating farmland of their liking about five miles from the original Shetler farm. It was located in "Soap Hollow," so named for the fact that soap had been manufactured there at one time. Here they built a substantial frame house in the style of the period, with the windows spaced for looks rather than for convenience. It was built as a duplex to accommodate two families, as many of the old houses used to be built in preparation for old age when the younger folks would occupy "the other side" of the house. He also erected a large barn several hundred feet west of the house. In addition there was a hog stable between the house and the barn, and a woodshed. Close by was the smokehouse. About fifty feet diagonally from the corner of the house on the east side, along the sloping hillside, the usual walled-in spring was located. A pine tree was planted on the hillside immediately above the spring, which in my time had become a magnificant overhanging twin pine.

Needing a "springhouse" to preserve perishable foods my grandfather was able to obtain the old abandoned log building that was once the first Miller schoolhouse. A picture of this appears in the "Family Album" in the photo section of this book. The old schoolhouse stood across the hill to the north just on the edge of the Joe Miller farm. The log structure was dismantled and moved to the new location just below the spring. The slope of the hillside made it possible with very little excavation to have a full cellar, which was also used as a springhouse.

In the back part of the cellar was the familiar wooden trough which, with its constant flow of running water from the spring, served well as a refrigerator. The springhouse was still in use when I was a boy and I recall vividly walking barefooted on the cool, damp, plank floor in the heat of summer. I also recall those distinctive springhouse odors! In the trough were numerous crocks of varying sizes with either wooden, slate, or flat stone lids, the larger ones for "separated" milk, the smaller ones for sweet and sour cream. Then there was the "butter crock" and larger crocks for storing meat, pickles, and other items. In addition to these were the swinging shelves suspended from the ceiling by wires to store other foods that needed less refrigeration. The purpose of suspending these was to prevent mice and rats from getting at the food.

The main floor of the structure, which had once been the schoolroom, was now converted into a shop. It contained the usual complement of tools used in that day, hand augers of varying sizes, planes, files, rasps, hammers, axes, and the old *Snitzelbank*. Sometime in the 1930s this building was dismantled. The farm, incidentally, is now (1980) owned by George Lybarger. The house and barn are still standing although most of the other buildings have long since been torn down. The house itself has been changed and improved by the various owners since my grandfather's time. Much of the original orchard is gone as is also the old mulberry tree. Just close to the spot where the tree once stood is a large pool, hidden from the road with an ornamental fence.

The typical farm of sixty or more years ago was a picture of quietude and plenty. In a day when a little went a long way the products of the small farm unit with its diversified farming was a lesson in subsistence. My grandfather's farm was one of these. Of the hundred acres or thereabouts, well over half was under cultivation. There were, in a typical year, 10 or more acres of wheat, 5 acres of oats, several acres of corn, and perhaps an acre or two of potatoes. Besides this, there was always a sizable truck patch and a garden close by the house. Then there was the family orchard with its many varieties of apples, peaches, cherries, pears, and plums. In addition there was a grape arbor close by the house with several varieties of blue, red, and white grapes, and a huge mulberry tree. Wild berries seemed to be plentiful along the fencerows and were used for jams and preserves. Some were canned for pie filling.

My grandfather's orchard, located on the hillside above the house, was a utopian delight. At apple-picking time piles of the several varieties were stacked on the earthen floor of the house from which the family could draw for their own consumption as well as to fill baskets to take along on the weekly marketing route in Johnstown. There was also an "apple hole" to store larger supplies of winter apples where they would be kept cold. This was simply a large rectangular box buried in the ground near the house and covered over with boards and leaves or straw or ground for insulation. The family would remove the fruit as the weather permitted, brushing back the snow in the heart of winter. I can remember those many lucious varieties—the Rambeaus, Smokehouse, Ewalds, Northern Spy, Pound, Banana, and other varieties not so popular today for commercial use.

Harvesting and threshing time were interesting experiences for everyone, though involving much work. Grain was cut with a horse-drawn reaper or "binder" after the farmer had first "cut the field loose" with a cradle, which meant cutting down by hand the outer rim of the field to avoid having the grain mashed by the machine. Men followed the binder to pick up sheaves as they were dropped and set them up in shocks. Corn was cut by hand with a large cleaver-type knife and set up in shocks to be husked later. When it was time for threshing the wheat and oats, or buckwheat, a crew with a steam engine and a huge separator and water tank moved in to "set up," usually the evening before the threshing day. The crew ate, and frequently slept, at the given farm where the threshing was to be done. Neighboring farmers helped each other on the big day. For a child this was a circus, watching the huge engine outside the barn driving the long belt that operated the separator inside on the threshing floor, and watching the men feed the machine. Tossing the bundles of grain into the machine and carrying away the sacked grain was all part of a long day's tiring and dusty work. The sumptuous meals at dinner and supper time seemed to compensate for this. Unbelievable quantities of food were eaten by the crew, the family, and neighbors who had come in to help.

Apple butter time also came in the fall. Apples were sacked and hauled to the nearby cider press to have them transformed into tasty cider and apple butter. A description of the process makes a story of its own. What cider was not consumed within a few days by the family as a beverage or sold for that same purpose on the route in town would be stored in a barrel to be turned into the winter's vinegar supply. The barrel was propped up on a wooden framework on the cellar floor and fitted with a tap for convenience. In a day when fancy salad oils were largely unknown to common people, vinegar was an important commodity for family use. A small vinegar jug was always kept on the table. The warm, spicy apple butter, brought home fresh from the cider press and ladled into crocks, was kept either for family use or was sold.

Recreation and social activities consisted mostly of such events as spelling bees, teachers' institutes, barn raisings, cornhuskings, sledding parties, and Sunday get-togethers. Cousin John Layman wrote an article for the local newspaper many years ago, in which he attempted to describe a cornhusking of the period. He wrote: "How those boys and girls would husk corn!" To him "their shouts of joy and laughter echoing along the hillsides, and those golden yellow ears of corn in neat mounds throughout the cornfield, were a sight to behold." He continued:

> When darkness came the boys and girls would be seen streaming toward the farmhouse kitchen, where tables were loaded with the best food the farmers' [wives] can bake; and that good old-fashioned country sausage! What a treat!

o   o   o

> Any corn not husked in the afternoon was hauled in on the barn floor where it had to be husked after supper before the barn party could start. After the barn floor was swept clean, lanterns were hung in safe places and the barn party was ready to start. These parties were never called barn dances, and no musical instruments were allowed excepting the mouth organ. Such numbers as "Shoot the Buffalo," "Skip to Maloo," and many others were played. Everyone on the barn floor helped to sing. These parties were under strict supervision and no smoking, swearing, or rowdyism were allowed. Gangs and rowdies from neighboring towns tried to break up these parties but they were quelled.
>
> Generally at midnight the farmer would take his lanterns down, which was the signal for the party to break up. The farmer was well satisfied with the corn that was husked, and the boys and girls with the fine supper and the good time.[10]

One very outstanding tragic event in my father's teenage

years was the Johnstown Flood of May 31, 1889, when the South
Fork reservoir broke. For days previously there had been heavy
rains completely saturating the ground, so that by the evening of
May 30 as the rain kept coming there was literally no place for the
water to go. The reservoir, held back by an earthen dam, had
been poorly constructed. It was owned by the South Fork Fishing
Club, an exclusive organization, which included in its
membership such noted men as John D. Rockefeller of New York
and Andrew Mellon of Pittsburgh. They had bought the old dam
from the Pennsylvania Railroad to create an artificial lake for
recreational purposes.

The railroad company had acquired it originally from the
Pennsylvania Canal system when that canal was abandoned. The
dam had been used in earlier days as a feeder to the canal in dry
seasons. Some time previous to this purchase by the sportsmen the
breast of the dam had been seriously damaged in a flood, and the
Club had not rebuilt it properly. It was in no way able to handle
such an extreme amount of water. On the afternoon of May 31
the dam finally broke under the strain, and the water moved
down the valleys in one massive wall of water, trees, and debris. It
destroyed and damaged property along the entire route to the
city. In the catastrophe the city itself was almost totally destroyed
and 2200 people lost their lives. The story of the famous flood has
been well told in several recent books.

The destruction that followed was beyond description.
Eighteen-year-old Samuel Grant Shetler went down to the city on
the evening of the first of June to view the ruins from a nearby
hillside. The scene that met his eyes was appalling. Rocks and debris were backed up against the old stone bridge (still standing,
1980), and people were trapped in the debris. Survivors were
hunting for relatives in hope that they would find them alive. It
was a picture of total desolation and grief which never left his
memory and to which he often referred in his messages after he
became a minister.

Some time later, at some young people's gathering or at
church, Samuel saw among the fair ladies a very young and

charming brunette whose love he sought. This was Maggie Jane Kaufman, actually a distant cousin. After a brief courtship they were married on his twentieth birthday, January 13, 1891, by Bishop Jonas Blauch in the Blauch residence at Krings. Maggie was then three months short of fifteen. But she was mature beyond her years. Her mother had passed away the year of the Johnstown flood, and for more than a year, until her father remarried, she, the eldest in the family and only daughter, was called upon to take care of her four brothers. She was not a fickle person, but took the tasks of life seriously and seemed to find in her new home the security a young girl without the counsel and concern of a mother needed.

The death of her mother had, in fact, been a sad consequence of the flood, at least indirectly. Her brother, Norman (J. N. Kaufman), who was one of the early missionaries to India, recorded this in his short autobiography written for the *Mennonite Historical Bulletin*. Grandpa Kaufman had a good friend who was a storekeeper in the city. After the flood this storekeeper allowed him to take home bolts of damaged dry goods, coats, shawls, and other articles that could be salvaged. These were washed and then spread through the meadows to dry. This was in June and his wife, Catherine, died in September from typhoid fever. Apparently she had contracted it from the flood goods. The immediate cause of her death, however, which her brother does not mention in his autobiography, was her exhaustion from a long walk to her home shortly after she had given birth to a child. Her body, weakened from her recent illness, could not take the rigors of this strenuous walk.

My mother often talked about her mother. She remembered particularly her singing as she went about her household tasks, an art almost forgotten by modern mothers. One of these songs which my mother, in turn, would often sing for us was "My Latest Sun Is Sinking Fast." At the time of her passing she thought her mother was rather mature, but in reflecting on this in later years she could hardly believe that she had died at 33!

To return to my parents' marriage—it was exactly a month

before their wedding (December 13, 1890) that both my father and mother had become members of the Mennonite Church. At that time it was the custom for people to wait until marriage to take this step, and, anticipating this, they had decided to make this important decision. The setting for this was an event which left a deep impression on the community. A series of evening meetings were being conducted by the young English-speaking evangelist, J. N. Durr, who had come into the area to help conduct an ordination. The ordination, which took place on Sunday morning, December 6, resulted in the call to the ministry of young L. A. Blough. On the evening before Durr had preached at a specially called service at the Stahl Mennonite Church. His stirring evangelistic sermon resulted in five confessions, and as a result of this meeting he was asked to continue for a number of nights. This was something new for the district, the first evangelistic meetings, in fact, for the Johnstown area. Durr preached at Stahl on Sunday, Monday, and Tuesday evenings, and at the Weaver Meetinghouse on the next two evenings, returning again to Stahl to conduct a special instruction service for the new converts. Altogether there were at the close of the week eighteen young people who had responded, among them my father and mother (then Maggie Kaufman). The baptismal services were held on Saturday, December 13. The correspondent in the *Herald of Truth*, the Mennonite monthly paper, stated, "It was indeed a time of rejoicing for us to see so many young souls forsake sin and cleave to that which is divine . . . ."[11]

6
Teaching as a Profession—The First Twenty-Eight Years (1887-1915)

On October 17, 1887, young Samuel Grant Shetler walked through the doors of the Kaufman one-room school located in Conemaugh Township, Somerset County, to begin his first year of teaching. He was 16 years, 9 months old.

To become a teacher at that time one needed only to have completed the elementary grades and to have passed successfully a teachers' examination given by the County Superintendent of Schools. To prepare for this the prospective teacher could either tutor himself or take advantage of a "summer normal" conducted by an experienced teacher and held in an area school building. The curriculum included advanced training in fields related to the common school subjects as well as more advanced subjects of high school and college level, depending somewhat on the Normal School teacher's training and abilities—courses such as psychology, rhetoric, botany, algebra, geometry, astronomy, and sometimes a language such as Latin or German.

In young Samuel's case he had attended one summer session under Professor Simon D. Elrick at the nearby Kiefer schoolhouse and had passed an examination given that July. Elrick, also a minister, remained a lifelong model to my father both as a good man and a capable teacher. Elrick later became principal of the

Meyersdale (elementary and secondary) School.

Beginning teachers were usually advised not to accept the home school since there were many former schoolmates in the group, and some of the bigger pupils, whose ages sometimes ranged to 20, might cause trouble.

His home school would have been the Miller school within sight of his home, so it was logical that he should take the Kaufman school which was several miles distant. Samuel's monthly pay that first year was $24.00. The average pay for "male teachers" in Conemaugh Township that year was $25.86, and for "female teachers," $25.50, according to the *Annual County Report,* the first report incidentally to have been published for Somerset County. Because Samuel was under 21 he had to turn all of his pay over to his father except the money he had to pay for board, and an allowance of a dollar a week for personal use.

It is both interesting and important to look at the times in which my father began his teaching career and to note the growth of schools and education of that period. This was the period known by historians as the "Romantic Period" in American history when many great men reasoned that America had come to maturity and was now ready to do almost anything. The population had grown remarkably. The center of population had moved from Baltimore to a point near Cincinnati. Progress was marching westward! President Harrison in one of his addresses stated that America was still by far the best country in the world. President Cleveland, in a not so optimistic appraisal, said almost prophetically in his last message to Congress in 1888:

> Our survival for one hundred years is not sufficient to assure us that we no longer have dangers to fear in the maintenance, with all its promised blessings, of a government founded upon the freedom of the people.... Upon some careful inspection we find the wealth and luxury of our cities mingled with poverty and discontent ... corporations, which should be carefully restrained creatures of the law and the servants of the people, are fast becoming the people's masters.

The country as a whole was looking to public education—then actually an innovation—to bring about the kind of social milieu that would solve the problems of society. This idealistic philosophy can be found imprinted in the statements of the educators and statesmen of the times, and in the school texts of that day. A strong moral influence in the schools was reflected in such standard reading texts as, for example, the McGuffey series, and the future did look promising. This was the day too when democracy was declared to be the magic key to unlock the doors to social progress and national glory. It was a kind of optimism, that was, however, all too simple.

When free public education came in 1834, not all residents of Pennsylvania had been ready to turn their children over to the state schools for their education. The area in which Samuel Shetler lived had been in fact one of the last in the state to adopt the new system, probably because of the strong Mennonite and Amish population. The change from private and "subscription" schools in this area took place in 1869. My grandfather in his day had attended subscription schools and his brother-in-law, Kore Kauffman, had taught in nearby Tire Hill. Subscription schools were simply community schools operated by a group of subscribers who had agreed to pay a teacher their share for educating their children. Mennonites and Amish, who for more than a hundred years had maintained their own schools, were very reluctant to turn over their pupils to a system of education which might jeopardize the principles and practices for which they had stood so long. One wonders now what their decision might have been had they foreseen the kind of innovations modern education was to bring in the century ahead, including the almost complete removal of religion from the schools.

The makeup of these early public school boards and teacher roster reflects the heavy Mennonite and Amish constituency of the area at the time. In 1895, for example, five of the six board members and four of the twelve teachers were of these faiths. Actually the character of the schools did not change much as long as these people and their God-fearing neighbors of other groups such as the Lutherans and the Dunkards remained the predominant element in the operation and control of the schools. The general atmosphere of the schools then was still definitely religious.

In the County Superintendent's *First Annual Report*, in 1888, Superintendent J. M. Berkey spoke of the schools as being "as a whole in a promising if not in a prosperous condition." Referring to "recent legislation, which had extended the minimum school term to six months (it had been five), he stated that he was pleased that all the districts in the county had fulfilled the requirements of the new law. The town of Berlin had, in fact, already gone to a seven-month term. Very little opposition had been noted, and teachers' wages had not decreased as a result of the heavier financial burden brought about by the extension.

To offset the increase in operation costs, the state had given an additional grant to each district. Local schools had to certify that they had met the requirements of the new law to be eligible for this appropriation. For the year ending on June 6, 1887, the county had received from the state $6,802.33, or an average of $26.13 for each school, an amount which roughly equalled the cost of the teacher's salary for the additional month of school. Berkey also hoped for the coming year "our teachers may have the encouragement of higher wages, and our schools the facilities for better work."

Berkey encouraged boards to pay teachers to attend the annual county institute. Some had already done this, allowing $7.00 for the full week.

During the 1887-1888 term new schoolhouses had been built in the county at a total cost of $6,247.50. In Paint Township a new district had been formed at Bethel (Hollsopple) and a two-story house erected there. Half of the schoolhouses in the county in 1888 had been built in the previous ten-year period. About half of the 40 schoolhouses in the county Berkey called unfit for use and hoped they would soon be replaced.

The superintendent also urged boards to provide good grounds and surroundings. His appeal seems to have foreshadowed modern school-ground landscaping and improved buildings and equipment. Referring to some of the better school grounds, he noted that about a dozen plots had been "neatly enclosed by a strong board fence," and in a few, shade trees had been planted, "presumably on Arbor Days." He noted, though, as a matter of regret, that the large majority of the schoolhouses did not have suitable surroundings. Some were built along the roadside with "scarcely room enough to stand"; some stood among rocks "because rocks could not be farmed"; "some grace the bleak and desolate hilltops, because two roads happen to meet there; some are found in the dark forest surrounded by gigantic oaks or wavy pines; many—very many indeed—could occupy some rough uncultivated spot that could not be utilized in any other way." Yet, he says, "here on these so-called school grounds the ten thousand children of our county are to get the pleasant recreation and healthful exercise they need for the prosy work of the schoolroom and from such attractions they are to gather inspiration for their happy school life. The picture," he continued, "was not to disparage, but to urge our people to consider the importance of the matter."

In his rather exhaustive report he went on to underscore the values of play and healthful exercise. Play, he said, is "an educational process and if rightly directed will do much to remove restlessness from the schoolroom . . . and promote better study." In almost poetic language he continued:

> When we learn to lead children through play up to work, we shall effect a happy change in our schools, and make the days spent in them the happiest period of life. Beautiful surroundings, morever, cultivate the higher nature and leave pleasant memories to brighten the pathway of afterlife.

Berkey encouraged teachers to make their schoolrooms attractive with "evergreens, pictures, and mottoes," which, he said, could be done at little expense but be an important factor in "aesthetic culture." He was looking forward to the future, when, through the help of teachers, boards, and citizens, a substantial number of buildings would be located on large and attractive grounds, suitable outbuildings would be provided, "and shaded windows and tinted walls," expressing thereby the conviction that "we are really interested in the boys and girls at school."

Education in 1888, as one can judge, was far from a prosaic, academic process with students confined within the four walls of a drab structure in an unattractive setting.

The typical equipment of the schools of that period is also reflected in Berkey's report. In the county's 110 schools all were supplied with Cornell's Outline Maps, but these, published "twenty-five years ago" (during the Civil War), were of little use now. Ninety-five each had a state map; 46 had globes; 38, modern reading charts; 16, solar system charts; 2 schools had encyclopedias and small libraries; 3, cabinet organs; 2, unabridged dictionaries; and one a physiological manikin. He noted with satisfaction that many teachers out of their own resources had added such items as "numerical frames", geometrical and arithmetical forms, dictionaries, and reference books. All the schools had blackboards, "though many not of sufficient size."

The 1887-1888 school term had 218 male teachers and 56 female teachers in the county. Of these, four held state normal school diplomas; four, permanent certificates; 56, professional certificates. One hundred and six had previously taught five or more annual terms and 48 had had no previous experience. About 20 had attended a state normal school, academy, or college, one or more terms, but without graduating. All the others had been educated in the public and local normal schools. Superintendent Berkey was urging the employment of more female teachers, especially for the primary rooms of the graded schools. He felt that "they are especially adapted to the elementary work, and as a rule more successful in that line than male teachers."

Commenting on teachers in general he noted, "Our teachers as a class are earnest, progressive, and faithful; as individuals they represent many grades of culture; as instructors, many grades of real worth." He was encouraged by the fact that many of them were giving more attention each year to professional training, general information, science, and literature, and as a consequence were becoming better qualified to teach "than those whose stock of knowledge is limited to the textbooks on the common branches."

He gave tribute to the young teachers who had just completed their first term's work (S. G. Shetler was one of those). He says, "While a few were careless and indifferent, lacking the zeal and energy so essential to success, many others measured up to their highest possibilities and (had) made a fair beginning in a noble work." He noted, however, that "longer experience will . . . give greater efficiency." Experience alone might not give greater efficiency, he observed, and deplored the fact that some who had been "fair teachers five or ten years ago . . . have turned into educational fossils, [becoming] fixtures in their district." A believer in merit pay, he felt that the educational interests of 40 or 50 pupils in a given room should never be sacrificed to the individual claims of poor teachers who cling to positions. To him a good teacher needed constantly to advance in the profession.

With such vision and insights in education, it is not difficult to understand why this particular educator later moved to an advanced position in a larger system—the Pittsburgh schools. My father, who knew Berkey well, not only as a superintendent but also as a congenial and understanding person, regarded him as a highly capable educator, and his own life and methods came to be greatly influenced by him as it also was by S. D. Elrick and his close schoolteacher friend and fellow minister, L. A. Blough. Both men had conducted summer normals which he attended.

The years from 1887 on proved to be years of opportunity and challenge for S. G. Shetler in the teaching profession. He held numerous positions in different areas and under different boards, and happily was recommended for various positions. To raise his professional standing he attended a number of summer normals and also tutored himself in additional subjects in preparation for further county teachers' examinations. Two of the normals he attended during this time were at the Kieffer schoolhouse already referred to, and another at the village of Jenner Crossroads, ten miles from his home.

For his second term of teaching, Samuel was back at the

Kaufman school, but the next term (1889-1890) he was assigned the home school. This was in the second Miller schoolhouse, which stood just across the hill from his home and across the road from the site of the original log structure just west of the former Freeman Thomas farm. Among his pupils that term and the following year were his sister Louisa; his first cousin Charles Kaufman; Louisa Blough (later Mrs. John Kniss); Lizzie Stahl (later Mrs. Ed Mishler); David and John Yoder; Ross Livingston; John Livingston, and others of the Jacob Livingston family; the David Berkey children; and members of the Sala family. In an interview with the late Charles Kaufman on the site of this school, 1962, he recalled with pleasure this early experience.

My father taught at the Miller school for two years and returned again to the Kaufman school for the 1891-1892 term. The next two terms (1892-1894) he taught at the Tire Hill school. By this time he was receiving $35.00 a month, the highest salary, incidentally, that was being paid that year by the township. Only three teachers received that amount. The teachers that term were: U. D. Miller, S. D. Yoder, W. N. Meyers, Norman Blough, H. A. Walker, John E. Weaver, J. C. Neff, J. N. Reads, J. J. Stahl, Daniel Kaufman, J. S. Zimmerman, and S. G. Shetler. Ulysses D. Miller, of Springs, Pa., was a brother to the (later) Bishop N. E. Miller. S. D. Yoder later became a Mennonite minister and Norman Blough, a Church of the Brethren preacher. The secretary of the board was Simon Lehman, who was also later ordained a Mennonite minister.

In the fall of 1894 S. G. accepted a position in the Benson Borough (Hollsopple) school, teaching both the upper and lower grades in one room, 63 pupils altogether. The board had had a problem that year to find a teacher for the lower grades, so he consented to take the entire school! The next two years, serving at the same place, he had help however, with M. H. Meyers and Norman Hoffman, teaching the lower grades in the respective terms. Serving also as principal those years he had 20 pupils in 1895-1896 and 24 in the latter term. N. H. Hoffman, in later years, became president of the Moxham bank in the city of

Johnstown. Father's income had climbed to a new $40 a month!

In 1897 S. G. was asked to come to the nearby town of Hooversville to serve as principal. The school there had been experiencing some discipline problems. With the help of a capable fellow teacher, J. M. Blough, who later became a minister and missionary in the Church of the Brethren, he was able during this term to bring about a different atmosphere in the school. During this term my father commuted daily, except in severe weather, driving the five miles back and forth in a sulky—a horse-drawn, two-wheeled cart which in that day might have been the equivalent to the modern motorcycle.

It was during this time, too, that he undertook to teach his first summer normal. This was in the summer of 1895. As described before, these normals provided a means of teacher training in a day when few had the opportunity to attend state normals or colleges, or even high school. The teachers' certificates had to be revalidated periodically, and additional training was expected on the part of the teacher. For a capable and enterprising teacher conducting a summer normal was a means of providing some additional income as well as of helping to raise one's professional status. The prospective teacher would simply announce his intentions of conducting a summer normal and begin to solicit students. It was not difficult to get 30 to 50 together for the period of the eight weeks from April to June.

One of my father's students during one of those early years was Joseph Johns mentioned earlier. He was living in 1971 and when interviewed he recalled walking each Monday morning from his home near the present North Fork Reservoir to Hollsopple, where the school was held, a distance of ten miles. He returned again each Friday evening. During this time he boarded with the Shetlers. He recalled quite vividly too the day tragedy struck that town during school hours. The boiler of the steam engine, used to run a sawmill on the hillside a half mile above the school, exploded and killed two men. The force of the explosion had shaken the building, causing the top window sashes, propped up by sticks, to drop down. Moments later someone arrived at the door to inform the teacher of the tragedy. In the midst of a test, the teacher told the students to stop where they were with their answers and fold their papers, and that they would be given credit for what they had already written. He told them that if they wished to do so, they could accompany him to the scene of the explosion, and that they were permitted to offer assistance, if needed. They were only to make certain that they would not be in anyone's way. The scene that greeted them was one of horror. Sydney Holsopple, manager of the hotel, who had walked up the hill that morning to watch the milling operations, had had the top of his head cut open. He died instantly. The other victim, who died some hours later, was Charles Holsopple, one of the operators of the sawmill. A piece of steel from the rent boiler had impaled his temples. Some of the students walked away and hung their heads over the fence to prevent fainting. It was a horrible experience.

Father taught altogether 24 summer normals, the last in 1919. The first years these were conducted at Holsopple, then at the old (second) Miller school, and in later years at the new Miller school (erected in 1900), the building which is now (1980) used as a residence.

Some interesting stories emerged from those days when a group of thirty to forty young people were packed into one small schoolroom to study the large variety of subjects of the normal school curriculum. The normal school, as previously indicated, was really a phenomenon of that period. While the young fellows and girls were all purportedly prospective teachers—though not all actually came to teach—they were nevertheless young, and some quite full of pranks.

One day one of these pranksters brought a frog to school. S. G. professed not to see it, meanwhile getting the students thoroughly involved with classwork to the point of drawing their attention completely away from the frog. In the meantime he looked around over the floor quickly to locate it, and, spotting it, picked it up and tossed it out through an open window. All the while he continued quite nonchalantly with his teaching.

In psychology class he told his students that a teacher can often detect offenders by their guilty looks. But at least one time his formula did not work. Young Milton Hoffman had stolen into the schoolroom one day during noon intermission and removed the clapper from the little handbell used to call in the students after intermission periods. When the discovery was made and the pupils had been called in by other means, the teacher told everyone to look around the room to see if they could detect the offender. During this brief interval, Hoffman, not to be outwitted, slyly, underneath the desk, kicked the legs of Dorsey Seese, the student in front of him. Dorsey's face reddened with anger, and everyone was sure he was the guilty one. The theory worked! Nothing more was said about this incident until the end of the school term when Dorsey, somewhat perturbed that he should have been wrongly accused for this misdemeanor, said in front of the whole group that there was something he wanted straightened out before everyone left for the summer. He had not stolen the clapper! The surprised teacher asked if the person who did it would please raise his hand. Sheepishly, Milton raised his hand, and the case was finally closed in the midst of considerable amusement, mostly at the teacher's expense!

Literally hundreds of young people attended normal school during those years, and many of these became teachers and school administrators. A long list of notable citizens of the area remembered with great appreciation the training they had received this way. Kent A. Bowman, for years the family physician, and Norman Hoffman, a teacher for a number of years and later a bank president, had been two of these. Others became business executives or followed useful professions or trades. Frequently through the years my father had the opportunity of meeting some of his former students and exchanging memories of those normal school years. A few have written testimonies for the last section of the book.

One of the side experiences of the summer normals was having student boarders in various homes in the community. The Shetler home was always a busy center during these times, and the fellowship and fun that went with these "dormitory" experiences would also make another interesting chapter.

Through the earlier years the local teachers' institutes, highly recommended by the county superintendent, became a recognized institution. They were the equivalent on the educational level of present-day teachers' conferences and seminars. They were also social events. Once a month, teachers, board members, parents, and young people would gather at a designated schoolhouse for the day's event. Here they would listen to teachers and others discourse on all kinds of topics or debate various issues. Some used this as an opportunity to develop their powers of oratory or to exhibit their knowledge (or expose their ignorance) on a variety of topics. These meetings served a good function, however, and did not lack for interest. The *Johnstown Weekly Tribune* for December 18, 1896, carried the program of one such institute that was scheduled to be held that week at the Saylor schoolhouse near Thomas Mills. Interestingly, the only teacher on the program given the title, "Professor" was twenty-five-year-old S. G. Shetler, which indicates somewhat his professional standing in the township, although by the standards of that time, others on the list would certainly have merited the same title. The scope of topics was fantastic, and considering the long list of speakers, even if each one spoke only 15 or 20 minutes, the day would have been more than spent. The topic, "Bimetallism" carried probably the same emotional charge for this period of the country's history—when citizens and politicans were discussing the question of a double gold-and-silver monetary standard—as a talk on campus riots or the Vietnam War would have carried in the period of the 1960s. And what "Professor" Shetler's talk on "The Character That Was the Battle of Life" was about, is anybody's guess. The entire program as listed in the *Tribune* ran as follows (copied from the original newspaper announcement):

PROGRAMME FOR A TEACHERS' INSTITUTE
at the Saylor Schoolhouse

What Should Directors Know About the Office of School Director? H. F. Brandt

A Year Among the Birds, S. D. Yoder
Kinds of Punishment, J. C. Neff
Promotion of Pupils, J. S. Zimmerman
Bimetallism, H. A. Walker
Child Study, J. J. Stahl
Training for Citizenship, W. A. Saylor
Business Education in Our Public Schools, J. E. Weaver
Simple Lessons in Hygiene, E. R. Blough
School Management, H. H. Mishler
Pleasure of Education, H. L. Swank
The Character That Was the Battle of Life, Prof. S. G. Shetler
Lessons from Nature, H. R. Livingstone
Oration, Daniel E. Heckman
Story of Pennsylvania, N. W. Hoffman
Hobbies in the Schoolroom, S. F. Hammer
Topical Talk, Sem Kaufman
The teachers are requested to bring along a copy of the *Ideal Music Book.*

—From *Weekly Tribune,* Johnstown, Friday, Dec. 18, 1896.

Teaching had definitely become S. G. Shetler's profession, although, as we shall see shortly, much of this was done outside the seven-month terms of the public schoolroom. In the early nineteen hundreds his churchwork began to eclipse his career as a public school teacher. Had he followed this career it might well have carried him to some top positions. The highest post he held, excluding his summer normal school teaching, was his principalship of the Hubbard, Oregon, elementary-secondary school, a job roughly equivalent to that of supervising principal in our current systems. A more complete account of this will be given in the section, "The Oregon Years."

His salary through the years increased gradually. He had started with $24.00 a month in 1887, but by the turn of the century he was getting $40.00 and in Oregon in 1915 this figure had doubled. He wrote on a picture post card from the West to his good friend Samuel Mishler in Pennsylvania, "... we are not coming back this fall. I have a school for next winter at $80.00 a month." The very manner in which he wrote this seemed to indicate his complete satisfaction with such high wages! It was an offer he could not afford to turn down.

Through the years Father seemed to maintain cordial and professional relations with his colleagues, frequently speaking at teachers' institutes and serving on various school committees. He had the privilege of serving under nine different county superintendents, seven in Pennsylvania, two in Oregon. In Pennsylvania these were: E. J. Berkey, E. E. Pritts, D. W. Seibert, John Fike, W. H. Kretchman, and Guy N. Hartman, of Somerset County, and M. S. Bentz of Cambria County.

S. G. Shetler as a Teacher

On the testimony of those who knew him best through the years, "Sam Shetler" (or S.G.) was a born teacher. His wily methods of holding the pupils' attention solved more than half the usual discipline problems. Nothing dragged when he was in charge. The familiar saying, "variety is the spice of life," characterized his teaching throughout. His idea of a good teacher was one who would always "keep a jump ahead of his pupils." For those of us who knew him well as a teacher, it seemed that he was often a good many jumps ahead. The surprise element kept the usual unwary youngsters wary, for no one likes to be made a fool of—too often!

The one-room school was itself an experience. For a teacher to handle all the subjects of the eight grades in one day was almost a juggler's act. It was necessary to have five-minute reading classes, six-minute arithmetic classes, ten-minute history classes, or however it worked out for that day. "Carrying over" classes for the next day was considered a mark of poor teaching. The good teacher was always expected to start each morning fresh with the regular schedule—at least most of the time.

The schedule began in the morning with beginners' reading, known also as the "chart class" (because originally charts with the alphabet and phonic drills were used). This was followed with the other lower grade reading classes, winding up with upper grade arithmetic by recess time. Geography classes came after the morning recess period, following a beginners' "number work" class, and some elementary lower grade geography. Number work for

Shetler included almost anything. It was a kind of m~~~matics-social studies-health-English combination—the forerunner, one might say, to the modern core course idea but of course on a very elementary level. Humorous answers by innocent first graders were a source of amusement for the older pupils who always had the privilege of tuning in on any recitation taking place in the front of the room on the "recitation seats." The afternoon usually started with a music period for the whole room, followed by the language classes. After the last recess came history. Sometimes history and geography were taught on alternate days, to save time. Spelling and handwriting were worked into the day when most convenient.

Friday afternoon in the old country school was always a special event and S. G. delighted in taking advantage of this change of routine. After the last recess there were indoor games or improvised programs. Pupils looked forward to this period with great anticipation. In later years art was often worked into this weekly period. It was expected that there should be at least one period of drawing per week, that is, if the teacher had any artistic ability at all. My father's ability in art was quite limited, but he had unique ways of conducting this class.

Discipline for him was of various sorts, but his method was not to keep pupils after school or to employ some type of deferred punishment. He would rather settle accounts promptly.

In one instance a boy was caught casting reflections around the room with a hand mirror. The young chap had not yet become wise to the Shetler methods. All the while the teacher was trying to locate the offender while professing to be busy teaching. When he finally spotted him he had him come forward with his mirror telling him that since he liked this so well he could stand there and do it for the rest of the day. This was amusing at first, but he soon began to lag in his "shining program." Told to keep on—since this was what he seemed to want to do—the boy continued for a little while longer, more reluctantly by the moment. Finally he broke down and cried. After a few final admonitions by the teacher he was allowed to return to his seat. A simple and effective disciplinary method used frequently was simply to "eye" a pupil. If one or two such silent confrontations did not do the job, he would resort to more severe measures, asking first, however, whether the pupil had seen him looking at him and whether he knew what this meant. For the tenderhearted mere eyeing would make them wilt. Sometimes, too, he would administer a *Kopfsneller*, the Pennsylvania Dutch term for flicking a finger sprung loose from the thumb against the offender's head. He made much use of the surprise element, and as he walked around the room pronouncing words for a spelling class for example, or tending the schoolroom stove, he would suddenly come up on the misbehaving pupil and give him a surprise Kopfsneller. The nearby pupils who saw this could only guess what in the world the poor fellow might have been up to.

While some of these methods may seem a bit outmoded today, there were at least no long-drawn-out counseling sessions to try to discover what kind of childhood traumas were coming to the surface or in what ways the child's emotional mechanisms were out of adjustment. His method was to be firm but not harsh, and whatever its faults, it usually proved effective.

To counterbalance this more negative approach, he would also extend extra privileges for those who cooperated well and did their lessons promptly. He would, for example, extend recess periods when sledding was good in wintertime or whenever pupils had done extra well on an assignment. All of this, with his constant use of humor and his fascinating teaching methods, added up to well-balanced classroom management. He captivated the average youngster and practiced good teaching. Educational psychologists, with all of their theories, might learn from observing some of these old schoolmasters.

S. G. was not to be outdone by his pupils. He was quick-witted. On one occasion a normal school student who had been trying to give the impression constantly that he knew *everything* was framed with a question which the teacher knew could not be answered. The student turned his head from side to side and remarked finally, "I used to know but I forgot." The teacher replied, "What a pity; you're the only one who ever knew and now you forgot!" The "Punxsutawney story" ranks probably among the best to illustrate his method. A new boy had moved in from the town of Punxsutawney in central Pennsylvania to Hooversville, a much smaller town. Coming from the "city schools," he professed to look down on the country methods of his new teacher. He constantly kept saying, regardless of what the teacher tried to do, "That's not the way we did it in Punxutawney." This was finally too much for S. G., and so one day he set a trap for him. He sent him to the blackboard to solve an arithmetic problem which he knew was far beyond him in difficulty. The boy kept working and working and working, passing the weight of his body from one foot to the other and scratching his head. My father meanwhile kept going about other matters casually walking by now and then, asking him, "Is that the way you did it in Punxsutawney?... Is that the way you did it in Punxutawney?" After the boy admitted that he could not do the problem he allowed him to return to his seat. That was the end of "Punxsutawney" for that boy.

But S. G. Shetler, however, also had a very tender heart and was concerned for his pupils. He regularly conducted morning devotions and had the pupils sing religious songs from the hymnbooks he himself supplied. This, of course, was a day when religion was not barred from the schools. He took a personal interest in the moral development of those who needed special help. While teaching in the Benson Borough schools he had a pupil who was a kind of ringleader of the group in mischief and at the same time was not too trustworthy. One day he sent him to the nearby post office for a postage stamp, giving him a five-dollar bill. When the boy returned, the teacher, without counting the change, which was deliberate on his part, put the change into his pocket. The boy was so impressed by this act of trust that he resolved to live up to this confidence. Years later, the boy, then a mature and useful citizen, told my father that this was the turning point in his life. He had been challenged to make something of himself when he realized that someone believed in him.

7

Making a Home and a Life—
Early Years in the Ministry
(1891-1903)

After Samuel Grant Shetler and Maggie Jane Kaufman were married in January 1891, the young couple lived for a time with Samuel's parents. Here their first child, Luella May, was born on February 7, 1892. In the fall of 1894 they purchased a home of their own in the nearby village of Hollsopple, to be nearer to his school. The house, a substantial two-story frame building (still standing, 1980), cost $1250. It stood directly across the street from the hotel, just close to the Baltimore and Ohio railroad station. These were some of the happiest years of their life as a family as my mother often recalled. They made many friends among the townspeople—the Casslers, the Borders, the Helsels, and others. Memories of those early years lingered in the memories of some of the older residents for many years.

My mother used to tell us stories of the many "tramps" who rode the freight trains in those times and who stopped off at various places along the route for handouts. If it is true that they marked the better homes along the route with an "X"—that is, the places where they fared the best—there must surely have been one on the Shetler house. A number of vagrants regularly stopped there. But my mother had one rule for all who cashed in on her generosity: they were always required to chop some firewood or do some other household chores before the meal. Her staunch background of hard work could not easily accede to welfare handouts! Incidentally, at that time passenger trains were also still operating between the mainline B. and O. Railroad which passed east and west through Rockwood in southern Somerset County and the city of Johnstown which lay to the north in Cambria County.

In Hollsopple three more of the children were born: Rosella Mary, May 12, 1895, and Ralph and Rena, twins, born June 11, 1899. A few months later the twins died of spinal meningitis—Rena, September 29, and Ralph, October 17. The story of those anxious days formed a very sad chapter in the life of the family. The tiny bodies were twisted with pain as the disease took its course, and the family experienced heartaches and sorrow as they saw the children pass on. The story was often retold. Hard as it was to give them up, my father often remarked that at least in the case of Ralph, God's providence may have been manifest. Had he lived he would have been of draft age in 1917 when many young men were being drafted and marched off to war and some conscientious objectors were being tested for their faith in the military camps.

Two other important events took place during the Hollsopple years. In 1894 S. G. Shetler was ordained to the office of deacon. He was then 23. A brief note in the *Herald of Truth*, the official church paper, submitted by "Little Levi" Blauch, a member of his home church who wrote many articles for the *Herald*, stated that on the twentieth of May a deacon had been ordained at the Stahl church, "the lot falling on Brother S. G. Shetler." The writer added, "May God help him to be faithful to his calling, and let us pray earnestly for him." In his new calling he tried to perform his duties faithfully. As an example of his compassion he took it upon himself to provide for a poor family in the community which some in the congregation felt was not worthy of help. His motto in his new role, as in every other undertaking of his life, was, "Whatsoever thy hand findeth to do, do it with thy might." Looking over the deacon records he kept, one gains some idea of the support for the poor in that period when there was no government aid. It was support which by modern standards seems quite meager.

Three years later, my father was ordained to the ministry. The story of that call was somewhat unique. He was not, for example, selected by lot from a list of candidates nominated by the church, which was the more-or-less usual method in Mennonite circles. Nor was the call initiated by the congregation. Jonas Blauch, who had been called into the Johnstown area some years earlier to serve as bishop, saw the need of providing leadership for the district. The Johnstown district was short of ministerial help, and Blauch saw the need of having a team of young English-speaking preachers in a time of transition from the German to the English language among Mennonites of the area. Accordingly he began to supply this need. Blauch himself was able to bridge this gap in this crucial period for the district, since he himself was fluent in both languages. In 1890 he had ordained L. A. Blough, a young schoolteacher, and now he took it upon himself to ask conference for permission to ordain Deacon Shetler to the ministry. The answer to his request came in the form of a resolution:

> Resolved that the Southwestern Pennsylvania Conference believes that God has qualified Bro. S. G. Shetler for the office of the ministry and we unanimously call him to that office in the fear of the Lord, and authorize Bishop Jonas Blauch to ordain him by the counsel and consent of the church.

A notable event took place soon afterward in the Stahl church which no doubt had a molding influence on the life of the new minister. The second Bible Conference to be held in the Mennonite Church was held here in 1898, the first having been held the previous year at Scottdale, Pennsylvania. Bible Conferences came to be a phenomenon in Mennonite Church life for years, as we shall note later. These were simply extended periods of Bible studies—usually of a week's duration, with the instructors representing some of the denomination's top leaders.

According to the testimony of those who attended Bible

Conference at the Stahl Church, 1898, this must have been a stirring event.[12] Those who served as instructors were: Daniel Kauffman, A. D. Wenger, J. S. Coffman, D. H. Bender, and M. S. Steiner. So good was the effect of the first week of daily sessions that it was decided by popular vote to continue a second week. In a day when personal schedules of churchleaders were not so crowded that they could not easily be altered, the speakers were all able to stay without any apparent conflicts in their programs. Likewise there was no heavy program of district events which conflicted nor were the people tied to jobs which would prevent their attendance.

There is no doubt that this two-week session of Bible conference became for S. G. Shetler a training school in teaching techniques, as well as providing for him the much-needed inspiration for his new task in the ministry. Observing these gifted preachers and teachers he undoubtedly tried to emulate them and gained from them also the deep convictions for the doctrines of the Bible and loyalty to the Mennonite faith. All this most certainly helped to prepare him for the Bible conference ministry that lay ahead for him.

While a new epoch had begun for him with the call to a life of service in the ministry, another epoch had ended with the family's decision to leave their home in Hollsopple and to establish a home near the Stahl meetinghouse. This took place in 1900, and will be discussed later.

Early Years in the Ministry (1897-1903)

S. G. Shetler was ordained to the ministry on Sunday, April 1897, at the age of 26 years, and on June 1, a Tuesday, he was called upon to preach his first sermon—strangely, a funeral sermon. The place was the Blough Church and the occasion the sudden passing of A. A. (Abe) Blough, who had been stricken in death by typhoid fever at the age of "35 years, one month, and 15 days." Abe, brother to preacher L. A. Blough, was a schoolteacher, and he had also been actively used in church work as a song leader and music instructor. It was a sad event. Young

Blough left behind a widow with a number of small children, the youngest, Stephen, still an infant. The widow who later remarried, is best remembered by the older folks of the community as the late Mrs. Silas Thomas. Stephen is still living at this writing (1980). It apparently seemed appropriate to the family to call upon the newly ordained minister, also a schoolteacher, to perform the funeral service, and it proved to be a good introduction to his ministry with the large assembly of area people present. His text for the message was Daniel 12:2, "And many of them that sleep in the dust of the earth shall awake, some to everlasting life, and some to shame and everlasting contempt."

In the years ahead S. G. Shetler became a frequent choice for preaching funeral services. He could seemingly always strike a very personal note in his message, drawing from life many illustrations to bring the message home to his listeners in a forceful manner. He spoke with emotion, frequently weeping as he spoke. He had learned to "weep with those who weep."

His first regular Sunday morning message was preached at the Weaver Church. At that time preaching appointments in the district were on a circuit. This was on June 6. The text for this service was John 1:29, a most appropriate theme to begin his ministry—"Behold the Lamb of God, which taketh away the sin of the world."

His third sermon, and the first at the home church, was preached on June 13 at Stahl. The text for this sermon was Jeremiah 6:16: "Thus saith the Lord, Stand ye in the ways, and see, and ask for the old paths, where is the good way, and walk therein. . . ." This seemed to be prophetic of his burden for the years ahead of trying to remain close to the traditions of the faith and the Word.

Interestingly, his sixth sermon was also another "first" for him, this being his first sermon in a church outside his own faith. This was delivered at the Roxbury (Johnstown) Methodist Episcopal Church on the evening of July 4. The text was Psalm 92:2, "To shew forth thy loving-kindness in the morning, and thy faithfulness every night." It was a repeat sermon of the one he had used that morning at the Thomas Church.

For the first number of years my father kept a careful record of all his sermons—the date, place, and text. This, incidentally, was the time when preachers were expected to preach on *texts*, meaning, a particular verse of Scripture. In his lifetime he preached approximately six thousand sermons, many of which he repeated numerous times. Some texts, for example, became classics: "What is that in thine hand?" (Exodus 4:2); "Hast thou entered into the treasures of the snow?" (Job 38:22); "Canst thou bind the sweet influences of Pleiades, or loose the bands of Orion?" (Job 38:31); "How shall I give thee up?" (Hosea 11:8); or "The harvest is past, the summer is ended, and we are not saved" (Jeremiah 8:20). To this day they are remembered by numerous persons across the church.

My father's first preaching experience outside his home conference area came very early in his ministry. Often in that period ministers made a visiting tour of churches in a neighboring county or state as the occasion afforded, all, of course, without previous arrangement. This is apparently the way this tour into central and eastern Pennsylvania was carried out. This trip helped introduce S. G. Shetler to the church at large and marked the beginning of an enlarged ministry. In the years ahead he was invited to speak again in these churches on many different occasions.

During this particular tour my father spoke in 24 different churches in a two-week period from August 20 to September 5, 1898. He was then 27 years old. His itinerary was as follows:

First Extended Preaching Tour Away from Home
(August 20-September 5, 1898)

Franconia Conference

1. Vincent, Chester County	August 20	Saturday
2. Coventry (Building 100 years old)	21	Sunday
Vincent	21	Sunday
Vincent	21	Sunday
3. Providence, Montgomery County	22	Monday

Lancaster Conference

4. Kinzer	23	Tuesday
5. Old Road	24	Wednesday

6. Weaverland (First evening meeting ever held
   in this church). . . . . .August 24 - 8:00 p.m., Wednesday
7. Groffdale . . . . .25 - 9:00 a.m., Thursday
8. Stumptown . . . . .25 - 2:00 p.m., Thursday
9. Paradise . . . . .25 - 2:00 p.m., Thursday
10. Strasburg . . . . .26 - 9:00 a.m., Friday
11. Byerland . . . . .26 - 2:00 p.m., Friday
12. Lancaster City. . . . . .26 - 7:30 p.m., Friday
13. Mechanicsville . . . . 27 - 2:00 p.m., Saturday
14. Rohrerstown . . . . .27 - 7:30 p.m., Saturday
15. Stone Church . . . . .28 - 9:00 a.m., Sunday
16. Landisville Church . . . . .28 - 7:30 p.m., Sunday
17. Masonville. . . . . .29 - 7:30 p.m., Monday
18. Florin Methodist Church . . . . .30 - 7:30 p.m., Tuesday
19. Good's Church . . . . .31 - 9:00 a.m., Wednesday
20. Slate Hill Church . . . . .31 - 7:30 p.m., Wednesday
    Slate Hill Church . . . . .September 1 - 10:00 a.m., Thursday
21. Mechanicsburg . . . . .1 - 7:30 p.m., Thursday
22. Churchtown (Cumberland Co.) . . . . .2 - 7:30 p.m., Friday

Mifflin County Amish Churches
23. Allensville Amish Church . . . . .3 - 8:00 p.m., Saturday
24. Belleville Amish Church . . . . .4 - 10:00 a.m., Sunday
    Belleville Amish Church . . . . .4 - 8:00 p.m., Sunday
    Allensville Amish Church . . . . .5 - 8:00 p.m., Monday

A Review of the First 751 Sermons

As already mentioned, my father kept a record of his first 751
sermons, the place, date, and text. A review of these shows some
interesting facts concerning his choice of texts, and the wide
extent of his ministry. He launched his ministry with the same
kind of crowded schedule that was to mark his entire life. He kept
his data in small notebooks. For some reason the second one is
missing, so that the dates covered in the two remaining ones cover
the periods from June 1, 1897 (the date of the first sermon), to
May 5, 1899, and again from March 1, 1901 (sermon 414) to February 15, 1903 (sermon 751). His own summary at the end of book
3 covers the total period from 1897 to 1903 and runs as follows:

Total number of sermons. 751
Funerals 60
Baptisms 29
Marriages 23

The average number of sermons for the first year (7 months) was

6.5 per month. For the next 22 months covered by book 2 it was 12 per month, and for the next two years until March 1, 1901, it was 14.3. He averaged each year for these five years in round numbers, 150 sermons (including 12 funerals, 6 baptisms, and 4 weddings).

The rapid increase in the number of sermons in the first few years reflects the widening extent of his ministry, which began to include his evangelistic services. These involved as a rule nightly services over a period of a week or two. A listing of the texts used with a brief analysis of the number of books of the Bible covered, as well as the frequency of use of the various texts makes an interesting study. There is also a record of his first 24 funerals from June 1, 1897, to May 5, 1899. The following data includes the "firsts" of S. G. Shetler's ministry and the churches in which he preached outside his own denomination in the first few years:

1. First sermon (and funeral), Blough Church . . . . June 1, 1897
2. First Sunday morning sermon, Weaver Church. . . . . June 6, 1897
3. First Sunday morning sermon at his home church . . . . . . June 13, 1897
4. First sermon at a church of another faith
   (Roxbury Methodist Episcopal, Johnstown, Pa.). . . . . . . July 4, 1897
5. First services outside Johnstown area, Rockton, Pa. . . . . . July 25, 1897
6. First wedding, Edwin Griffith and Mollie Blough
   (in the Johnstown area) . . . . October 23, 1897
7. First evangelistic meetings, Martinsburg, Pa. . . . . April 1-6, 1898
8. First communion service, Casselman Church, near
   Grantsville, Maryland . . . . May 29, 1898
9. First topical sermon (subject "Foot Washing," John 13)
   Weaver Church . . . . June 5, 1898
10. First German Service, Miller Amish Church, Johnstown
    area . . . . July 1, 1898
11. First baptism, Amanda Yoder, wife of Joseph Yoder,
    at Davidsville, Pa. . . . . August 10, 1898
12. First sermon outside conference area (text Ephesians 3:15), Vincent
    Church, Chester County, Pa. . . . . August 20, 1898
13. First evening service ever held at the Weaverland
    Mennonite Church, Lancaster County (text
    John 1:29) . . . . August 24, 1898

14. First series of meetings (presumably of an
    evangelistic nature) in his home district,
    Weaver Church ....December 23-25, 1898
15. First Bible Conference, Folk Church (now
    Springs, (Pa.) ....January 1, 1899
16. First Sunday School Conference in which he
    served ....October 13, 14, 1897

Sermons at Churches of Other Denominations—June 1, 1897 to May 5,
1899

1. Roxbury Methodist Episcopal Church, Johnstown, Pa. . . .July 4, 1897
2. Bethel (Hollsopple, Pa.) United Brethren Church . . . .August 15, 1897
3. Roxbury Methodist Episcopal Church,
   Johnstown, Pa. . . . . .August 29, 1897
4. Union Chapel, Westmont, Johnstown, Pa. . . . . . .September 12, 1897
5. Union Chapel, Westmont, Johnstown, Pa. . . . . .December 5, 1897
6. Union Chapel, Westmont, Johnstown, Pa. . . . . .March 26, 1898
7. Union Chapel, Westmont, Johnstown, Pa. . . . . .March 27, 1898
8. Bethel (Hollsopple, Pa.) United Brethren Church . . . . .April 16, 1898
9. Union Chapel, Westmont, Johnstown, Pa. . . . . .June 19, 1898
10. Bethel (Hollsopple, Pa.) United Brethren Church . . . . . .June 20, 1898
11. United Brethren Church, Lovett, Pa. . . . . .June 26, 1898
12. Miller Amish Church, near Johnstown, Pa. . . . . .July 1, 1898
13. Bethel (Hollsopple, Pa.) United Brethren Church . . . . . . .July 6, 1898
14. Middlecreek Dunkard Church. . . .(3 services)   July 30, 31, 1898
15. Florin Methodist Church, Lancaster County, Pa. . . . .August 30, 1898
16. Bethel (Hollsopple, Pa.) United Brethren Church
    (2 services) ....October 2, 1898
17. Union Chapel, Westmont, Johnstown, Pa. . . . . .November 6, 1898
18. Hollsopple Reformed Church . . . . .February 12, 1899
19. Hollsopple Reformed Church . . . . .February 19, 1899
20. Union Chapel, Westmont, Johnstown, Pa. . . . . .March 26, 1899[13]

S. G. Shetler as a Preacher

Almost from the beginning of his preaching it became apparent that the new minister had an unusual gift for "riveting" a

text in the minds of his listeners and of holding the attention of both young and old. He had, as the late Grant Stoltzfus of Eastern Mennonite College remembered him, "acumen"—"a sharp and penetrating and widely perceptive mind" which captivated people's minds.[14]

S. G. Shetler was thoroughly at home in the pulpit, using a unique style that marked his preaching. His delivery was not the dry didactic style of many lecturers, nor did he use a kind of monotonous "ministerial" drone that lulls people to sleep. He spoke fast and made constant use of inflection to accentuate certain phrases he wanted people to remember. Soon after his ordination my father had gone to Preacher Gid Miller of Springs, whom he admired as an interesting and practical speaker, for advice. Gid remarked, "Preach the Bible and when you're through stop." He often referred to this and in his ministry practiced it.

Although he was not an orator in the classical sense, he is interestingly remembered by one well-known Mennonite attorney, Samuel S. Wenger of Lancaster, Pa., as one of the two "orators" he had heard in his youth: "William Jennings Bryan and S. G. Shetler!"[15]

My father made much use of pathos and humor and could sway an audience from tears to laughter in a matter of moments. He used this ability not altogether without design, yet not merely to manipulate his audience. He often referred to the old saying, the "well of tears and the fountain of laughter lie close together." If a person's attention could be gained by humor, he could also be moved to tears—tears for his own spiritual condition. To him it was thus a means of reaching the heart and not merely an end in itself. Though using humor as a means of facilitating communication, he certainly did not make use of light humor or levity. Modern speakers frequently use jokes to loosen up an audience, but their messages seldom produce tears. Tears perhaps do not fit too well to the sophisticated mood of our times.

It would be interesting to know how much the rhetorical style of the period might have been reflected in my father's own pulpit style. This was the era of such great pulpit orators as Henry

Ward Beecher, Henry Drummond, G. Campbell Morgan, S. Parkes Cadman, John A. Broadus, Ernest Roland Wilberforce, Henry Van Dyke, Thomas De Witt Talmadge, Charles Hadden Spurgeon, Lyman Abbot, Philip Brooks, and Dwight Lyman Moody. He rarely referred to big-name preachers and theologians in his preaching, however. He preferred to quote Bible characters. Nevertheless, it is not unlikely that he had on occasion read some of the sermons of those great men which were frequently printed in the newspapers and magazines of the day. As I recall, he had a book of Spurgeon's sermons and also a book of quotations, not to mention other Bible helps, such as commentaries.

His sermon preparation was simple, consisting chiefly of studying a particular passage of Scripture and deducting practical points. Or he assembled a battery of well-chosen verses to fit some topical outline he had prepared. His thorough familiarity with the Bible made it easy to find verses to illuminate the points he wished to make. He was more textual and topical in his approach than exegetical or expository, though the latter methods were by no means foreign to him. It was simply that he seemed to prefer the other methods. The brief notes he used would make most students of homiletics feel insecure. They were usually written on a very small sheet of notebook paper, or sometimes on the clean side of a used envelope. They were simple and clear with the points stated very concisely. A few of the many sermon outlines preserved appear in the appendix. Illustrations which he pulled from his wide experience and reading and which he thought were particularly suited to a particular message were listed at the bottom of the sheet. A glance at these would refresh his memory and he would then select the ones he felt he wished to use for the occasion.

His sermon preparation time may have taken anywhere from a half hour to several hours depending on the topic or occasion. Asked to preach, as he so frequently was on short notice, he would not worry if he was not prepared—that is in the conventional sense. He might simply jot down some points while on his way to the church or even while another speaker was on the floor when he was asked at the last minute to fill in for some other speaker or to take an added assignment. This would never bother him. He would never refuse simply because he did not have time to prepare. It was, in fact, a rule with him never to turn down any request unless he had very good reasons for doing so, believing that God would supply the need.

All this is not to say, however, that he always spoke off the cuff with minimal preparation. There were those times when he became quite deep, and, when the occasion demanded, he could deliver a very systematic and well-developed message. Basically, however, he was the "people's preacher" and his messages were aimed at the pew and not at the intelligentsia. He had no room for lengthy read sermons couched in stilted terms, and he was so natured that he could not content himself with a lot of research and the development of lengthy propositions.

My father's library was not very large, but he had the basic tools needed to study. I know he made use of a Greek lexicon, and, as mentioned, a good concordance and commentaries. Sources outside the Bible were for him as a matter of principle, truly secondary, and although he considered them valuable reference material, he did not make use of many quotations. The magazines he used included, through the years, some of the news magazines currently published, copies of which he would frequently buy at newsstands while waiting for a train. He was a subscriber to *Pathfinder,* a news magazine, somewhat comparable to our present *Newsweek.* He also received several farm and family magazines. I do not recall that he subscribed to very many religious periodicals outside our own church publications, which he read faithfully. For a time he was a subscriber to the *Christian Herald.*

While he might not necessarily be characterized as a scholarly man, my father was nevertheless academically alert. He constantly tried to keep abreast with new ideas and with the times. At the same time he was not one to accept readily every new idea that came floating along. His measuring stick was always, "Does it (the idea) stand the test of Scripture?" He was particularly sensitive, too, to word meanings, and tried to keep his English in line with current usage. Much of his freshness he gained from association with other ministers and teachers in his school and church work and from lectures at the yearly County Teachers' Institutes. These included such notables as the American writer Hamlin Garland, Evangelist Sam Jones, and the well-known Baptist preacher who delivered his famous lecture "Acres of Diamonds," Russell Conwell.

In speaking he tried to follow the accepted principles of rhetoric and homiletics. His use of various figures of speech was deliberate. As indicated, he was a stickler for the use of correct English and he avoided farfetched and bookish illustrations. Instead, his illustrations were generally drawn from his years of experience as a pastor, teacher, and evangelist. He also had the unique ability of camouflaging the characters of his personal stories in such a way that a person involved in the story could be seated right before him and not be able to identify himself. He also used himself in illustrations, frequently in the third person, without the audience being aware of this. He would refer, for example, to "a man whom he had known for many years," who was very selfish, and then went on to illustrate how this selfishness was demonstrated, all the while talking about himself.

S.G., as he was commonly known, was noted for his rapid-fire speaking and for his sometimes shrill voice, which occasionally frightened small children. But there never was any guessing as to who was speaking or what the speaker was trying to say. His movement on the platform and gesturing helped to keep the eyes of his listeners fastened on him in rapt attention.

The late Bishop Oscar Burkholder of Canada remembered hearing S. G. Shelter for the first time at Breslau in the early 1900s, in the same church where he himself later served as pastor. Upon entering the service he saw seated on the rostrum the short, slender young man who was to be the speaker for the evening and began to wonder whether it had been worth coming. But when the youthful evangelist took his place behind the pulpit young Burkholder's mind began to change rapidly. The stirring message so captivated him that by the time the sermon ended, he resolved to change his plans for his life career. Burkholder at the time was not a member of the church.

My father's preaching was certainly not without its faults. Some felt he frequently made an overuse of humor and pathos. He, in fact, on several occasions publicly acknowledged his "weakness" for humor. Actually, his most appreciated sermons were some of those without much of laughter or tears. He tended too, in later years, to repeat himself and to use too frequently the same illustrations before the same audiences, unaware of doing this apparently. In spite of his own free use of gesture and humor, he was opposed to "clowning" in the pulpit. Largely for this reason he could not appreciate Billy Sunday's methods, and he discouraged attendance at his meetings when the famous evangelist conducted his Johnstown campaign in the fall of 1913. It is not unlikely that he had this in mind when he wrote in *The Christian Worker's Manual*, published two years later: "When Satan can get some minister to turn the sacred stand into the platform or stage or a theater, and can get the minister himself to appear as an actor instead of as a man of God, burdened for the welfare of never-dying souls, one victory is won by the destroyer of souls."

According to the testimonies of many individuals, as well as my own personal evaluation, the human qualities that made his preaching great and that characterized him as a preacher were these: He was a textual preacher using short and pointed texts that could easily be remembered and would leave a vivid impression. He inspired persons to appreciate their own abilities, however limited, and to work with what was at hand. He gave the common people a sense of belonging. He deepened everyone's appreciation for the church and its doctrines. He had an unusual gift for driving conviction into the hearts of the unsaved. He used a lucid, clipped style, sparkling with live illustrations. He never wrote out his sermons and spoke with very few notes but with deep persuasiveness in a direct forthright manner. He used simple words that everyone could understand. He was in every sense the layman's preacher.

As both a grammarian and public speaker, he was always ready, when appropriate, to give helpful advice to young ministers who had had very little formal training. He helped them, too, in overcoming mannerisms.

Few men are blessed with as good a memory as he possessed. He was especially adept at recalling Scriptures and quoting them from memory. But he could also turn to a particular passage in a moment. Holding his well-worn, thumb-indexed Bible in his left hand he would turn to the specific Scripture he wanted to refer to with a characteristic flip of his hand, the Bible seemingly always opening exactly at the right place. This always impressed his audiences.

Only one time, however, was he unable to find his text as he attempted to begin his sermon. Not to be embarrassed, he finally simply opened his Bible at random and quoted the text as well as he could from memory. In relating this anecdote numerous times through the years, he said that as luck would have it, that same day his dinner host related a story of a minister who one time could not find his text! My father laughed with the rest of the guests at this very amusing incident, not revealing that this had been his own problem that very day!

My father's ability to recall names was outstanding. Many times in my own ministry I have been bluntly reminded that apparently I did not have the same talent! Dale Carnegie said that the sweetest word in the English language is one's own name, and the Apostle Paul said, "Greet thy friends by name." It is a great point of contact. My father, however, actually made a science of memorizing names. It was not all sheer talent. He kept strict records of all the families he visited in his evangelistic services. These lists for his forty years of service include 33,770 names. Before returning to a given locality he would simply get out his little folded sheet of paper on which he had written the names for that particular congregation, trying to visualize the changes in appearance the years might have brought. Imagine the look of surprise on a person's face, particularly a youth, when he was greeted by name at the church door or in his home.

In a letter to Bishop L. J. Heatwole in 1903 he asked for a more complete list of the family names of the church near Dayton, Virginia, where he had just concluded a series of meetings. Apparently as he was reviewing the list he was trying to fix names and faces in his mind. In one of the many lists of names on file there is one particular entry that holds very special interest for me. I remember his showing this to me one time in the last years of his life as he was going through his records. In 1910 when he was holding meetings at Minot, North Dakota, he tried to get a complete list of all the families of that region and was told there were some Mennonite families living at Coalridge, Montana, just across the Dakota line. In the list was the name of a little two-year-old girl, Florence Hazel Young, daughter of Fred and Janie Young. Little did he imagine at the time that twenty-two years later this same little girl would become his daughter-in-law!

As already indicated, my father's ministry away from home began to blossom about the turn of the century. In the years between 1900 and 1903 he held revival meetings in Pennsylvania, Maryland, Ohio, and Indiana. These meetings were, of course, in addition to a busy schedule in his home area. The pattern that one observes in going over his schedule for the years from 1903 on is quite similar. In those years when he was not teaching school, roughly from 1904 to 1912, he held revival meetings in the early months of each year and revival meetings and Bible conferences in the fall. From April to September he was at home. During eight of these weeks each year, from mid-April to mid-June, he conducted his summer normals, and the remainder of the summer he was engaged in truck farming.

It has been possible to reconstruct almost entirely his yearly schedules, but for obvious reasons we cannot include all of those. The schedule for 1902 is reproduced in its entirety in chapter 9. It is quite typical of the early years of his ministry and should afford some idea of his work pattern. Several more of these early years will be covered in summary form in the next chapter. A few of his retirement years' schedules will be reproduced in a later chapter. The comparison between his early years and later years is striking.

With but little variation he maintained a rigorous program of church and school activity from 1897 to 1942.

In 1903, when my father was 32 years old, he was voted for as a candidate for the office of bishop of the Johnstown area churches. The lot, however, fell upon James Saylor who was three years his senior. The ordination took place on May 23, and on May 25 my father wrote in a letter to Bishop L. J. Heatwole in Virginia, "On Saturday Bro. James Saylor, one of our ministers, was ordained bishop. We believe this is quite satisfactory to the church."

Twelve years later, however, he was ordained to this office in Oregon. Saylor served the Johnstown area churches for many years and outlived my father by more than 20 years. At the time of his death, Saylor was the senior bishop of the Mennonite Church in the United States and Canada. In some of the last years of my father's life he and Bishop Saylor served conjointly in the oversight of the new Mennonite congregation in the city of Johnstown.

In February 1903, Samuel and Maggie's oldest daughter, Luella, aged 11, was baptized at the Stahl Church. She was one of a large class of converts, including also her uncle Harry B. Kaufman. My father and mother lived to see all of their children baptized into the Christian faith and become active members of the Mennonite Church.

8
Evangelist and Bible Conference Speaker

As far as is known, the first revival meetings held in the Mennonite Church were held by John F. Funk and Daniel Brenneman, two Mennonite leaders, at the Masontown (Pa.) Church, January and February, 1872. At these meetings John N. Durr, an eighteen-year-old youth from nearby Greene County, was led to Christ. At this time, very interestingly, he was also ordained to the ministry. Young as he was, however, he was not considered a novice but as one who had stability and potential leadership qualities. Less than two years later, he was ordained to the office of bishop. In 1876 Durr was able to help found the new Southwestern Pennsylvania Mennonite Conference (now Allegheny Conference). This was done under the direction of several bishops representing what might be considered the mother conference, the Lancaster Mennonite Conference.

In December 1891, the new bishop came into the Johnstown area to hold "continued meetings" in the style of Funk and Brenneman. At these meetings Samuel G. Shetler and Maggie Jane Kaufman, with sixteen other young people, accepted Christ and subsequently became members of the Mennonite Church.

When my father was ordained to the ministry in 1897 he immediately felt that he should use his gifts in the area of evangelism as opportunity afforded. There is no doubt that he desired to emulate J. N. Durr, John S. Coffman, A. D. Wenger, and others whom he had come to hear in the early years of his life and ministry. These men were at the time outstanding evangelists in the denomination. In time he also came to be one of these himself. John C. Wenger, in *The Mennonite Church of North America* (1966) lists S. G. Shetler as one of the "outstanding evangelists of the past seventy-five years."[16]

As noted in the previous chapter, his first revival meetings were held at Martinsburg, Pa., just one year after his ordination, from Friday, April 1, to Wednesday evening, April 6, 1898. The texts from which he preached were: Psalm 13:6; Genesis 3:9; 1 Kings 10:19; Luke 15:24; Joshua 2:21; Psalm 37:25, and John 14:21. These texts would be used many times in later revivals.

In the years ahead he came to conduct revival meetings in more than 200 churches in the United States and Canada. In the course of these meetings, he visited in more than 8,000 homes, an accomplishment likely unequaled by any other evangelist in the entire history of the Mennonite Church.[17] John Wesley, the famous English evangelist, had visited many homes in his long ministry. It was said that "the households which entertained him [Wesley] were captivated and boasted of the honor ever after." So many evangelists of our time prefer not to do much, if any, home visiting, concentrating on the platform messages. Contacts they do make outside the building are usually with the pastor or with church officials. The "common man" is slighted. Visiting in homes and getting acquainted with the families can be a grueling task, when after visiting all day, the evangelist has to appear at his best for the evening service. But it makes it easy to communicate in the public setting.

Frequently in the winter months revival meetings were held in connection with Bible conferences in which other speakers served. For some years my father conducted evangelistic services and Bible conferences during major portions of the year, reserving only the summer months for his teachers' normal school and his modest truck-farming operation.

The Bible conferences were a phenomenon of the Mennonite Church in the early part of this century. Their effectiveness is still recognized, however, by many denominations, and in some parts of the Mennonite Church. There was an era, however, in which they seemed to flourish in a marked way. During that period at the end of the nineteenth and the beginning of the twentieth centuries they served as a training school for many future church workers. At that time Mennonites were still basically a rural people and were able to take time off to attend church services during weekdays. Many of these revival meetings and Bible conferences were held in the winter months when farm work was slack.

Considering the large part these two institutions played in the life of the church, S. G. Shetler's role in both, it seems appropriate to take a more detailed look at them.

Revival Meetings

Many recall with a certain nostalgia the fervor and interest that went into the revival meetings of that period. During a given revival series, chores on the farm were completed early in the evening and a note of expectancy filled the air as the typical Mennonite family prepared for the evening service. Sometimes people would drive for miles each evening in the family buggy, surrey, or buckboard, and later the car. The meetinghouse was usually packed, which lent to the excitement and emotional atmosphere. The whole community turned out, including many "outsiders." This was, of course, in a day when there were very few other activities in a community.

Each evangelist had his own style and routine. This for S. G. included either children's meetings or pre-sermon talks (sometimes both) followed by a short, stirring evangelistic message. The service always closed with an invitation to accept Christ, which, in my father's case, was never drawn out.

S. G. Shetler was remembered, among other things, for his punctuality. Many ministers waited until most of the congregation had gathered before the minister would announce the open-

ing hymn, but not he. When the designated time for the opening
of the meeting had arrived, he would begin the meeting, even if
the home preacher himself had not arrived. Stragglers soon
learned that if they were not there on time, they would miss
something. He was a man of variety, too, and kept things moving
from the first song to the benediction, which, incidentally, was
also on time! He did not believe in dragging out any service,
much less a revival meeting. The main objective was to move
people toward love of—not hatred of—Christ and the church.

When S. G. took his place behind the pulpit and announced
his text the atmosphere seemed to be electrified. It is difficult to
explain, but as many still recall, including the writer, he could
send a thrill through the congregation with the mere announcement of the text. Just the way he read it—and it was usually
short—made it stand out boldly as God's Word for that hour.
Richard Martin, himself a pastor and evangelist, wrote (1971),
"He seemed to breathe the very air of divine revelation."[18]

Frequently conviction seemed to seize those who were not
"right with God," almost from the beginning of a service. By the
time the invitation was given there was no need of coaxing to get
responses. His method of announcing an invitation song, almost
with the last word of his message, was also very effective. The
spirit of the message seemed to flow right into the song.

My father was perhaps weakest in his method of dealing
with converts, that is, on the level of personal counseling and dealing with an individual's own problems. He did not have "after-
meetings," but simply gave each one who had made a public
commitment a brief word of encouragement afterwards. His main
work was in the pulpit. Toward the end of a given series of meetings, however, he would have the "class" of converts come forward each night to occupy the front seats for special instructions
on the Christian life. In this way the whole audience could benefit
from the teaching. In his long campaign in Ontario in 1908 he
instructed, in an all-day meeting, the hundred converts which had
come from the various churches of Waterloo County. These meetings for converts were both of a doctrinal and practical nature

with an aim at motivating everyone to become staunch Bible Christians. It was impressive to see a group, sometimes a very large group, come forward to occupy the front benches for this part of the meeting. Sometimes through this others were inspired to "join the class."

What made his sermons live was his dramatic use of timely illustrations taken from his personal experience in evangelistic work. Another favorable feature, already mentioned, was his handling of the Bible in the pulpit. He could turn rapidly from one Scripture to another. He quoted few men, but many Bible verses. He never spoke in platitudes. He had a remarkable way too of reaching older people and hardened sinners who seemed unreachable. The records show that his converts included a wide spread of age-groups. I shall never forget one meeting in my home area when the building was packed on a Sunday night and the last stanza of the invitation was being sung. In that audience sat a middle-aged father, highly respected in the community but not a Christian. For years there had been concern for him. The song was drawing to a close, when to the joyful surprise of many, he rose to his feet to accept Christ. The whole audience was stirred and many wept. It was an unforgettable evening and it demonstrated the kind of spirit which drew people to his services night after night.

The unusual combination of natural abilities with a definite emotional element coupled in turn with a skillful use of the Word of God under the power of the Holy Spirit made my father's meetings very powerful and effective. Although his own part in the meetings was certainly not to be minimized, S. G. Shetler never conducted "Shetler" revivals. Interestingly, too, a high percentage of those who confessed in his meetings also became accessions to the church and members of the Mennonite Church. As stated numerous times, he never made apologies for the teachings of his church, which he insisted were also Bible teachings and hence to be kept by everyone, not only by Mennonites.

In later years "boys' and girls' meetings" became a powerful adjunct to his revival meetings. These will be discussed later.

Bible Conferences—The Story of a Man and an Era

As already stated, Bible conferences played an important role in the life of the Mennonite Church for many years, and my father's name came to be associated with these in a major way.

The exact time and place of the first Bible conference is not known, but there were several such conferences held toward the end of the 1800s. It used to be stated that the first one was held at Scottdale, Pennsylvania, in 1896, but John S. Coffman, who served as an instructor in that meeting and also at Johnstown a year later, wrote in the preface of the little booklet, *Outlines and Notes*, prepared after the latter meeting: "For several years some of the ministers of our Mennonite congregations have been holding Bible conferences at various places for special study of Scripture subjects."[19] Apparently the Scottdale conference was quite outstanding and for that reason came to be remembered above the earlier conferences. It also came to serve as a model for later meetings.

The promotion of this new type of Christian educational ministry in the church can well be attributed to Aaron Loucks, pastor of the Scottdale Church, who arranged for the conference at his home church. In 1894 he had enrolled as a student at Moody Bible Institute in Chicago, where he sat under the teaching of some prominent Bible teachers of the time. Observing the Bible conference work carried on by such men as R. A. Torrey, Loucks conceived the idea that this kind of teaching would fill a real need among the rank and file of the membership of his own church. He began to promote conferences in his home church and conference district.

Instructors for the Scottdale conference (Dec. 1896-Jan. 1897), besides Coffman, who was from Indiana, were M. S. Steiner of Ohio and D. H. Bender of nearby Springs. The "Second Annual Bible Conference" for the Mennonites of southwestern Pennsylvania was held, as already indicated, at Johnstown at the Stahl meetinghouse from December 17, 1897, to January 8, 1898. The same men served here who had served at Scottdale, in addition to two new instructors: A. D. Wenger of eastern Pennsylvania and Daniel Kauffman of Missouri. It was a powerful team of young church leaders and they left a great impact on the respective communities. Their use of systematic outlines for the teaching of the Scriptures was something new and as Coffman wrote, concerning the Johnstown conference, "The desire became general to have the outlines published in a convenient little book." This resulted in the booklet *Outlines and Notes*, which was published that same year, a copy of which the writer has in his cherished possession.[20]

The third annual conference for the Southwestern Pennsylvania Conference area was held at Springs, Pennsylvania, from December 1898 to January 6, 1899. The same team of instructors was used, adding still another, J. A. Ressler of Scottdale.

The pattern had now been set. The churches involved in this experimental stage had proved to the church at large that a new movement had begun which was entirely worthy of support. Not all areas of the church were, however, ready to accept immediately this new kind of teaching agency. As the records indicate, although the conferences were started in the latter part of the 1800s, it took a number of years until they became widespread. But by 1905 there was clear evidence that the movement was under way. In the November 23 issue of the *Herald of Truth*, Editor John F. Funk wrote:

> Bible conferences seem to be the order of the day. We have received a program of the Bible conference to be held at the Martin Meeting House near Orrville, Ohio, December 6-13. The program names J. S. Shoemaker, S. G. Shetler, and D. D. Miller as instructors.

Almost from the beginning the church papers published occasionally lists of announcements of coming conferences. The first lists were quite short. In 1901, for example, only three conferences were listed. Most of the conferences through these first years were announced through the "Personal Mention" columns of the *Herald of Truth*, but beginning in 1906 lists were regularly published through the fall and winter months. As new announcements came in they were added to the list and old ones dropped after the meetings were held. The longest single list appearing between 1906 and 1916 (when they were no longer published in the lists) named 24. Typical of these Bible conference announcements is one appearing in 1907 in the *Gospel Witness* (October 23):

Bible Conferences

Following we give a list of the places and dates of a number of Bible conferences. We shall be pleased to publish a full list of these important meetings to be held during the fall and winter. Our readers are hereby requested to send in the dates of conferences not listed below.

Masontown, Pa., Nov. 4-9.
Pleasant View, Stark Co., Ohio, Nov. 18-22.
Leetonia (Ohio) Church, last week in Nov.
Oak Grove, M. H., Wayne Co., Ohio, Thanksgiving week.
Freeport Church, Stephenson Co., Ill., first week in Dec.
Walnut Creek, M. H., Holmes Co., Ohio, second week in Dec.
Nappanee, Ind., Dec. 2-7.
Goshen, Ind. (Clinton A. M.), Dec. 9-13.
Tiskilwa, Ill., Dec. 10-13.
Fulton Co., Ohio, third week in Dec.
Church near South English, Iowa, third week in Dec.
Special Bible Term, Goshen College, Nov. 26-Dec. 24.
West Liberty, Ohio, Christmas Week.
Carver, Mo., Christmas week.
Martinsburg, Pa., Holiday Week.
Goshen College, Goshen, Ind., Dec. 26-Jan. 1.
North Lima, Ohio, Dec. 30-Jan. 4.
Mt. Zion, M. H., Morgan Co., Mo., New Year's week.
Belleville, Pa., week beginning Jan. 27.
Berlin, Can., no date given.

Beginning in 1908 the names of the instructors were included with these announcements, which makes it relatively easy to determine who the men were who were most active in Bible conference work during the heyday of the era. To obtain a fair sampling I took the longest single list published each year during the Bible conference months, October to December. Using this data from the years 1908 to 1916, the names of 108 different men appeared as instructors. Many of these were listed only once or twice, some of these represented "home talent" in the respective areas where the conferences were held, not men in the center of the movement. The places the conferences were held have not been tabulated. Actually Bible conferences were held over the entire Mennonite Church in the United States and Canada.

Out of this total list of 108 names I have listed the 34 whose names appeared three or more times. Following is the list in order of frequency:

S. G. Shetler	22	I. J. Buchwalter	4
D. D. Miller	19	L. J. Miller	4
Daniel Kauffman	15	J. L. Stauffer	4
Eli Frey	15	E. B. Stoltzfus	4
Abram Metzler	12		
J. E. Hartzler	12	The following are	
S. H. Miller	11	listed 3 times:	
Noah H. Mack	9		
S. E. Allgyer	8	E. J. Berkey	
S. F. Coffman	8	A. Hershey Leaman	
J. S. Hartzler	8	A. D. Wenger	
I. W. Royer	8	John S. Mast	
J. S. Shoemaker	8	A. I. Yoder	
J. E. Zimmerman	7	C. Z. Yoder	
J. S. Gerig	7	J. B. Zook	
D. G. Lapp	6	J. P. Berkey	
		A. M. Eash	
		J. P. Bontrager	
		E. D. Hess	
		B. B. King	
		C. F. Derstine	

There is no particular significance to this ranking except to show in a general way who the main leaders of the movement were when it was at its height. Although all of these men served many times more than the figures indicate, their relative position in the table would probably vary but little. It should be noted, too, that two of the foremost early Bible conference leaders died rather prematurely, J. S. Coffman in 1899 and M. S. Steiner, in 1911. It should also be observed that others served who were not listed in the church papers from which my own calculation was taken.

It is more difficult to obtain accurate data on the earlier period, that is, prior to 1908, since there were very few printed lists and these, short. Searching through the various news items and

"Personal Mention" lists of the earlier church periodicals, the *Herald of Truth* and *Gospel Witness*, one can, however, get some information about those who served in that period.

From the data collected of this earlier period, the following names occurred most frequently, the numbers in the parentheses indicating the frequency of the times they were listed: Daniel Kauffman (6); D. H. Bender (6); J. S. Shoemaker (5); J. S. Coffman (3); M. S. Steiner (3); S. F. Coffman (3); L. J. Burkholder (3); I. J. Buchwalter (2); I. A. Wambold (2); S. G. Shetler (2). Other names also appearing once; J. A. Ressler, D. J. Johns, Noah (N. O.) Blosser, and John Blosser.[21]

For many persons who read over the names of the men of this interesting era of North American Mennonite history, it will be just a page from the past. However, I am startled to realize that of the 44 men listed from 1897 to 1916, I personally knew 30 of these and heard 23 of them speak in public. I had A. D. Wenger as a teacher at Eastern Mennonite School, and after I was ordained had the privilege of serving on weekend Bible conferences with four of them: S. E. Allgyer, E. J. Berkey, J. L. Stauffer, and my father. I also served in the same conference district for a number of years with Daniel Kauffman and J. A. Ressler, and knew intimately Noah Mack, S. F. Coffman, I. W. Royer, L. J. Miller, and C. F. Derstine. For me these men represent more than names out of history.

One can determine roughly the peak years of the Bible conference movement simply by charting the total number of conferences listed each year in the official church organ.

This appears as follows:

1897 1	1904 3	1911 18
1898 2	1905 6	1912 17
1899 2	1906 16	1913 20
1900 2	1907 19	1914 24
1901 3	1908 24	1915 14
1902 5	1909 22	1916. . . . . . 15[22]
1903 3	1910 16	

Although there were no longer published lists of announcements after 1916, Bible conferences had by no means come to an end then. They continued through the 20s and into the 30s and even beyond, but by that time the movement as such, had spent itself. There was no longer a regular list of fall-and-winter conferences, and the format of the conferences had changed. Many became "weekend" conferences. A spot check of *Gospel Herald* announcements for some of the years after 1916 shows that in 1921 fifteen conferences were held, more or less of the old pattern, in 1928, 17, and in 1935, 12. By 1950 only six are mentioned in the field notes. It is interesting to note that after 1916 the announcements of the winter Bible schools had begun to replace the Bible conference lists. A new kind of teaching agency had taken over, an agency which also in due time was destined to reach its peak of popularity. It should be mentioned, however, that in some areas of the church Bible conferences continued to be held far beyond the actual period of the movement. Among these were the same churches where the first conferences had been held—Scottdale, Johnstown, and Springs. In the Johnstown area, the Bible conference is still an annual affair with considerable interest. Conferences have been shortened, however, and day sessions eliminated to accommodate the schedules of a modern working world. Interestingly, too, three of the men who had served in the very first years of the movement were still frequent speakers in the declining years of the movement: Daniel Kauffman, S. G. Shetler, and S. F. Coffman.

Format of the Early Bible Conferences

The format of the original Bible conferences was intriguing. They were definitely one of the chief "teaching agencies" of the time. They were held for varying periods of time ranging from several days to a week or more, and as stated previously, they were often held in connection with revival meetings. Even when they were not, they represented a unique combination of Bible teaching and evangelism. It is not unusual to read in a report of a given conference that a number of souls confessed Christ. Coff-

man in *Outlines and Notes,* the booklet he compiled in 1898 after
the Johnstown conference, gives us a picture of the format used
then. He writes:

> Three lectures were usually given each day. One hour was given to train-
> ing in singing, and another hour to prayer and exhortations and spiritual
> talks. In the evening Gospel sermons were preached and an evangelistic
> effort put forth....[23]

As noted earlier, there were usually three sessions each day.
Mennonites were largely rural then, and in the winter months
farm work was not pressing. This meant that daytime attendance
was usually quite good. As part of the program, "queries" were
handed in by members of the audience to a "query manager,"
who in turn, would hand these to the respective instructors to be
answered in the public meeting. The speakers made copious use
of "outlines" and "charts" which would be seen well by the
audience.

The various points were reinforced by Scripture verses
handed out in the opening of each address. The speaker would
simply call out each passage he had included in his message,
chapter and verse, and wait until some person in the audience
repeated it. This signified that he was "taking the verse" and that
he would read it at the appointed time in the message when the
speaker called for it. Giving out verses was usually done in a brisk
manner, speakers frequently chiding the audience gently if
responses lagged. Sometimes a speaker might ask the person who
read the verse to offer some comment, or he might, somewhat
cunningly, direct a question at the reader to add some point of
interest. This manner provided tremendous audience participa-
tion and interest.

Note-taking was encouraged. One thing that made these
conferences so fascinating was the fact that these men, somewhat
more gifted and trained than the average Mennonite preacher of
the time, were using systematic "outlines." This itself was new for
many people. John S. Coffman in *Outlines and Notes* describes
the nature of the presentations:

> In order to make the subjects treated as plain and impress[   ] s possible,
> the speakers arranged their talks logically and proved each position by the
> Scriptures. The outlines were written out and presented before the class of
> learners so that each one could copy them for future use if he desired to do
> so.[24]

The "class of learners" incidentally included the whole congregation, although the original purpose of these conferences had apparently been to serve a more limited group. Coffman wrote in his
preface:

> These conferences have been attended by many ministers of the Gospel,
> but principally the younger preachers and beginners in active Christian
> labors. Besides the ministers there have been in attendance many
> brethren and sisters who are Sunday school superintendents, teachers, and
> workers who desired to be better equipped for their work and their duties
> in the church.[25]

While most of the outlines were apparently written on the
blackboard for the members of the audience to copy, some of the
instructors began in time to use previously prepared charts. Coffman's booklet, *Outlines and Notes*, gives a very accurate
representation of the nature of the kinds of systematic outlines
used. Looking over these one sees a striking similarity between his
outlines and those used later by my father. It is a safe deduction
that since my father had been ordained only a year before, he
drank in those studies with more than average interest. It seems
that when he himself began to enter the same work he deliberately attempted to follow Coffman's method of using brief
and concise points.

To facilitate chart-making for his Bible conference work, my
father, early in his ministry, bought a printing set made up of rub-
ber stamps with letters of some size. He printed his outlines on 3-
by-4-foot pieces of cloth which could be easily folded and taken
along in his suitcase from conference to conference. These charts
in time came to cover the whole gamut of the topics he used. It
was a convenient method of having his message ready for his
many talks, though he constantly added new ideas and illustrations along the way. He also prepared duplicated sheets contain-

ing the titles of some of his most frequently used topics, which he could mail to churches which had contacted him for a conference. A copy of the list included the following 37 titles:

Temperance	Anointing with Oil
Eternal Punishment	Sanctification
Christian Discipleship	Woman's Sphere
Practical Christianity in the Church	Holy Spirit (2 talks)
Evils of the Tongue	Relation of Church to
Judgment on Earth	Government (2 talks)
Final Judgment	Covetousness
Christ's Mission	Giving
Spurious Investments	Angels
Devotional Covering	Humility
Life Insurance	Regeneration
Rural Missions	Self-Denial
Evil Spirits	Resurrection
Worldly Gatherings	Secrecy (Lodges)
The Good Shepherd	Communion
Swearing of Oaths	First John
Marriage (2 talks)	God
Sincerity	Fasting
Philemon	Education

It is not certain when these duplicated sheets were prepared. Apparently it was done rather early in his Bible conference work. It includes only one book study, and I know he had more of these. However, it does show rather well the wide range of topics discussed. One of his aims in all of his preaching and teaching was to try to be "balanced" and to avoid "riding hobby-horses."

The subjects discussed by the various speakers in many Bible conferences of the period, as gleaned from numerous announcements and reports in the church papers, were as follows (the arrangement is not significant):

Preparation for Christian Service, Communion, Plan of Salvation, Marriage, Faith, Law and Grace, Baptism, Child Training, Nonconformity, Conversion, Future Destiny, Covetousness, Devotional Covering (Veiling), Secret Societies, Life Insurance, Spurious Investments, Women's Place, Practical Christianity in the Home, Christian Regulations and Ordinances, Nonresistance, Sociability in the Church, Duty of the Congregation to the Ministers, Holy Ghost, Popular Evils, The Unequal Yoke,

Missions, Love, Christian Character, Humility, The New Birth, Proper Observance of the Lord's Day, Forgiveness, Worship, Personal Work (Evangelism), Sincerity, Evil Speaking, Obedience, Prayer, The Christian's Relation to Government, Unbelief, Christian's Duty to the Church, Worldly Amusements, Christian Discipleship, Secular Employment, Parental Training, Worldly Gatherings, Relation of the Laity to the Ministry and the Ministry to the Laity, Modest Apparel, Relation of the Church to the World, Giving, Unity, Education, Missions, The Young Disciple, Christian Liberty, Heaven, Birth and Early Life of Christ, Foot Washing, Temperance, Practical Piety in the Home, Repentance, Sanctification, Prophecies Concerning Christ.

Analyzed, these topics covered the whole range of Bible doctrines dealing with salvation, God, Christ, the Holy Spirit, the church, prophecy, the future life, as well as the ordinances and "restrictions" of the Mennonite Church. There were also numerous topics on the Christian life and practical piety.

In a day when there was not so much emphasis on training and higher education, and when the average person was not saturated with all kinds of information through literature and the news media, these Bible conferences served a most important function in the church. They were strong motivating agencies. While the manner in which certain topics were handled showed a certain naiveté and some oversimplification, there was never any problem knowing where an instructor stood on a given teaching or on a particular issue of the day. And people were also not confused with a lot of theological jargon so frequently present in modern teaching.

Furthermore, combining the Bible conference with revival services, as was frequently done, a balanced program of evangelism and doctrinal teaching was provided for the general constituency unequaled today. Many have on occasion raised the question whether this type of conference could be held successfully today. Granted that there was an era when they seemed to have special significance in the life of the church, I have no reason to believe that they are totally outdated. We know that there are denominations which are presently conducting very similar Bible conferences with great success and some are being held in our own church.

One of the strong points of the earlier conferences was that they frequently involved a *team* of capable men, not merely one guest speaker. In the course of a week of meetings of this sort a momentum was built up that was overwhelming. Imagine what would happen today—and it has—if a team of capable church leaders participated in an extended conference. Today, it seems, when we do have conferences which employ a staff of instructors they are usually designed for a limited group of church workers or leaders, rather than for the constituency. Ironically, in a day when we profess to be magnifying the importance of the churches at the grassroots level, we seem to be doing less teaching at this level than ever. It was largely the laity who profited from these early Bible conferences, not merely a small group of "specialists" and invited guests.

The total impact of these conferences is difficult to measure, but as a contemporary Mennonite leader has noted, they "left a lasting mark upon the church. Many souls found Christ ... churches were thoroughly indoctrinated in the simple nonresistant faith. Mission interest increased, and men were brought to a deeper consecration of life...."[26]

Children's Meetings

A very special interest of S. G. Shetler, and also an integral part of his revival services were his "boys' and girls' meetings." I cannot determine when my father held the first of these, but we know he had already conducted some in the early 1900s.

Children's meetings were usually conducted each evening, sometimes on alternate evenings, prior to the evening evangelistic message. They served several purposes, one of which was to create interest in the revival meetings themselves. Once the children started attending the captivated boys and girls gave their parents no rest until they brought them each evening. Parents and older people needed no special prodding, however, as the boys' and girls' meetings appealed to all ages. As you will note in the testimonies at the end of the book, many remember him best in this capacity.

My father had a unique way of holding children's attention with his object lessons. While an occasional critic would suggest that children remembered the objects instead of the lessons they were intended to teach, he felt there was ample biblical precedent for object lessons in both Testaments. Using a variety of objects— string, nails, envelopes, English walnuts, and what have you—he attempted to drive home some spiritual truth or ideal. They were modern parables on the children's level.

S. G. was quick in his actions and sometimes used almost a magician's techniques. Seldom did his procedures fail, and if they did, he had a way of pulling himself out of such predicaments without making it too obvious. One time in Virginia, however, he worked himself into a "jam" with his lesson in which he tried to show the evils of alcoholic drinks. In this lesson he offered money to the youngster who would be willing to eat or drink any of the items, not mentioning that one of the glasses contained whiskey. To show the dangerous nature of alcoholic drinks he struck a match and lit the whiskey. Only by great restraint could he keep one daring girl from drinking the burning fluid. Surprised himself that anyone should attempt this he gave the girl some money, but not the full amount he had first promised, a matter which caused just a little criticism. He was actually not one to break promises, so this has to be chalked up to his list of "failures."[27]

Part of his teaching technique was to ask many questions and to try to elicit a constant stream of answers from the children. This kept interest at a high pitch. Children are very frank in saying what they think and he played on this. "How many of you help your mother do the dishes?" he would ask, with a few hands going up here and there. "Why don't you all help? Isn't that one of your favorite chores?" The children would come through with a long, "No-o-o!" Then he would ask someone "Does your father help do dishes?" When the child answered, "No," some father in the audience was on the spot to the amusement of the audience and, of course, to the father himself.

Urged for years by many teachers of children to write a book on object lessons, he finally undertook the project collaborating with his son. The book, *117 Object Lessons for Boys and Girls*, by "Shetler and Shetler," came out in 1941, published by Mennonite Publishing House, Scottdale, Pennsylvania. Dedicated jointly to the memory of Maggie Jane Shetler, whose "intense interest in object lessons for children" had inspired the writers, and to the "boys and girls of the United States and Canada" whom the authors had served "on numerous occasions," the book enjoyed wide sales going through four editions.

The book was arranged to cover a wide variety of themes suitable on various occasions, and included such titles as: "Clean Within and Without," "Dead Letter Office," "Soiled Cup," "Clipping the Conscience," "The Greedy Family," "The Good and Bad Church," "A Drugstore," "Borrowed Things," "Two Faces," "Lost and Found," "Gifts Without Money," and "Small Important Things."

For example, the lesson, "Dead Letter Office," began with a description of the Dead Letter Office in Washington, D.C., showing how unclaimed letters with no return or identification are opened there. Pretending that he had before him a stack of such letters (letters previously prepared), the teacher was directed to have the various boys and girls act as clerks and open and read them. The group was to say then whether they could tell something about the character of the various writers from the contents of the letter. The lesson had a real point, of course; one *can* often tell something about the character of people by what they write. Letters given as examples of the type a teacher might prepare for the lesson were:

Date_____

Dear friend:

Our church is having a visiting minister to give a series of talks on Bible subjects. I am writing to you to invite you out for services on this coming Sunday. Hope you can come. Bring some of your friends along.

Sincerely,

Date_____

Dear member of the "gang":

We are planning another midnight robbery on June 7. Meet me at the corner of Smith and Clinton streets in Jonesville. Hope to crack a large safe. Will give you the usual share. Come well armed.

Your pal,
Smithy

Ideals stressed in the various lessons included love for the Bible, obedience to parents, helpfulness around the home, regular church attendance, giving one's heart to Jesus, good behavior in the house of God, honesty, eating what is set before you, and playing without fighting. There was no attempt to teach lessons that would apply only later in life. The objective was to help boys and girls *now*.

9
Churchwide Service
(1900-1912)

The Times at the Turn of the Century

Looking back at this most interesting period of American history at the beginning of the present century, one catches a bit of the enthusiasm and spirit that characterized the life and thought of the times. It was unquestionably the day of unlimited opportunity for both the kingdoms of this world and the kingdom of Christ, and no one was losing any time in trying to exploit all the potentials of this new era.

The "age of big business" was coming into its own with factories turning out quantities of machines and store goods. All the blessings and curses of the industrial system were beginning to be realized in a marked way. Expansion was to be the key to progress. Inventors were opening up to the populace a wonder world of gadgets and devices that boggled the mind and robbed the purse.

The automobile, invented at the close of the nineteenth century, was becoming the possession of the common person, including rural, conservative Mennonites. Vachel Lindsay, the noted American poet, while working one summer among the Mennonites in the harvest fields of Kansas, observed what he considered an amusing incongruity, plain Mennonites—women with neatly tied bonnets—riding to church on Sundays in their new "Jerusalem buggies." The Virginia Mennonite Conference troubled somewhat by the new "machine," passed a resolution stating that "it is right to use automobiles when it can be done to the glory of God, but that we condemn their extravagance and display, and their use in seeking pleasure instead of divine worship."[28]

Railroads too were entering their heyday and were rapidly expanding their facilities to every nook and corner of the land. Mennonite leaders began to make use of these in a major way to meet their widening circle of appointments miles from their homes. Trips that once took days or a week to reach a destination could now be accomplished in hours or a day. The new Union Station in Washington, D.C., was completed in 1907—at the time the largest building ever constructed for that purpose. During those years of expansion great efforts were made by railroad companies to encourage people to use the new Western railroads, even through church publications. In one single issue of *Herald of Truth*, for example, as many as six "ads" appeared trying to entice people to travel by the various rail routes to the West, offering attractive excursion rates. Railroad companies were trying also to use their facilities as a means of drawing settlers to promising unsettled areas of the West.

The new "aeroplane" invented by the Wright brothers in 1903 was coming to be recognized as a possible future mode of transportation. A newsman reported that aerial navigation, while just in its infancy, had already made sufficient headway that there was a need for establishing safe "harbours for the great airships." Maps were to be made "to show places of safety, such as great gravel pits, protected nooks along the hillside or behind thick woods, where the ship may alight in safety until the storm is over."

Political, social, and economic problems were beginning to confront the nation. The power of labor unions and the violent tactics in their struggle against capitalism were underscored. An important bridge over a navigable river that could be raised for boat traffic, operated by nonunion men, was dynamited for the fifth time on February 4, 1907. Unfair business practices by wealthy capitalists were making headlines. This was the "gilded age" when the wealthy were exploiting every means, legitimate and otherwise, to make their millions. Thirty-two-year-old Cornelius Vanderbilt was making three million dollars a year exclusive of his income from his 23 patents. John D. Rockefeller, another of the "robber barons,"[29] was being prosecuted by the Federal government for his unfair price discrimination and monopoly in the oil industry. Ida Tarbell, in her history of the Standard Oil Company (1904), exposed the corrupt practices of that industry, and Upton Sinclair laid wide open the unethical practices of the meat-packing industry in his startling book, *The Jungle* (1906). In Chicago, in 1908, 60,000 hungry people were without money and work, and in New York there was a poor people's march with thousands of "tenement dwellers" demonstrating in the streets because of their plight.

"Women's lib" and terrorism did not exactly originate in the decade of the 1970s. Already in the early 1900s women's suffrage was becoming an active issue. Those most vocal in the movement went so far as to engage in terrorist activities. A comment in the *Gospel Herald* (May 22, 1913) referred to this:

> The suffragettes of London have been showing such pernicious activities as placing bombs under the homes of prominent men opposing their movement that it is proposed to put London under martial law for the protection of property. The question naturally arises, what would be the consequences if the ballot were placed in the hands of a class showing such lawlessness?

Crime in general was beginning to make its inroads. From 1902 to 1907, 43,000 persons were killed in the United States by violence, surpassing the number killed on the battlefield in the Civil War. Of the violent deaths and murders, 651 had been through lynchings.

While highway accidents had not yet been a matter of concern, railroad accidents had become a serious problem. In the same period (1902-1907), 46,500 had lost their lives in this way. And in one year alone (1912) deaths through accidents in the coal mines of the nation was 2,360!

Urban development, too, was becoming a high priority item. In 1915 the city of Philadelphia was asking voters to approve a $90 million loan for the purpose of developing various enterprises. Almost prophetically Editor Kauffman of the *Herald* wrote that "this loan business has gotten to be quite a fad among the leading cities of the country," and that this might be one of the things that "will help fulfill the prophecy that someday America will become a bankrupt nation."

Secularization of the schools had also become such an issue by the turn of the century that a drive to "get the Bible back into the schools" was introduced. Dr. Samuel Windsor Brown of Columbia University in 1912 wrote his classic work, *The Secularization of American Education*, in which he showed how that either by legislation or court decision, religion had been gradually removed from the schools.

Toward the close of the decade the war clouds were beginning to hang over Europe. Prime Minister David Lloyd George of Great Britain saw the folly of the military craze that was proving to be such a burden upon nations. In a report to Parliament he said, "The cost of armaments is the largest and most sterile increase in expenditure, and I can not see any prospect of this menacing development coming to an end unless some change takes place in the attitudes and policies of the nations concerned." David Starr Jordan, eminent American educator and student of international affairs, noted that European governments were under "bondage of the Rothchilds since the Battle of Waterloo and were so in debt to them that it would be impossible to pay them off." In Germany a serious scandal connected with the move for greater armies and navies was uncovered. Charges were brought against the Krupps, the powerful industrialists, for paying a liberal sum to newspapers in France for the purpose of inciting hatred on the part of the French against Germany. That war was proving to be expensive was shown in the increase in pensions. A new pension law in the USA in 1907 had authorized a payment of $12.00 a month to the widows of soldiers who had fought in the various wars. This item involved a national expenditure of $12 million annually—a staggering figure for those days.

In the religious world eventful changes were also taking place. December 1908 marked the beginning of the ecumenical movement with the organizing of the new "Federal Council of Churches of Christ in America" (forerunner of the National Council of Churches). More, than 30 of the American Protestant denominations, totaling a membership of more than 17 million, were represented in the new organization. Modernism, too, had made its debut, with its candid rejection of long-cherished views of biblical authority and inspiration. The Church Mission Society of India in a 1912 issue of the *Bombay Guardian* protested the invasion of modernism to the point that it was undermining the churches of India.

Era of Expansion for Mennonites

It was "in times like these" that the Mennonite Church launched its churchwide, and in fact, worldwide program of evangelism, its Bible conferences, schools, and missions. This was the time for expansion. The impediments for spreading the gospel had been removed in modes of transportation and communication. The psychological and spiritual atmosphere of the times was also beginning to remove impediments within the church, such as the use of the German language and ruralisms which had no special biblical sanction. Higher education in the Christian context had been initiated with the founding of a church college at Goshen, Indiana, and short-term winter Bible schools. It was, as one might put it, the beginning of the "golden age" for American Mennonitism.

In this very period a new group of progressive (yet conservative) Mennonite leaders, Bible teachers, and evangelists was coming to the forefront and making an impact on the church. Many of these have already been noted in the previous chapter. Among these was S. G. Shetler.

The years between 1900 and 1912 represented for him a period of active engagement in churchwide evangelism, Bible conferences, and other church work that took him from his home for major portions of time. During this period, as the records seem to indicate, he taught only one term of public school. A "Field Note" in the January 2, 1907, issue of the *Gospel Witness*, official church organ, reflected the busy program of activities in which he was engaged:

> S. G. Shetler of Johnstown spent last week at home. Bro. Shetler is getting to be as much a stranger to his home congregations as to some congregations hundreds of miles away.

During this decade two of the major evangelistic campaigns of his life were held, one in Waterloo County, Ontario, and the other in Rockingham County, Virginia. Literally hundreds of persons were added to the church through his evangelistic efforts in various parts of the church.

In addition to his revival meetings and Bible conferences, he also served on a number of denominational boards and committees. He was secretary of the Southwestern Pennsylvania Mennonite Conference; a director of the denominational Board of Charitable Homes and Missions, forerunner to the General Mission Board; and a delegate to the General Conference several times. In addition to these, he was a member of the Book Examining Committee of the Mennonite Book and Tract Society, forerunner to the Mennonite Publication Board, and also a member of an *ad hoc* Investigation Committee of Mennonite General Conference to evaluate the work of the various denominational boards and institutions.

I have chronicled in detail his program of activities for 1902, which is quite typical of the other years of the period, simply to show how much he was involved, both in the work of the local church and in the church at large. The remaining years of this particular period, beginning with 1904, I have handled in summary form.

1902 Schedule

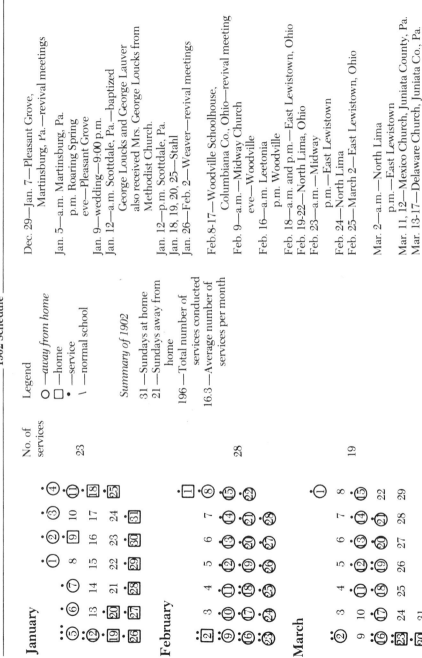

Legend

O — *away from home*
□ — home
• — service
\ — normal school

Summary of 1902

31 — Sundays at home
21 — Sundays away from home
196 — Total number of services conducted
16.3 — Average number of services per month

	No. of services	Events
January	23	Dec. 29—Jan. 7—Pleasant Grove, Martinsburg, Pa.—revival meetings
		Jan. 5—a.m. Martinsburg, Pa. p.m. Roaring Spring eve—Pleasant Grove
		Jan. 9—wedding—9:00 p.m.
		Jan. 12—a.m. Scottdale, Pa.—baptized George Loucks and George Lauver also received Mrs. George Loucks from Methodist Church.
		Jan. 12—p.m. Scottdale, Pa.
		Jan. 18, 19, 20, 25—Stahl
		Jan. 26—Feb. 2—Weaver—revival meetings
February	28	Feb. 8-17—Woodville Schoolhouse, Columbiana Co., Ohio—revival meeting
		Feb. 9—a.m.—Midway Church eve—Woodville
		Feb. 16—a.m. Leetonia p.m. Woodville
		Feb. 18—a.m. and p.m.—East Lewistown, Ohio
		Feb. 19-22—North Lima, Ohio
		Feb. 23—a.m.—Midway p.m.—East Lewistown
		Feb. 24—North Lima
		Feb. 25 — March 2 — East Lewistown, Ohio
March	19	Mar. 2—a.m.—North Lima p.m.—East Lewistown
		Mar. 11, 12—Mexico Church, Juniata County, Pa.
		Mar. 13-17—Delaware Church, Juniata Co., Pa.

Mar. 16—a.m.—Fairview Schoolhouse, Juniata Co., Pa.

p.m.—Delaware Church, Juniata Co.,

Mar. 18—Fairview Schoolhouse
Mar. 19—a.m. Lauver Church

p.m. Lost Creek Church, Juniata Co.

Mar. 20, 21—Lost Creek Church
Mar. 23—a.m. and p.m.—Blauch Church
Mar. 30—Thomas Church

Apr. 4—a.m.—Weaver Church—funeral
Apr. 6—Elton Church
Apr. 13—two weddings—4:00 and 6:00 p.m. (residence)
Apr. 20—wedding 11:00 a.m. (residence)
Apr. 21-June 13—normal school

May 3—Weaver Church
May 4—a.m.—Weaver Church eve—Blough Church
May 11—eve—Shaffer Schoolhouse
May 31—funeral (residence)

June 1—Elton Church
June 7, 8—Mullen Schoolhouse, Schellsburg, Pa.
June 15—a.m.—service in a home

p.m.—Blauch Church
June 21—Folk Church (Springs), Pa.
June 22—a.m.—Casselman Church—Grantsville, Md.

eve—Oak Grove
June 22-28—Oak Grove Church, Grantsville, Md.—revival meetings
June 29—a.m.—Folk Church, Springs, Pa.

p.m.—Oak Grove Church, Grantsville, Md.

eve—Folk Church, Springs, Pa

April   6

			:: 4	5
:6:	7	1	2	3
:13:	14	8	9	10	11	12
20	21	15	16	17	18	19
27	28	22	23	24	25	26
		29	30

May   5

				•3
:4:	•11			10
18				17
25				24
				31

June   16

•1	•7
•8	14
:15:	•21
22	•28
•29	30

July

		1	2	3	4	5
6	7	8	9	10	11	12
13	14	15	16	17	18	19
20	21	22	23	24	25	26
27	28	29	30	31		

July 13—Blauch Church
July 20—Stahl Church
July 27—Weaver Church

No. of services: 3

August

					1	2
3	4	5	6	7	8	9
10	11	12	13	14	15	16
17	18	19	20	21	22	23
24	25	26	27	28	29	30
31						

Aug. 11—Logania Church, Perry Co., Pa.
Aug. 12—Lampeter Music Hall, Lancaster, Pa.
Aug. 13—Lampeter Music Hall, song and Bible meeting
  Subject "The Child," Subjects—"Solomon's Temple," "The Life of Church"
Aug. 14—a.m.—Millersville Church
  p.m.—Stone Church
  eve—Lancaster City mission
Aug. 16—visited and ate at Industrial Welsh Mt. Mission, Lancaster Co.
Aug. 16—p.m.—Stumptown Church, Lancaster Co.
  eve—Red Well Church, Lancaster Co.
Aug. 17—a.m. and p.m. Groffdale Church, Lancaster Co.
Aug. 26—Scottdale, Pa.—Sunday school conference. Subject: "Letting the Light Shine."
Aug. 28-29—attended church conference, Scottdale, Pa.
Aug. 30—funeral in a home
Aug. 31—Shaffer Schoolhouse—evening

No. of services: 15

September

	1	2	3	4	5	6
7	8	9	10	11	12	13
14	15	16	17	18	19	20
21	22	23	24	25	26	27
28	29	30	31			

Sept. 7—Blauch Church (eve)
Sept. 13—Elton—funeral
Sept. 14—Tire Hill of the Brethren (eve)
Sept. 17—funeral—Tire Hill Church (Charles David—son of David and Sallie Mishler)
Sept. 21—a.m.—wedding at residence
Sept. 28—Union Chapel, Johnstown, Pa.

No. of services: 6

October

Oct. 2-7—Mullen Schoolhouse, Schellsburg, Pa.
Oct. 12—Tire Hill Church of the Brethren (eve)
Oct. 16—Emma Church, Indiana
Oct. 18-28—Shore Church, Indiana—revival meetings
Oct. 19—a.m.—Clinton Church
        eve.—Shore
Oct. 22—a.m.—Forks Church
Oct. 29—Nov. 5—Emma Church—Indiana—revival
        meetings (?)

November

Nov. 6—Maple Grove, Ind.
Nov. 7—Elkhart Church
Nov. 8—Clinton Amish Church
Nov. 9—a.m.—Clinton Amish Church
        eve—Clinton Brick Church
Nov. 10—Emma Church
Nov. 12—Pike Church, Allen Co., Ohio
        M. E. and B. Bd. meeting, also Mennonite
        Book and Tract Society
Nov. 13, 14—Delegate to General Conference
        Pike Church
Nov. 15-21—Pike Church, Ohio—Bible conference
Nov. 22-26—Pike Church—revival meetings
Nov. 27—Salem Church, Allen Co., Ohio—
        Thanksgiving service
Nov. 27-30—Salem Church, revival meeting

December

Dec. 2—funeral—Weaver Church
Dec. 7—Kaufman Church
Dec. 10-17—Freeport Church, Ill. revival meetings ?
Dec. 14—a.m.—Freeport
        p.m.—home of Benjamin Shoemaker
        eve.—Freeport
Dec. 22-27—Folk Church—Bible Conference
Dec. 28—Folk Church

October 25

1 2 3 4
5 6 7 8 9 10 11
12 13 14 15 16 17 18
19 20 21 22 23 24 25
26 27 28 29 30 31

November 31

1
2 3 4 5 6 7 8
9 10 11 12 13 14 15
16 17 18 19 20 21 22
23 24 25 26 27 28 29
30

December 19

1 2 3 4 5 6
7 8 9 10 11 12 13
14 15 16 17 18 19 20
21 22 23 24 25 26 27
28 29 30 31

1904

My father's schedule from January to March, 1904, began with a six-week term of Bible school at Goshen College, Goshen, Indiana. My mother, who seldom accompanied him in his tours, was with him during this extended period, and also their daughters, Luella and Rosella. Luella was then 11 and Rosella, 8. Unfortunately my mother had to spend a good portion of her time at Goshen under quarantine because of a contagious disease she had contracted along the way.

My father served as principal of the Bible school, but also conducted a revival meeting on campus. The church paper recorded the event:

> During the winter Bible term in January and February, 1904, S. G. Shetler conducted a series of meetings at the college during which fifteen people confessed Christ. On the last Sunday of February David Burkholder of Nappanee held baptismal services in Assembly Hall. Only five were baptized; some preferred to be baptized in a stream by an Amish Mennonite bishop. Accordingly Bishop Daniel Johns baptized them on Saturday, April 30, 1904.

As an interesting sidelight to the Goshen story, many years later Luella and her family came to reside in Goshen and she saw her six sons and daughter graduate from the college.

Immediately after this six-week stint my father conducted meetings at the Salem Church near Dalton, Ohio, preaching also on Sunday morning, February 21, at the "Martin Meeting House." On February 26, he preached in German at the nearby Sonnenberg Church on the theme, "Building a Spiritual House," using for his text, Luke 14:30. That same evening (February 26) meetings were begun at the Bethel Church in Medina County, Ohio, which lasted presumably a week. Then in March he began meetings at the Longenecker Church in Holmes County.

April found my father back home in time to begin his summer normal. In May an article of his appeared in the *Herald of Truth* on the "Ascension." It was a well-written presentation, probably one of his best. Following the end of the eight-week normal he conducted a week of revival meetings at the Rockton

Church in Clearfield County, Pennsylvania (June 18-26), where his brother-in-law, J. N. Kaufman, later a pioneer missionary to India, was pastor at the time.

A theme my father had worked on at some length was "Woman's Sphere in the Christian Church." He had used this in his outline studies in Bible conferences, and it is likely that the editor of the *Herald*, knowing of this, had asked him to write the series. Already in 1904 "woman's place" was a topic of concern in the church. From September to November three articles appeared on this theme.

The fall months found him back on the revival meeting trail. He spent six weeks in the Missouri congregations. From September 8 to October 3 he was in Cass County, Missouri, at the Bethel and Sycamore churches. These were followed in turn with a series at Cherry Box (Shelby County) and at Palmyra, closing there on October 19.

At home less than two weeks, he left for a Sunday school meeting at Hanover, York County, Pennsylvania, and on November 3 for a series of meetings at Newville, Cumberland County, Pennsylvania, which began on November 4. The same month he conducted meetings also at Allensville and Shiremanstown. He returned home briefly and headed westward to Ohio to the Bethel Church at West Liberty, where he preached a series of evangelistic messages in connection with a Bible conference. The speakers for this conference were J. S. Shoemaker of Freeport, Illinois, and D. D. Miller of Indiana. The conference and meetings closed on December 21 letting him return home for the Christmas holidays.

1905

In the early part of 1905 my father was at home, filling some local appointments. By this time he had become a regular contributor to the denominational magazine, *The Herald of Truth*. Another article appearing in the April 19 issue, "The Busy Time," describes interestingly the kind of schedule of activities he maintained constantly. It throws light too on the kinds of activities the rural people of the times carried on, including, for example, the summer "warfare against the flies!" He speaks of springtime as a busy time, including such activities as "plowing, sowing, planting, pruning, grafting, hoeing, fencing, renovating" and the housewife being busy with "housecleaning, lawn-decorating, getting ready with screens for a summer's siege of warfare against the flies . . ." (Apparently the day of household insecticides had not yet arrived!) In the article he points out how some people are too busy—having no time for the things of the Lord.

In August the busy evangelist was back at Rockton, Pennsylvania, for another series of revival meetings and in September at Allensville and Barrville for the same kind of work.

A field note in the *Gospel Witness*, (November 8), the new official church publication, stated that

> Bro. Shetler of Johnstown, Pa., stopped overnight in Scottdale, October 30 on his way to Medina County, Ohio, where he expects to be engaged in meetings the next two weeks. As a member of the Investigating Committee to report on church institutions at the General Conference, he looked into the work of the Mennonite Tract Society and of the *Gospel Witness.* From here he went to the Old People's Home in the same mission before beginning meetings in Medina.

For a number of years General Conference appointed "Investigating Committees" to evaluate the different denominational institutions. D. D. Miller and John Nice served with Shetler on the particular committee mentioned above. Their detailed report was presented at the Fourth Biennial General Conference held at Berlin (Kitchener), Ontario, November 16, 17, 1905. The committee, as commissioned, had investigated the Evangelism and Benevolent Board; the Book and Tract Society; The *Gospel Witness* Company; the Chicago Mission; the Mennonite Board of Charitable Homes and Missions; the Old People's Home at Rittman, Ohio; the Orphans' Home, West Liberty, Ohio; and the Fort Wayne (Indiana), Canton (Ohio), and Kansas City (Missouri) missions. This was a huge undertaking. Just prior to the meeting of General Conference the "technical meeting" of the Mennonite Evangelizing and Benevolent Board was held at the same place

(November 14, 15). At this meeting S. G. Shetler delivered a sermon on Isaiah 54:2, "Lengthen thy cords, and strengthen thy stakes."

The revival meetings referred to in Medina County had been held just previous to the biennial General Conference. These were held at the Bethel and the Guilford churches.

1906

As the reconstructed calendar for 1906 shows, this was probably one of the busiest and most fruitful of my father's career. It included his Virginia "campaign" in which there were many converts. During the year he spoke or held meetings at 20 churches outside his home district, including 10 revival meetings, and 4 Bible conferences. He also participated in a Sunday school conference. In addition, he conducted 7 funerals in his home district, one of which was that of his beloved friend and colleague, Bishop Jonas Blauch.

The year had started with an assignment on the annual Ontario Bible Conference, January 1 to 5, in the Kitchener area. The other instructors in this conference were: E. S. Hallman, S. F. Coffman, Israel R. Shantz, I. J. Buchwalter, and Norman Stauffer. From here Buchwalter and Shetler went to Vineland, Ontario, for another Bible conference. My father served with "I. J." many times through the years and the two remained close friends. The next place of service was at the Oak Grove congregation, Smithville, Ohio, where 21 souls responded to the call. As reported later in the *Herald*, the "weather and roads" were not very "favorable," but the attendance was "good." Apparently Bible conference was again combined with the evangelistic meetings. Mention is made of "day meetings when Bro. Shetler teaches by outlines." The subjects were: "The Good Shepherd," "Heaven," "Holy Spirit," "Practical Christianity in the Home," and "The Tongue."

The month of February saw him in his home conference district area at the Folk (Springs) Church. A tragic event took place during the meetings which resulted in an unusual outpouring of the Spirit. A young married brother, Christ Beachy, fell to his death while making repairs on the chimney of the church building. The event threw a deep solemnity over the church. The result was that by the end of the meetings 52 persons had responded, including his own daughter, Rosella, who had accompanied him to the meetings, and George Cutrell, who in later years served in an important capacity at the Mennonite Publishing House. His son, Ben Cutrell, is presently (1980) manager (publishing agent) of the same institution.

In March S. G. began his five-week campaign in the Shenandoah Valley, holding meetings at the Weaver, Bank, Trissel, and Zion churches, with an ingathering of 58 souls. John Alger, Lewis Showalter, and Samuel Shank, who in 1972 were still serving as deacon and ministers, respectively, recalled quite vividly these 1906 meetings. All three had been members of the class of converts. Alger remembered the pre-sermon talks, something new for those times. He remembered too that the people were quite impressed with his fresh approach to preaching, the animated spirit, the young evangelist's natural gift in speaking, and his understanding of how to present his message. He was impressed especially with my father's memory for people's names. He made a mistake, however, with young Alger. When Sam Shank stood one evening to confess Christ, the evangelist called out Alger's name, instead, in acknowledging the confession. Hardly off the platform after the service, he realized his mistake and apologized to Alger, saying somewhat tactfully, "Well, you might come some other evening," which he did.

But Alger had some problems of his own which had to be cleared first. In the home later he told the evangelist that he did not consider himself a sinner. My father carefully explained the two types of sin, the "Adamic" and the personal, and new light shone through. The 13-year-old youth could accept this, and he made his decision.[30] Alger later came to serve both as deacon and, for many years, chairman of the board of trustees of Eastern Mennonite College.

Lewis Showalter also recalled my father's ability to remember names. Everyone was amazed how that after a few nights he could name people as he gave out Scripture references to have read audibly in the audience in his pre-sermon talks. People were impressed too with his use of the Scriptures. Commenting on the total impact of these meetings after these many years, Alger said, "He strengthened our faith and beliefs in the Bible that we should read it to be more perfect in the use of the books [of the Bible]. He introduced us to Bible study and to a study of the doctrines."[31]

After these very interesting meetings S. G. returned to his normal school work for the summer. The May 2 issue of the *Gospel Witness* reported:

> Bro. S. G. Shetler has again entered the teachers' profession. He opened a teachers' normal at the schoolhouse near his home on April 23 with an enrollment of 30 students. A number more are expected soon. We wish our brother success in his work.

After a busy schedule of summer activities, he returned again that fall to evangelistic and Bible conference work. The first of his series of meetings was held at the Thomas Church in his home area. There were six confessions. In October he held two revivals in Indiana, at the Forks and Clinton Brick churches. The places where he served in Bible conferences were: Rockton, Pennsylvania, Warwick River, Virginia, Salem Church, Elkhart County, Indiana, and the Mennonite Chapel, Hancock, Ohio. Elva Shank who had heard my father at the Warwick River Church remembered distinctly three of his texts: "The throne had six steps," "Can I hear anymore the voice of singing men and singing women?" and "As an eagle stirreth up her nest. . . ."[32]

1907

My father was in Fulton County, Ohio, in January for a Bible Conference, where he was assisted by D. J. Johns of Indiana. From March to April he conducted meetings in various Lancaster Conference churches.

In an article in the *Gospel Witness*, dated May 1, 1907, titled

"Which First?" he expressed his concern for establishing priorities in reading materials. He says that "in his last eight months of evangelistic work" it had been his "pleasure to get into many homes," and that while he had observed that few homes are without a newspaper, "many are without a church paper." He asks, "Which first?" the newspaper with its "daily grind (of) murder, robbery, etc., or a good church paper?" He made a strong plea to have a brother in each church responsible for the promotion of church literature, to take care of subscriptions, and to get free subscriptions for worthy poor. He was much opposed to having people get "non-sectarian and other church papers" which frequently "advise to do something entirely contrary to our own good" and which did not line up with "the Word." Each home needs to decide for itself which kind of paper should be first, he said.

On August 23 two of his good friends, J. N. Durr and John M. Mosemann, were guests in his home. In September he held meetings at Lost Creek Church in Juniata County and the Port Trevorton Church in Snyder County, both in Pennsylvania. He also stopped at the Marion Church in Franklin County for some services. In this same month the Book Examining Committee met at Scottdale to perform their assigned duties. The original committee was comprised of D. D. Miller, George R. Brunk, and S. G. Shetler, but since "D. D." and George R." were "so far away" (Indiana and Missouri), A. D. Wenger and D. H. Bender were appointed as substitutes. The committee met "and went over the books in the manner stated in the announcement" (referring to an earlier announcement in the *Gospel Witness*). The news note continued, "It is the aim of the Society (Book and Tract Society) to handle only such books as are safe for all to read and tend to intellectual, moral, and spiritual upbuilding of the reader." The job confronting the committee was formidable and they were aware of it as the following report in the *Witness* indicates. One is impressed, however, with the diligent concerns of the church at this time regarding sound literature. Following is a copy of the committee's report:

Book Examining Committee

We believe that it is generally known that at the last meeting of the Book and Tract Society three brethren were appointed as a Book Examining Committee.

Wishing to handle good books only, it is the purpose of this committee to examine all books catalogued and sold by the Society.

The question has been raised whether the committee reads every book in its examination. This is not done with all the books, as anyone of literary knowledge well knows how much time would be required for this. Various methods have been used to utilize time.

Some books such as *Josephus, Martyr's Mirror*, etc., are standard works. So far the books by our own authors have been recognized as excellent reading matter.

Books about which questions have been raised have been closely examined. Some new books have been carefully read. Some books have been accepted on the recommendation of other brethren.

Thus we feel safe in recommending any work catalogued by the Society. There are a few minor differences in some of the books, but not of such a nature as to be considered dangerous. When the theme or a number of expressions were objectionable, the book was rejected.

The profits of the book business are divided among the various church institutions, and we therefore trust that the brotherhood will remember the work of the Society in its efforts for good.

S. G. Shetler
A. D. Wenger
D. H. Bender
Committee

Two revival meetings and five Bible conferences made up a major part of the schedule from October to the end of 1907. The two revival meetings were: Weaver (in the home district), October 9-20, and Howard-Miami, near Kokomo, Indiana, in November. The Bible conferences were at Masontown, Pennsylvania, and Pleasant View, Stark County, Ohio, in November. In December Bible conferences were at Nappanee, Indiana; Tiskilwa, Illinois; and West Liberty, Ohio (Bethel Church), closing at the latter place on December 31. J. S. Shoemaker served with him at the Bethel Church and Daniel Kauffman at Nappanee. I. J. Buchwalter had also served with my father at Masontown.

The revival meetings at Kokomo followed immediately after General Conference, to which he had been a delegate. The other Pennsylvania delegates were: Bishops Abram Metzler and Aaron Loucks, and ministers Levi A. Blough, D. H. Bender, and John M. Yoder.

While it is impossible, and unnecessary, to attempt to include in this biography the many comments made by those individuals who reported S. G. Shetler's revival meetings and conferences in the various issues of the denominational organ, a few here and there in our story are certainly permissible in order to verify the interest and concern of the church in the work that was being accomplished under the blessing of the Lord. The report of the Nappanee meeting is quite typical:

Nappanee, Ind.

To the Readers of the *Witness*, Greeting:—During the week of Dec. 2-8, a Bible Conference was held at Nappanee by S. G. Shetler of Johnstown, Pa., and I. J. Buchwalter of Dalton, O. These meetings were well attended and highly instructive. Many from other districts and other denominations attended. The doctrines of the church and Bible were made very plain. At the evening services some powerful sermons were preached by the brethren, and four souls confessed Christ. May the Lord richly bless His Church and brethren who so faithfully teach His word.

While my father had great success in evangelistic work he also had experiences which yielded no "visible results." Levi Blauch, the faithful correspondent from the Johnstown area (incidentally an uncle of Roger Blough, a former president of U.S. Steel) reporting on the revivals at the Weaver Church in October said,

"With all the praying, pleading, and admonishing, sinners turned a deaf ear towards the truth."[33]

In addition to the other articles appearing in 1907, my father also wrote a lengthy article for the doctrinal section of the *Witness* on "Evils That Threaten the Church and How to Counteract Them." It appeared in seven installments from November 27 to February 28, 1908. He frequently spoke on this topic in Bible conferences and he exhibited a gift of discernment which was recognized in the church. Typical of his optimism, however, he said in his introductory paragraph,

> Everywhere the congregations of our beloved church are seeing and fearing some great evils which are gradually destroying souls. These precious souls are children from our own homes. Discussing this subject, of course, is looking at the dark side, and I do not want to depress or discourage anyone. Let no one say that these evils will overcome us anyhow, and we might as well give up.

He covered many of the "evils" which the church has always faced, such as "worldly amusements," unscriptural marriages, and the "chronic ills which many churches and individuals face." He deplored those who thought too lightly of existing evils, noting that some church officials are frequently "not courageous and firm enough to fight a great battle for the Lord," thinking "it will go better after a while." Afraid of hurting someone's feelings they "frequently sanction evil by their silence."

He was concerned about the inroads being made by modern philosophy and the influence of "erroneous education" and modernistic theology. There were too many who were beginning to challenge the plain teachings of the Scripture. He spoke of the "divinity professors" of the University of Chicago "who had joined the number of those mentioned in 2 Peter 3:3," quoting some of their writings on the second coming. One professor had written that "in the large circles of Christian thought the old eschatology is gone, probably never to return." Challenging this, he raised the question, "Is it any wonder that many of our children have been lost to the faith when they sit under the instruction of such men for several years?"

He referred also to Alexander Dowie, the divine healer who had misled many people, and to "Christian-coated skepticism" which was threatening the church "more than the teachings of Rogert Ingersoll or Tom Paine." Such expressions as "Customs have changed," "These things are not all necessary," and "The Scripture is not all inspired," were simply catch phrases that were deceiving many. He also deplored laxness in church government and the practice of "liberal" churches of admitting individuals regardless of their spiritual standing.

He concluded his series in his usual way on the "bright side" with two installments on how to remedy the situation. He recommended a good program of using sound teachers.

1908

The year 1908 proved to be another very fruitful year in evangelism. In January and February my father conducted meetings at four Ontario churches: Weber, Strasburg, Berlin (Kitchener), and Breslau. Church leaders gathered at Goshen, Indiana, in January to create a new Mennonite Publication Board, and although he would normally have been present for this historic event, he had foregone this privilege to take care of what came to be probably the outstanding campaign of his career. With the organization of the Publication Board, my father was placed on the newly formed Publishing Committee. A number of field notes in the *Gospel Witness* reflected the impact of the Canadian meetings. The one in the February 5 issue read:

> After closing a series of meetings at the Strasburg Church, Waterloo County, Ontario, on January 19, Brother Shetler began meetings at Berlin (the present Kitchener) in connection with the Bible Conference at that place. Bro. M. S. Steiner and a number of other brethren assisted in the work at the latter place. According to the latest reports the Lord was wonderfully blessing the work and many souls were led from darkness to light.

The next issue (Feb. 12) stated:

> From Berlin, Canada, comes the good news that fifty-eight persons took a stand for Christ during the meetings held recently at that place by Bro. S. G. Shetler of Johnstown, Pa. We trust that all will prove faithful servants for the Master.

And then again, March 4, the *Witness* reported:

> Bro. Shetler closed his evangelistic work in Canada by taking part in an all-day instruction at Berlin on Feb. 20, where nearly a hundred converts

had gathered. We are informed that about all of these will be received
into the church in the near future. May they indeed be servants who will
grace their calling and exemplifying the doctrines of Christ in their lives,
and be used of the Master in enlarging His church upon the earth.

While the paper reported "nearly a hundred converts," there
were actually exactly a hundred. A list of these appears in the appendix. The fact that "about all" were to be received into church
fellowship was not an unusual result of his meetings. His
confessions usually resulted in accessions, since he drove home the
need for having church connections if one is to succeed in the
Christian life. And his emphasis on the Bible doctrines upheld by
the Mennonite Church led his converts to make that the church of
their choice.

That this percentage of accessions at Kitchener was indeed
more than ordinary is evidenced by an editorial in the *Witness*
(October 30, 1907) in which the editor expressed some concern for
the gap between confessions and accessions in evangelistic meetings. Of the 158 confessions in one conference district of the Mennonite Church in 1906, only 116 had become affiliated with the
church. The editor continued, "When less than 75 percent of
those who make public confessions unite with the church . . . it
looks as though there were something seriously wrong with the
work."

Bible conferences had become quite an established institution by 1908, but there was need now for some guidance. In his
wide experience with these meetings my father had something to
suggest to the planners. He did this in an article published in the
Witness, May 23. He pleaded for a wider range of time than the
holidays for these conferences which he noted was obviously
"choice time." It was hard for any given instructor to plan all of
his conferences to fit into the holiday season. He wrote: "We
know of one instructor (likely himself) who has 24 calls already
before March 1909." He suggested, too, that only two daily
sessions be held instead of three. The first could start at 9:30 or
10:00 a.m., closing at 1:00 and the second at 6:00 or 6:30, closing
at 9:00. Where people live closer together perhaps three sessions

could be held. He suggested also opening on Wednesday rather than on Monday to allow travel time for the instructors without necessitating travel on the Lord's Day.

His comments on the value of the Bible conference are worthy of note, since these comments were made during the era of Bible conferences. An evaluation of these were also given previously. He wrote in this instance:

> Many souls have found Christ in these meetings. Leaders in the church have come closer in touch with each other. There is more uniformity in teaching the Word. The churches have become better indoctrinated. A number of popular church members [meaning those in churches outside our own] have been made to realize that we base our belief on God's Word, and some have come to unite and labor with us. It has resulted in much Bible study. The mission interest has been increased. In a number of places public opinion as to our standard as a church has been favorably raised. Many evidences of a deeper consecration have been seen, and considerable worldliness has been cast aside. An earnest desire for more knowledge of God's Word [has resulted].

He states that there would be at least 35 conferences held during the next year (1908-1909).[34] As indicated earlier it is impossible to measure the tremendous impact of the movement.

The same month S. G. Shetler had written another article titled "Evangelistic Observations." It was a careful analysis of what it takes to have an effective evangelistic service. He noted that the number of confessions in a meeting is not important, rather the spiritual condition of the church and "if that is not as it should be there will be no confessions." What he considered a "favorable situation" for a successful revival service included such considerations as: good attendance, many children just old enough to accept [Christ], "perfect harmony in the church," praying fathers and mothers, a good Sunday school, Spirit-filled ministers, a church that is in close touch with "outsiders," easy access to the church, good weather, "souls starting to confess from the beginning of the meetings and in turn inviting others."

During the year he held revival meetings and Bible conferences in four Illinois churches, in four Iowa churches, in Maryland, Ohio, Michigan, Minnesota, and Pennsylvania, besides participating in two Sunday school conferences. On August 16 he preached the dedicatory sermon for the new Glade Church in Garrett County, Maryland. At this same place he conducted revival meetings with 14 confessions. In a card sent to the editor of the *Gospel Herald* from Fairview, Michigan, December 19, he said, "Souls are confessing. I could live in Oscoda County, Michigan."

In November he and my mother had an interesting experience from which he drew a number of illustrations for the messages through the years. They accompanied the newly appointed missionaries, Mary Burkhard, Elsie Drange, and Eva Harder to New York and watched them embark on the *Adriatic* for India. He commented in a news note to the *Herald* that "the missionaries seemed anxious to get to their field of labor...." Incidentally, Elsie Drange, a convert of the Chicago Mission, was to become the wife of my mother's brother, J. N. Kaufman, who was at the time a missionary in India.

1909-1913

There was but little change from the regular routine in the years between 1909 to 1913. My father returned again to Ontario in 1909 for several meetings and also to various states from the East to the Midwest. From Nappanee, Indiana, he had to return abruptly to his home on account of illness, something extremely rare in his ministry.

In the summer of 1909 he had the occasion of visiting the Chicago Mission (incidentally the first "Home Mission" in the Mennonite Church) and reported that the work "looks encouraging." He was a close friend of A. Hershey Leaman, who served there as superintendent for years.

In September of that year he was given the honor of delivering the dedicatory address at the opening of the new academy at Hesston, Kansas. He had gone there from Science Ridge, Illinois, where he had been holding meetings. Mary Miller, in *A Pillar of Cloud,* the history of Hesston College and Bible school, relates the event in her book:

In an evening service on Tuesday, September 21, 1909, Hesston Academy
and Bible School opened its doors and was solemnly dedicated. George R.
Brunk conducted the service and S. G. Shetler spoke on "What seest thou
in thine house?" T. M. Erb reported a "splendid sermon" and a "large
crowd"![35]

Allen Erb, a son of Bishop T. M. Erb, the first treasurer of the
school, was present that evening. In 1971 he related his memories
of the event, remarkably recalling some of the details of my
father's sermon. Shetler, with several other men, had been
consulted in 1908 about the possibility of assuming the principalship of the new school in the West but had declined. Instead, his
lifelong friend and colleague in the Southwestern Pennsylvania
Conference, D. H. Bender, was chosen for the job.

In November my father wrote an article on "The Government—Our Duty Toward It," No. 15 of a series, "Gospel Lights
on Timely Topics." Many in the church came to recognize S. G.
Shetler for his clear and sound understanding of church-and-state
relationships.

In 1910 my father made his first contact with the churches of
Augusta County, Virginia. He was to return to this section of the
church numerous times in the years ahead. At Groffdale Church,
Lancaster County, Pennsylvania, in late summer, he preached his
2000th sermon, on the text 2 Samuel 19:35, one of his favorite
texts. He preached the dedicatory sermon of the Pleasant Grove
Church near Salix, Pennsylvania, August 28, using for his text 1
Kings 9:3, "I have hallowed this house, which thou hast built, to
put my name there for ever." He also preached the dedication
sermon for the new Pleasant View Church near Schellsburg, Pennsylvania, that fall. The fact of his busy schedule is noted on a
card sent to Bishop Benjamin Weaver of the Lancaster
Conference in which he stated in his typical, abbreviated style:

Your postal received. Will fill appointments as arranged. Am so
busy I can hardly get ready in time.

And then a short personal note,

Little Margaret [then only one year old] has not been well
for the last week.
Wish you all well.

Yours in love,
S. G. S.[36]

The year 1911 found him again in Canada, serving a number
of churches, and also in Ohio at several places. In the latter area
he was "accompanied by his wife and two small children" (Goldie
and Margaret). In Holmes County they visited their Shetler relatives.

In August 1911 Daniel Kauffman and my father were
instructors in a Bible conference at the Blooming Glen Church in
the Franconia Conference in eastern Pennsylvania. It was the first
meeting of its kind in this conference and it drew large crowds.
Rhine Benner remembered (1971) riding each night to this meeting on a hired "hack" which carried sixteen passengers. There
were two seats that ran lengthwise on the sides of the carriage.
The fee for the round trip between Souderton and Blooming Glen
was 25 cents.[37]

It has been pointed out by some Mennonite writers that the
aim of Kauffman and Shetler in this conference was to "bring the
bonnet back" on the sisters. But Benner, recalling the whole
event, said this could by no means have been considered the aim
of the conference, at least as he perceived it. Instead, he said,
there was well-rounded teaching on every phase of the Christian
life. It is true, as he recalled, that the church of that area had at
that time departed somewhat from the general practices of the
church on nonconformity including such matters as the failure to
wear the conventional bonnet. The teaching of the Scriptures,
however, aroused such conviction in the members that there was
at this time a general return to a more nonconformed position.[37a]

I recall my father referring to these meetings frequently.
This was an example of how a church's departure from the faith
need not be considered a "lost cause" as many ministers are prone
to think in similar circumstances. He cited the return, in this
instance, to simplicity in attire, which did include the bonnet, but

he did not consider this by any means a "bonnet" conference. No doubt the leaders of the church who had planned for this meeting did have some definite concerns for the church which may have been shared with the speakers, but whatever their motives, we do know that it was neither Kauffman's or Shetler's method to preach anything but a balanced message. Neither of them, for example, came from a "plain district." Whatever the motives of the planners of the meeting or of the speakers themselves may have been, we do know that this particular conference left nothing but a good influence in the Franconia Conference for many years. Some of the older people in recent years have testified to the impact these men, under the power of the Spirit, left upon the Blooming Glen Church of that era.

Additional light on my father's balanced nonconformity teaching comes out in his comments on that subject made at a Bible conference at Elida, Ohio, in November of that same year. "Nonconformity to the world," he said, "should always be discussed from a Bible viewpoint and not from a church or custom viewpoint." Speaking of dress in part of his message, he stressed the fact that "the Bible does not say how a garment shall be made, but it does say that the believer's apparel must be modest." If the heart is right he said, "all else *will* be right." There was certainly nothing provincial or "cultural" in his approach.

The early part of the following year (1912) was taken up in additional Bible conferences in Ohio, Indiana, and Michigan. Churches served in these respective areas were: Clinton, Central, and Lockport, in Fulton County, Ohio; Yellow Creek in Elkhart, Indiana; and Bowne, in Kent County, Michigan. At Yellow Creek there were 35 confessions; J. K. Bixler served with my father for four days of that conference.

Teachers' normal school that summer was large with 51 students. During July and August there were some appointments for special meetings in eastern Pennsylvania at Mount Joy, Elizabethtown, and Lancaster.

In June of that year, a son, Sanford, was born, and the family of five—four daughters and one son—was now complete. As noted earlier, a set of twins had died in infancy.

In September my father's routine changed again. Once more he returned to the school room, this time to teach in the Church Grove (public) school in Richland Township in Cambria County. This meant a long drive each day with horse and buggy, but his daughter, Luella, was teaching at the Blough school near Krings Station, which was on his route, so this made it convenient for both. Luella was teaching her fifth term of school which was also her last.[38] In December of that year she married Harry E. Miller of Springs, Pennsylvania. For my father this year of teaching was a kind of interim job, since the following year, December 1913, he with the family, moved to Oregon.

Prior to the new assignment in Oregon, however, my father returned in September 1913 to the Shenandoah Valley of Virginia for an extended period of revival meetings. He served in the Northern District at Lindale, Zion, Trissels, and Brenneman. Elizabeth Showalter, then six, says these were the first revival meetings she remembers, and that they made a deep impression on her. Her brothers, Luke and Michael, became Christians in these meetings. She remembers too that there seemed to be a "stir of rejoicing" when George Mason and his wife, a young couple of the area, came into the church. Mason's wife was "not from the Mennonites," and "to have some one like this to accept the call in those days was worthy of comment." Young as she was, she says, "the feeling came through to me." Recalling these memories in 1972, she noted further that "Shetler's use of illustrations and his choruses" were of popular appeal—a break from the usual type of preaching of those times, and "as a child I felt the excitement of the elders." She said that when she heard some of S. G.'s stories in later years she remembered having heard them at this revival.[39]

Mark Showalter, another esteemed church worker of the area, also recalled these meetings, though he too, was quite young. He remembered, too, Shetler's excellent ability to recall names. In 1917, while living for a while in eastern Ohio, he attended his meetings at Leetonia, Ohio. My father, sitting in the "amen corner," noticed two young men coming in and at once recognized Mark. Using an illustration from Virginia that evening in his sermon, he made special mention of this young man from Virginia being present, and after the service addressed him by name. This made a lasting impression on young Mark.[40]

In October my father held evangelistic services at South English, Iowa, which coincided for part of the time with the Publication Board Meeting (October 25-27). The editor of the *Herald* made special mention of this in the November 6 issue:

> The evangelistic services held before and during the Board meetings are deserving of special mention. For over a week Bro. S. G. Shetler had been faithfully proclaiming the Word. A number of precious souls had already confessed their Savior. Each evening, after an hour's discussion of some subject pertaining to literature, a stirring sermon was preached which drove the truth home to attentive congregations.[41]

At the General Conference at Kalona, Iowa, immediately after the Publication Board Meeting, my father was elected assistant secretary. Through this office and his later position as moderator, he came to serve for a number of years on the executive committee of the Publication Board. At the Kalona meeting he and George R. Brunk spoke on "The Mission of Literature in the Work of the Church." Both emphasized the need of guarding against "poisonous" literature and of choosing the "right kind" of books.

In an article in the *Gospel Herald* appearing December 4, titled "The Two Sides of an Evangelist's Life," one can gain some idea of the strains he was beginning to feel in his heavy program of carrying on his evangelistic work away from home and also in making a living. He notes that if you live in the city there are some advantages, but the cost of living is high. In the country it is cheaper but more work and chores are involved. He was no doubt thinking of the work load on a family when the evangelist is away from home. Whether the family had given any consideration at all to moving back to town is not known. He wrote:

> The cost of living can be much reduced by having a garden and truck patch. Very well! The evangelist plants corn, tomatoes, potatoes, beans,

etc., and then goes out for six weeks' work. One of two things will take place, either the wife and children must fight the weeds, or the whole family must hear the remark, "He is too lazy to raise his own eatables."

He writes further:

1) Dear Reader, where shall evangelists live? and 2) who shall train the children?
The children of evangelists are just as human as any other children. They need the same careful training. To leave all this to the beloved wife is more than any true-hearted evangelist cares to do. Besides, his children are very closely watched. The mistakes his children made are nearly always considered worse than if made by other children.

He then raises still another question: What relation shall he bear to the home congregation?

No one congregation will prosper very well, when under the care of a pastor who is almost continually in other fields. Such a congregation keenly and rightly feels her loss and continually begs the pastor to preach at home. To be in a congregation without pastoral duties, robs him of the important and necessary experience in church government to do successful work elsewhere.

He further speaks of the matter of the evangelist's use of money when traveling. He compares the evangelist's travels to that of a tourist who enjoys a fine night's rest in a Pullman coach and eats in the diner.

He who is sent to gather in the lost spends many long hours in depots. At nights he takes a nap between the conductor's "all tickets." For breakfast he takes contentedly to a sandwich bought on the train or to the last of the lunch box that he has carried under his arm for the last two days.

At the church itself where he is carrying on the evangelistic meetings there are some problems: meeting the expectation of the congregation, and whom to visit. Visiting alone can be a strenuous undertaking. But it is important.

If time permits it is wise to visit every home where there is one or more members, homes of unconverted, and homes of people belonging to other churches.

Recalling the earlier section on his heavy home visitation program in connection with his revival meetings one knows what he is talking about. The whole article gives good insights on the problems and strains that an evangelist of that day faced at home, away from home, and enroute.

Shortly after this article appeared, the long move to Oregon took place, the story of which appears in Chapter 11.

10
Eight Important Years
(1913-1921)

The years between 1913 and 1921 were crucial for S. G. Shetler. During this period the minister-educator, now in his forties, was confronted with some of the most important decisions of his life. During this period, too, he came to hold the highest positions both in his educational and church careers. And it was during these years that he conducted the last of his summer normals for the training of public school teachers.

In church, S. G. Shetler was ordained to the office of bishop in 1915. In that same year the *Christian Workers' Manual,* of which he was coauthor, was published. In 1917 he was elected moderator of Mennonite General Conference, the highest official post in the denomination.

In the educational field he was asked to become principal of a new church academy to be opened in Virginia—Eastern Mennonite School which was later to become Eastern Mennonite College. Similar contacts had been made earlier as to the possibility of his serving in the same capacity at Hesston Academy and Bible School in Kansas. In Oregon he was elected principal of the Hubbard schools, the highest position he ever held in the public schools.

This was also the World War I era, and much of my father's

145

time during that period was taken up in counseling conscientious objectors, helping them secure proper recognition from the government. In August 1917 he was appointed by Mennonite General Conference to serve on a committee of three to interview the secretary of war of the USA in behalf of the Mennonite conscientious objectors.

This eight-year period might also well be designated the "Oregon Years," since nearly half of this time, intermittently from 1913 to 1921, was spent on the West Coast. While there he helped establish the Pacific Coast Bible School and a short-term winter school. He became a key figure in helping to bring about a merger of the Western Amish Mennonite Church and the Pacific Coast Mennonite Conference.

Call to Become Principal of the New School in the East

Soon after the turn of the century there was considerable sentiment for the establishment of a school somewhere in the eastern part of the United States for the training of Mennonite young people who at the time were being lost to the church through higher education and other influences. Elkhart Institute (Goshen college in 1903) had already been founded in 1894 in Indiana.

Sentiment for the new school was crystallized in December 1912 when a group of brethren from Virginia at a meeting held in Denbigh decided to establish a school with a "prevailing religious influence in defense of the simple Gospel." Here students would be trained who would develop "physically, morally, intellectually, and spiritually." The account of the founding of this school and the search for suitable men to head up the new institution is told in interesting detail in Hubert Pellman's history of *Eastern Mennonite College—1917-1967*. What follows is drawn largely from his book.[42]

The first hint that my father was to be asked to accept a position of leadership in the new school was given in a letter L. J. Heatwole of Dayton, Virginia, had written to his family while he was in Denbigh helping to work out some details about the school. He wrote in a high note of expectancy, "It is expected that Dan Kaufman and J. S. Shetler (meaning S. G.) will be asked to take charge of this school—and the Loucks family at Scottdale, which is worth half a million, is expected to support the school with a good donation."

Bishop Heatwole, who was a member of the planning committee, had a deep concern for the church and noted that in the period between 1900 and 1915, "much of the best talent of the church was lost to the church." A church school, according to these concerned leaders, would help stop this gap.

During 1913 efforts were made to secure S. G. Shetler to serve as the principal of the new school. Pellman notes that "the faculty committee tried hard but unsuccessfully to persuade S. G. Shetler, Mennonite teacher and evangelist from southwestern Pennsylvania, who at the time was 'on the Pacific slope' " to become the principal. "Conservative, able, and prominent in the church," Pellman writes, "he was eminently qualified for this position." While he does not mention my father's educational background at this point, academically he had the equivalent of a college education, and with his years of conducting teachers' normals he had what appeared at the time to be the ideal background for such a position.

The search for a "capable and conscientious" principal continued through the spring and summer of 1914. S. G. Shetler and Daniel Kauffman "were implored to consider the matter seriously, but neither accepted the position." On February 6, 1915 the first annual meeting of the board took place, at which time it was decided to go ahead with plans in spite of the difficulties they were encountering, not the least of which was to secure a principal. Soon after this meeting, vice-president of the board, George R. Brunk, Sr., who was also a member of the faculty committee, wrote to J. J. Wenger outlining the situation and giving his approach to the problem. He said, "The first thing is to find a man to head the school, and the second thing is to find money to put into the school and the rest will be easy." He stated further that "unless someone like D. K. (Daniel Kauffman) or Shetler becomes the head and promotes the thing it cannot go forward but will drag as it has."

Not much progress was made in 1915, but the board, still hopeful that either Kauffman or Shetler would say, yes, let the matter rest for some months. In December plans were made to lease the main building at Assembly Park near Harrisonburg, Virginia, for one or two short Bible terms. It would be conducted like an original Bible term conducted at Hayfield Mansion near Alexandria in January of that year. In fact, out of this effort the board hoped the new school would emerge. Daniel Kauffman had served as principal. The Assembly Park building was subsequently leased and served as the facility for several more winter terms of Bible school.

My father had been asked to serve on the Bible school faculty and consented to do so for two weeks in 1917. He wrote to L. J. Heatwole on December 4, 1916, "I have promised to come to the Mission Board Meeting and will therefore be at the opening of the Bible term. Cannot stay longer than the two weeks formerly promised. Am leaving for Cumberland County [Pa.] today. Pray for us." Signed, "S.G."

The final call to accept the principalship of the new school was made on April 19, 1917, the board having met in January to formulate plans for the actual opening of the school in the fall. The resolution, which Pellman refers to as a "mighty last summons," was as follows:

> Resolved, since S. G. Shetler, of Johnstown, Pa., is the unanimous choice of the Faculty Committee, Board of Trustees, Virginia Conference, and all brethren in the East, so far as opportunity has been given for an expression, we hereby declare that S. G. Shetler is this day chosen as head or principal of the Eastern Mennonite School to be located at Assembly Park, near Harrisonburg, Virginia, and that it is the desire of that body that the school be opened the coming September, 1917, but if not practicable at that time, then a time in the future to be suggested by the principal now elected.

A copy of this resolution was sent to Shetler, with a letter stating that a furnished cottage would be provided for him and his family on the school grounds. "But Shetler did not accept," says Pellman, "and the leaders in Virginia finally ceased calling." It was J. B. Smith of Elida, Ohio, who became the first principal of E.M.S. when it opened its doors officially that fall.

At this point in time it may seem difficult to understand why such an important call was not accepted, but there are always extenuating circumstances which condition such decisions. In this case, my father's widening ministry in the church, his call to the West Coast, as well as the new situation thrust upon the church because of the war at the time the "mighty last summons" came in 1917, all certainly had some bearing in helping to make such a move seem inadvisable. Family considerations also entered the picture.

Through the years, however, he remained sympathetic to the school as it developed into a major institution, and he served there on various occasions. Among other assignments through the years, he served as a part-time Bible instructor in the short-term Bible school in 1917. In 1928 and 1929, respectively, he delivered the baccalaureate and commencement addresses.

Coauthor of a Ministers' Manual—1915

In 1915, Volume I of a *Christian Workers' Manual* was published by the Mennonite Publishing House. Volume II, on the Sunday school, was ready before its companion volume had been published two years earlier. Noah E. Byers of Goshen College had been the author of that book. Volume I, on *The Ministry*, was the work of three writers, who, like Byers, had been assigned the task by Mennonite General Conference. They were: J. S. Shoemaker, of the Illinois Conference; S. G. Shetler, of the Southwestern Pennsylvania Conference; and John W. Weaver, of the Lancaster Conference. The three authors, however, were selected not only on the basis of geographic representation, but also apparently as qualified representatives of the ministerial calling. The publishers stated in the preface of the book:

It is our conviction that the authors of this volume have a message that can be used by the Spirit, not only for the benefit of young ministers, but for the strengthening and upholding of many a veteran in the church of Jesus Christ.

The writers of this volume need no introduction to the reader. They are well known throughout the church as men who are sound in the faith and aggressive leaders in the cause of Christ. That God may bless this effort to the ingathering of many souls and to the strengthening and confirming of many Christian workers is our wish and prayer.

Out of a total of ten chapters Shetler wrote three; Shoemaker, five; and Weaver, two. Shoemaker's chapters were: "The Minister as a Man," "The Minister as a Pastor," "The Minister as an Example," "The Preacher's Equipment," and "The Christian Home." Weaver wrote: "The Minister as Preacher," and "Evangelistic Work of the Church." Shetler's contribution was: "The Young Preacher's Problems," "Problems for All Preachers," and "Encouraging Features in the Minister's Experience."

Typical of so many of his sermons, after discussing the "dark side" (in the two chapters on the minister's problems), he closed on the "bright side" in his third chapter on "Encouraging Features." The contents of these three chapters characterize quite well my father's concept of the ministry as gained from his wide experience and the Scriptures. These chapters definitely reflect his own practice and deserve more than passing attention here.

His approach, first of all, was practical, not theoretical. Some of the problems he dealt with in his first two chapters were:

How to Win the Confidence of the People
How to Meet Unfavorable Criticism
Relation of Junior to Senior Minister
How to Solve the Financial Problem
How to Keep Worldliness out of the Church
How to Care for Young Converts
How to Reach and Maintain a High Standard of Spirituality

"Encouraging Features in the Minister's Experience," discussed in his third chapter, included the following:

The Peace of God Within the Soul
The Consciousness of Being in the Master's Service

The Assurance of the Spirit's Guidance
Daily Access by Prayer to the Throne of Grace
Victory Through Faith Over the Powers of Darkness
The Support of a Consistent Brotherhood
The Zeal of Noble-hearted Young People
The Increase of His Kingdom
The Hope of a Glorious Return

Some of the ideas presented in the various chapters are summarized below:

While a minister should not enter the pulpit as a "monarch of all he surveys," neither should he enter as a "fettered man," chained with a number of stiff rules or "false modesty." To see one put on a "sanctified look," and walk with "religious step," to "sit as if he feared a particle of dust might defile his sacred personage," to him seemed totally inappropriate. Yet a minister should be tidy.

      o   o   o

Possessing a comprehensive knowledge of the Bible was paramount. Some ministers, he felt, "study more outside knowledge" than they do the "inspired Word." He believed the Bible had something for all. Here he used his oratorical style, then quite popular. "In the Scripture may be found food for the artist, the naturalist, the poet, the agriculturist, the machinist, the linguist, the scientist, the philosopher, etc. There may be found comfort for the comfortless, encouragement for the discouraged, a warning for the unruly, strength for the helpless, an invitation for the sinner, and increased knowledge and power for all who will do his will."

      o   o   o

He deplored two-facedness and believed that trying merely to side in with someone one time and with another on another occasion was a breach of good ethics. Rather one should have settled convictions based "on the pure Word of God which will have much weight with any man of principle."

      o   o   o

Changing pastoral charges frequently for him was not the mark of a good preacher. "To continually change places . . . indicates an unsettled state of mind." He advised, too, against trying to fill too many roles, such as trying to be at the same time evangelist, pastor, teacher, and mission worker. "Be slow in choosing your work," he admonished, "then stay by it, aiming to do it well."

      o   o   o

He was not opposed to change, but for him, trying to follow every new fad, instituting new tactics, methods, or themes which became the fad for a short time and "which die like a mushroom" was not good policy.

o   o   o

Although he did not like the idea of paying a preacher "nine dollars to preach a sermon," as one small congregation he knew was doing, he felt a minister's work should not be hindered constantly because of a lack of funds. This too he had seen. He said, "There is no reason why a faithful servant of the Lord should be muzzled with a debt on only a small, comfortable home. How can a minister 'study to show himself approved unto God' when he must work hard six days out of the week?" On the other hand, while he advocated ministerial support, he believed that "working with one's hands" was a good quality of a minister. He felt that if a minister has a family "it is a blessing for them not to be dependent on others."

o   o   o

Opposed to long sermons, he recommended that preachers should "cut out of such sermons apologies, excuses, repetitions, nonessential parts, references to self, and such like, and you will have a good, practical sermon of proper length." He recognized, however, that there were times "when the sermons need to be lengthy," and deplored the "present-day tendency" to have services very short, so much so that "sometimes very little Bible [is] heard."

o   o   o

He was strong on the idea of involving many individuals in the work of the church "even if it is only to lift the offerings or visit some sick person at the suggestion of the pastor." And in all this a "word of encouragement" to persons "when they attempt some task as giving a talk or teaching a class" was important to help them grow in the Christian life.

o   o   o

Flattery and ostentation and titles for preachers had no place. Quoting the "Word" he reminded readers of Job's statement: "Neither let me give flattering titles unto man," and of Christ's words to the Pharisees, "But be not ye called Rabbi: for one is your Master, even Christ; and all ye are brethren."

o   o   o

One of his ideals was to have old and young working together. Again in somewhat oratorical fashion he wrote: "Happy is the state when an aged minister whose silvery locks indicate many wintry snows . . . and a young minister just entering the great battlefield, can go hand in hand winning souls for Jesus."

°   °   °

My father's concern for maintaining a sound and balanced position against worldliness comes out clearly in the book. He wrote: "Churches whose origin date back to a century or more have tried to keep worldliness out. Even some of later origin have taken the same ground. One by one they have lost the battle, and worldliness in some form or in all of its forms has robbed them of much power. Many pastors and other workers of the so-called popular churches lament this fact and frequently refer to it. The question may be asked, 'Are any churches to be found which are entirely free from worldliness?' But one answer is to be found [and that is], No." That he looked beyond mere outward forms, however, particularly fashionable dress as the only index of worldliness, is readily gathered from sentiments here and there in the book. He referred to the Bible's condemnation of "strange apparel," the wearing of gold for ornamentation, and similar adornments "against which God has pronounced his displeasure. . . ." But on the other hand he said, "Some churches have taught plain clothes, plain clothes, and have left other forms of worldliness sap out the very life of the church. Unfortunately, in the reaction to this overemphasis, the plain clothes are discarded. The mistake," he hastened to point out, "was not in the plain clothes, but in not guarding against other forms of worldliness."

Typical of his short, pointed subtopics used throughout his chapters is his list of suggestions on "How to Counteract Erroneous Doctrine":

1. Watch closely the teaching of your own members.
2. Watch the literature.
3. Note the early seed.
4. Present sound doctrine.
5. Rebuke sharply.
6. Reject the heretic.

As in all of his sermons, he used no long drawn-out propositions, but instead, pointed ideas couched in simple language. These he accompanied with lucid illustrations and then "clinched" the thoughts with Bible verses.

His last chapter on "Encouraging Features in the Minister's Experience" reveals the basic optimism which he carried with him through life. He noted that God was "the great equalizer," always balancing the problems of life with encouragement. There is, he said, a peace of God within the soul. For him the consciousness of "being in the Master's service" was a rewarding thought. "What a satisfaction," he wrote, "to really know that the service in which one is engaged is the Master's."

He observed the encouraging things in the church, "the growth in the last few decades for which we have reason to rejoice." He noted that "new fields had been attempted and congregations organized," and that "greater doors of opportunity lie ahead on every side." For him it was a great thought that there was hope "for the future day when men would rejoice 'in the day of Christ' that they had not 'labored in vain.'"

How widely the *Christian Workers' Manual* was read by ministers cannot easily be determined. Its style and format would probably be considered rather stuffy for our time, but what these men wrote came from their life experience and represented their highest ideals for the ministry in a day when formal training and "depth discussions" on theological issues had not yet become a part of the church's repertoire. Their ideals and suggestions, in short, epitomized rather well the thought patterns of that day, and there is no doubt that much of what they wrote still applies today. Something about their direct and simple style made their teaching and writing beautiful, even if it was not always profound or lacked literary finesse. At any rate this particular book undoubtedly helped build the church of that day just as the publishers had hoped it would.

11

The Oregon Ministry
(1913-1916 and 1920-1921)

First Period of Service, 1913-1916

In December 1913, at the invitation of Bishop J. D. Mishler of Hubbard, Oregon, S. G. Shetler, with his family, moved to Oregon to assist in the work of the Hopewell congregation and the Pacific Coast Mennonite Conference. Mishler, who had known my father for some years (his wife, the former Mary Hostetler, had been reared in Somerset County, Pennsylvania, saw in him a potential leader and helper for the thriving work on the West Coast.[43] Some prolonged effort had been made to persuade him to come West, which is reflected in a report by Mishler to the *Herald* (April 24, 1913):

> We are glad to say things here are in a growing condition, and also glad that Bro. S. G. Shetler has finally decided to come to this western field the latter part of this year to labor for a season. He will bring his family and stay a year, which we hope will be a help to the cause in this western field.

The "western field" was still relatively new. In fact, the first settlers having arrived there only at the end of the previous century. Because of the distance from the eastern churches and a certain degree of isolation, any influx of members, let alone leaders, was obviously welcomed.

The trip West in those days was in itself an event. En route the family stopped half a day in Chicago with the Mennonite mission workers of that city. Taking the northernmost route from there by way of the Great Northern Railway, they stopped at Kalispell, Montana. Here, by previous arrangement, services were held with the Mountain View congregation where Jacob Roth was pastor. At Roth's insistence, it had been planned that Shetler was to conduct services "in the English language" and also baptize a class of applicants for church membership. These young converts had been the fruits of the labors of young evangelist Isaac Mast of North Dakota, who had held meetings there in September.

During this two-day stopover at Kalispell, Shetler's daughter, Rosella, then 18, met her future husband, John M. Bachman, a young man of the area. John's sister, Fanny, had been one of the five baptized.

Arriving in Oregon shortly after the middle of December, the family immediately adjusted to the new environment and took up the tasks assigned. The new place of residence was a comfortable house just outside the town of Hubbard and close to the school where Goldie, aged 8, would attend. Margaret was then 4 and the writer 18 months old. The contentment of everyone with the new home is shown in two short notes written shortly after being established at Hubbard. One was written to the *Gospel Herald*, the other to Walter Mishler, a young man of Johnstown. To the *Herald* my father wrote:

> So far our work in the western field has been pleasant . . . as parents we rejoice that the children stood the trip so well and are so happy among new associates in home, school, and church. Remember us in prayer to Him who is able to answer.

To Mishler he wrote on a card dated February 28: "We are all well and very glad that we came West. Children have not been homesick at all. They do not want to go back."

Several other *Herald* items reflected the feelings of both those who were left behind at the home church and of those of the new group at Hubbard. Levi Blauch of Johnstown, who was a frequent writer to the *Herald's* correspondence columns, wrote shortly after the Shetlers left, "One special loss the district had is the moving away of Bro. S. G. Shetler and family. May a kind heavenly Father bless him and family while away." And two weeks later the Hopewell Church correspondent reported in the same columns:

> Brother S. G. Shetler and family arrived here safely for which we are thankful and with the exception of colds have been enjoying good health. We feel that their presence has already been a blessing to the community.

As might be expected, my father soon became involved deeply in church work both at the new "home church" and also in other parts of the conference district. Impressed with the "western field" he again wrote in the *Herald:*

> We are glad to report that in each congregation visited so far we have found those who are interested in and concerned about the welfare of the church. Have also found that the same satanic influences are at work here as elsewhere.

From December 29 to January 3, 1914, a Bible conference was held at Hopewell with S. G. Shetler and J. P. Bontrager serving as instructors. The next two weeks he was the Albany and Fairview churches serving in the same capacity with C. R. Gerig. In February and March he held revival meetings at Nampa, Idaho, and at Kalispell, Montana. At that time both of these areas were part of the Pacific Coast Conference. Later that spring he held revival meetings at the Bethel Church near Hubbard. My father often told of a sad event which occurred in connection with the Nampa meetings. He had just stepped off the train at Hubbard upon his return from Idaho, when a telegram was handed him. The Nampa pastor, David Hilty, had suddenly passed away and my father was to return immediately for the funeral service. Having just left Bro. Hilty in seemingly good health, this sudden passing was an abrupt reminder of the uncertainty of life. He often referred to this in his evangelistic messages.

During June and July he conducted evangelistic meetings at

five churches in the Canadian province of Alberta: Mount View, Mayton, Salem, West Zion, and Clearwater. From there he returned to the states, holding meetings at two North Dakota congregations: Minot and Spring Valley. Later that summer he conducted evangelistic services at the home church, Hopewell.

In the meantime the family had settled down to the familiar domestic routine of rural families of the time—gardening and canning of fruits and vegetables and the daily chores of feeding livestock and milking. Canning season was brightened with the abundant supply of the lucious Oregon berries and cherries and other fruits. Members of the family joined in berry picking and to aid the family budget Rosella and my mother worked part-time in the onion fields.

At the annual meeting of the Pacific Coast Conference, October 1, 2, 1914, at the Hopewell Church the new minister was recognized in various ways. There was a resolution which read:

> Resolved that this conference express our sincere thanks and appreciation by a rising vote to Bro. S. G. Shetler and family for their sacrifice they have made in leaving their eastern home, and while in our midst, to help us in this great work; and whereas we see the need of more workers in this western field, be it therefore
>
> Resolved that we as a conference earnestly invite them to continue their labors.

This resolution was not made in a blind hope that the family would stay, beyond the promised year, since it was known by this time that my father had accepted a teaching position in the schools of the area. He had received an offer he felt he could not afford to turn down. He had written about this in May 22 letter to his friend, Samuel Mishler. The letter was written from Filer, Idaho, where he was holding meetings at the time: "We are all well at home. Harry's like it fine, and we are not coming back this fall. I have a school for next winter at $80 a month." "Harry's" was a reference to his son-in-law and daughter, Harry and Luella Miller, and their small son Harold, the Shetlers' first grandson. They had come to Oregon to live some time previously.

A number of responsibilities were assigned the new minister

from the East at the October conference. He was elected moderator, a post which he held for two years; he was elected district evangelist and a delegate to General Conference. He was also placed on a committee to revise the conference constitution and discipline. The report of this latter committee was unanimously adopted at the next annual meeting of conference in 1915 at Filer, Idaho.

In preparation for this work of revision the committee had acquired copies of the constitutions of all the major Mennonite conferences. In reviewing these my father was so impressed with the churchwide unanimity in doctrine and practice, that he wrote an article for the *Herald* (September 2, 1915), titled, "We Are One." It might be observed that it is altogether possible that there never has been a period in North American Mennonite history when there was such sincere unanimity in faith and practice in all areas of the church as in the early decades of the present century. For the historical value this may have here, I am giving the full text of his article, which was written from Johnstown in the summer of 1915.

We Are One
By S. G. Shetler

For the *Gospel Herald*

The Pacific Coast Conference desiring a Constitution and Discipline for their own district, appointed a committee of three brethren to formulate the same for consideration at the Church Conference to be held at Filer, Idaho, Sept. 27 and 28, 1915. The committee obtained the Rules and Disciplines of all the other Mennonite Conferences in America that have printed disciplines. Besides this they obtained from some conferences the printed minutes from the time of organization. The purpose of obtaining these was for the help to be obtained from them, and also that we might be in harmony with other conferences. After examining and studying these disciplines and minutes, we were much impressed with the following:

1. On all the vital and fundamental doctrines upheld by the Mennonite Church for centuries, they are one.

2. All are agreed on the gospel teaching in a life separate from the world.

3. Active work for salvation of the lost by means of evangelistic and mission work is supported by all.

4. None of them hold the discipline as a means of salvation, but as a means of godly edification and strengthening of the brotherhood.

Our heart throbbed with joy as we noticed this unity in the churches from coast to coast.

"Behold, how good and how pleasant it is for brethren to dwell together in unity." The question came to us, How could such unity come about?

Surely the love of God prompted the brethren in their respective fields of labor to so adopt a system of rules, based on the Lord, and thus a unity that we can truly say, "We are one."

Johnstown, Pennsylvania

At the 1914 conference at Hopewell action had also been taken to approve J. D. Mishler's request for the ordination of a bishop at Hopewell to assist him. Subsequently, on February 28, 1915, upon the approval of the congregation, S. G. Shetler was ordained to the office of bishop by Bishops J. D. Mishler and J. P. Bontrager.

Since plans had been made for an extended stay in the West, because of the serious illness of Grandmother Shetler in Pennsylvania, a decision was made to return to Pennsylvania for the summer months. With a marked note of anticipation he wrote again to the *Herald,* March 1: "The time is fast drawing nigh when we shall start on our journey eastward. These have been fifteen months of varied experiences and we feel grateful to God for caring for us both materially and spiritually." The Hopewell correspondent's note to the *Herald* for the April 15 issue stated that "S. G. Shetler's school will close Friday, April 2, and he and his family will start the following Monday for their home in Pennsylvania to remain during the summer months."

In order to visit some of the Mennonite churches in the Southern part of the United States, a decision was made to take the "rim route" via California, Texas, Louisiana, and the East Coast. A stopover was made at Porterville, Los Angeles, and Pasadena, California. At the latter places, respectively, Aldus Brackbill and Parke Lantz were ministers. On a Wednesday evening a preparatory and communion service was held in the Brackbill home.

The town of Arolsen in the principality of Waldeck-Pyrmont, Germany, birthplace of Christian Schöttler (1804), as it appeared in 1967.

S. G. Shetler as a boy.

Jacob and Amelia, parents of S. G., 1915.

Maggie Jane Kaufman, later Mrs. S. G. Shetler, as a young girl.

S. G. Shetler, 1886 or 1887.

S. G. Shetler as a young man of 18 or 19 in 1889 or 1890.

The original Shetler home near Stahl meetinghouse, around 1900.

Goldie, Margaret, and S. G. Shetler in 1911 or 1912.

On the way to Oregon, 1913—Rosella, Mrs. Shetler, a porter, Goldie, Margaret, and Sanford.

Sanford and his nephew, Harold Miller, in a buggy at the Shetler homestead about 1916.

S. G. Shetler family picture (about 1918). Back row: Harry Miller and Luella (holding Allen), Goldie, Margaret, Rosella and her husband, John Bachman. Front row: Grandfather Jacob (holding Clyde Miller), Harold Miller, S. G., Sanford, and Maggie.

Family picture about 1928.

Holsopple Grade School, 1899, with teacher S. G. Shetler at the left and Luella in the front row at the far right.

Conemaugh Normal at the Miller school around 1900, with S. G. Shetler seated near the top (book in hand).

Winter Bible term at Goshen College in 1904. Third row: Ruth Buckwalter (?), Ella Musselman, Howard Moor, H. F. Reist, Anna Kauffman, Sam Zook, C. E. Bender, S. G. Shetler, Conny Buler, Eva _____, Second row: Abram Herr, Mrs. Kauffman, _____, Mrs. Shetler, C. R. Wolford, Clara Reist (?). First row: N. E. Miller, Sam Yoder, _____, Hess, _____, Christ Hooley, John Byler.

The summer 1906 Conemaugh normal class held at Miller Elementary School, with teacher S. G. Shetler at the left.

The Hopewell Church, Hubbard, Oregon, 1920.

Pacific Coast Bible School at Hopewell Church, 1921.

Johnstown Bible School, 1923, with S. G. Shetler at left.

J. Irvin Lehman, S. G. Shetler, and D. A. Yoder at Archbold, Ohio, in the late 1930s.

D. A. Yoder, A. J. Metzler, and S. G. Shetler at Archbold, Ohio, in the late 1930s.

173

Summer Bible school at Coatesville, Pennsylvania (Lancaster area), in 1938, with an enrollment of 470 pupils.

Opposite page: Summer Bible school at Pinto, Maryland, 1936. Ernest Bennett is to the left of the tree at the near corner of the church.

Johnstown Bible School faculty, 1940. Back: Aaron Mast, Nelson Kauffman, Elmer E. Yoder. Front: Paul Roth, Christmas Carol Carol Kauffman, S. G. Shetler.

In another of his many notes to the *Herald*, he wrote, "The brethren at Tuleta, Texas, had so strongly urged us to stop, but we feared to tarry long" [because of the urgency to getting to his mother's bedside]. The fact was the schedule had already been upset because of a freight train wreck which had blocked the tracks and delayed them for seventeen hours. This in itself had been quite a trying experience. It was extremely warm, and in those days trains were not air-conditioned. To help alleviate some of the discomfort, dampened towels were hung in the open windows of the train, an example of my mother's ingenuity. The train passed through Lake Charles, Louisiana, on a Sunday morning, but because of the delay they had experienced they could not stop here either as had previously been planned.

Describing the trip home my father wrote some time after their return:

> We left our field of labor in Oregon, April 7, and stopped only at a few places on account of the illness of my mother, whom we were anxious to meet again.
>
> The journey from Oregon to Washington, D.C., was new to us, and thus the time passed speedily, yet we were all eager to get to Johnstown.
>
> At Johnstown the family was met at the station by H. J. Custer and wife and J. T. Eash and wife, who took us in their autos to my mother's home.

It was a moving scene, no doubt, as he describes the meeting of loved ones:

> Our heart was filled up with gratitude and praise to find Mother still living. Though it was one o'clock at night, yet we spent the moments in pleasant conversation.

He noted further, "We already feel that the time will be entirely too short to fill calls and to visit until the middle of August when we will again start westward."

In a letter to the *Herald* in June he makes further reference to the trip home and the reuniting with friends. In this he noted that his first preaching appointment in the home district was at the Kaufman Church on April 25, and the second at Stahl that same day. With affection he wrote: "The latter is the congrega-

tion where we were members for 23 years. It seemed like home to
see the many familiar faces." And though the family had come
home to Johnstown for the summer, his away-from-home
schedule continued unabated. He writes at length:

> On June 2, wife, little son, and I, started for an eight days' work in some of
> the eastern counties of the state. The next day the Sunday school meeting
> was at Hanover, York County. The attendance and interest showed that
> the church is at work.
>
> The next day we enjoyed ourselves in a similar meeting with the
> brotherhood in the Marion Church, Franklin County. The next day the
> Amish Mennonites churches of Chester and Lancaster counties held their
> first Sunday school meeting. It was a source of great joy to see both old
> and young take such an active part in the meeting. Every available seat
> was occupied and a number had to stand. The next morning, June 6, we
> were taken to the Conestoga A. M. Church, where we attended church
> and Sunday school. We enjoyed our visit to this congregation. In the
> evening we once more had the pleasure of speaking to a full house in
> Lancaster city.

He refers to the "Brick Church" near the town of Willow
Street as being in a "thickly settled community and the church active." Here, too, another "crowded house listened to the gospel."
This was apparently on Monday evening. A Sunday school meeting was held on Tuesday at Rohrerstown, and on Wednesday
forenoon he spoke at the Goodville Church. In the evening he was
at Groffdale where once again he says there was a "crowded
church" with an "attentive audience." He notes further that on
this trip he received much "information, help, and encouragement by meeting 12 bishops, 55 ministers, and 20 deacons." He
was further encouraged by the fact that a "number of the most active and consecrated feel keenly the responsibility of the work and
desire much that all might adhere more closely to the doctrines of
the Bible." Then he states a deep conviction of his, often
repeated: "The evangelistic, mission, and educational work is
judged by the church in general according to the product
received." He had by this time seen the church at the grass roots
level as well as the institutions and was able to see the problem
from both sides. There were those back home who were some-

times disappointed with some of the young people they had sent out, while, at the same time, he had also heard the argument of the institutional staffs that they could only work with the young people sent to them. Whatever allowances one would wish to make on either side, to him, however, the real test of the success of a church institution would always be the end product.

One of the significant contributions of the new Oregon pastor had been to help initiate a church building program at the Hopewell congregation. The small frame building had outgrown its usefulness, and so plans were made in 1915 to erect a larger structure. Prior to his trip east in the summer of 1915, a solicitation program had been set in motion. During the summer he took the liberty to solicit money for the project and in this he was quite successful.

In a long letter to the *Herald* about his eastern Pennsylvania tour, referred to above, he thanked those who had donated money for the new building. Impressed with the need in Oregon compared with the seeming abundance of facilities in the East, he wrote: "A great contrast has placed itself before us. Hundreds of people assemble in the east, while in the far west we are few in number. If the roof were taken off [a church building] about four church buildings of the far west could be put inside one of the large buildings of the east."

But his solicitation program was also carried on by mail, as the records seem to indicate. From the list of contributions in the Hopewell treasurer's records for that year, one gathers that he contacted a number of churches where he had previously held meetings. Donations came in from North Dakota, Illinois, California, Indiana, Ohio, Michigan, and Pennsylvania. The churches of the Johnstown area also responded well. From June 1915 to January 1916 receipts for the new building totaled $1,462.14, a sizable figure for those times. The total cost of the structure, exclusive of much donated labor, was $2,200. Of the total cash receipts, my father had collected from friends and churches $466.54. It is not known how much of the other donated money sent in came as a result of his contacts. Some interesting names in the list of donors were Preacher John F. Charles, Mountville, Pennsylvania; Preacher Joseph Lehman, Chambersburg, Pennsylvania; Martin B. Miller, Bainbridge, Pennsylvania; J. C. Frey, Archbold, Ohio; H. F. Reist, Scottdale, Pennsylvania; Abner Holderman, Wakarusa, Indiana; D. S. Weaver, Hesston, Kansas. Congregations also sent in offerings. Those from the Lancaster Conference, who sent in their contributions through the Eastern Mennonite Board of Missions and Charities, were: Kraybill, Mt. Joy, East Petersburg, Chestnut Hill, Salunga, and Landisville. Richfield, a central Pennsylvania congregation, also sent in an offering.

The summer of 1915 passed all too rapidly. It was far from a vacation in the usual sense of the word. My father's busy schedule continued. However there seemed to be time to visit some of the close friends of the area during the four months from April to August. Among these were the John Speigle, Sam Mishler, Moses Mishler, Silas Thomas, D. S. Yoder, and Levi Knavel families. Grandmother Shetler, while far from well, was improved enough that it was not thought inadvisable to return to the West.

In August my father attended General Conference at Archbold, Ohio, and was reelected assistant secretary. During the last part of that month the family started on its return trip to Oregon, stopping off in Cass County, Missouri, for revival meetings and in Filer, Idaho, in early September for the annual meeting of the Pacific Coast Conference. Reporting the trip again in the *Herald*, he wrote: "After a month of travelling we felt relieved to again be in the western home." He noted that in the meetings held at Hopewell to decide on the plan, size, and location, "perfect harmony prevailed." Work on the new building had in fact already begun at the time of his writing, and once again he wished to thank the "brethren and congregations in the East for their contributions."

As part of his new official duties as bishop, he ordained a deacon at Hopewell and also helped in an ordination at Albany.

By this time my father had stepped into a new teaching position. He had been elected principal of the Hubbard schools, which included both the elementary grades and high school, both of these schools were housed in a sizable new two-story brick structure, quite modern for the times. He had carried with him to the West Coast a recommendation from his former county superintendent in Pennsylvania which he was able to use to advantage in whatever job might turn up. It is probable that he had already used this the previous year. The recommendation read as follows:

> Somerset, Pa.
>
> This is to certify that Pro. S. G. Shetler of Hubbard, Oregon, has taught in the schools of Somerset County, Pa., for a number of years.
>
> Professor Shetler is a gentleman who stands high in the esteem of all those with whom he comes in contact. He is a man of strong character and unusual ability. He is earnest, conscientious, and faithful in all that pertains to his duties. He readily wins and holds the interest and respect of all his pupils and patrons. He is one of those who controls without any apparent effort.
>
> I consider Professor Shetler well qualified for any position in the schools and congratulate any board upon being so fortunate as to procure his services.
>
> Respectfully submitted,
> (Signed) *S. W. Seibert*

In his new position as "supervising principal," there seemed to be excellent rapport with his students, his teachers, and the citizens of the town. Years later, in visiting this same community, I found a number of persons in the town of Hubbard who still vividly remembered him as a teacher and minister. This fact seemed almost incredible considering his very short tenure there.

It was unfortunate that this job, scarcely begun, had to be terminated, but on January 1 news of grandmother's very critical condition reached the family, and the work in the school and church had to be abruptly ended. Arrangements had to be made immediately to leave for the East. The uncertainties of the involvements in the whole experience made it seem advisable to terminate the work on the West Coast. Sad, both for his mother's apparent terminal illness (she passed away that same month) and also for leaving behind a work he dearly loved, the family left for their destination shortly. On his last day of school he called the students together in an assembly and told them of his leave. As he often related the story in later years, many students were moved to tears as he bade them farewell.

My father preached his farewell sermon at the Hopewell congregation on Sunday morning January 9 to a full house. He preached again that evening at which time eight souls confessed Christ. Goldie, then 10, recalled (1978) that at this meeting she herself was under deep conviction to accept the call but thinking she was too young did not make it known publicly. The local correspondent, reporting this memorable event in the *Gospel Herald*, wrote:

> Many were the tears that flowed that day. We cannot understand why he should be called away when he is needed so much in the West.... May God bless and keep them. We are glad for the time the brother and family have spent in the West, hoping that if it is God's will they may return to the West, as he has been a great help in the cause. We shall indeed miss them in the church, in the conference, and in the school, where he was loved and respected by all.

Returning to Pennsylvania my father once more resumed the old routine of conducting revival meetings and carrying on small-scale truck farming for a livelihood. The war years, however, added a strange new twist to the regular schedule and also added certain pressures and anxieties so different from anything he and the family had ever experienced. The story of these experiences will be told later.

In the meantime he also continued his churchwide ministry. The early part of 1917 found him in two areas in which, according to the records, he served probably oftener than anywhere else; Columbiana, Ohio, and Lawrence County, Pennsylvania. He also served in that same year, both in the spring and fall, in some of the Illinois congregations where he had so frequently served in earlier years.

In the fall of 1918 he returned once more to the schoolroom in the local area public system. The summer of 1919 marked his last term of summer normals. This type of teacher training was being phased out by the state, thus ending a most colorful era in Pennsylvania's educational history.

Second Term of Service in Oregon (1920-1921)

Once again in 1920 the Hopewell Church in Oregon prevailed upon S. G. Shetler and family to come to the West. This second and last term of service was to be only for one year. The family left for Oregon on the last day of May. Just before leaving, Cloyd and Earl Mishler, two young men of the home (Stahl) congregation stopped at the house to present a beautiful going-away gift from their family—the David Mishlers—a large thermos bottle for use on the trip, a surprise gift much appreciated.

The trip west this time was via the Northern Pacific Railway from Chicago. The family was accompanied on this trip by three Johnstown area young people, Lloy A. Kniss,[44] Howard Stahl, and Nora Blough (Mrs. Morgan Yoder). Both Lloy Kniss and Nora Blough were schoolteachers. These three gifted and spiritually minded young people not only gained a wealth of experience for themselves, as they later testified, but they also added a lot of spice to the trip and subsequent family life in Oregon. Like previous trips, the whole journey was long and tedious, yet it was also filled with some interesting and exciting incidents. En route the family took in some sights between the long waits between trains. One exciting episode might have ended in tragedy. Kniss, with some others of the group, had left the train at one of the stops, but delayed his return. By the time he got back to the train it was already moving slowly out of the station. Not to be left behind he caught hold of the long, vertical bars on the sides of the door of his coach, and hung on tenaciously as the train was gathering speed. Fortunately the conductor saw him just in time, opened the door, and let him inside, rebuking him, however, for his dangerous attempt.

To avoid excessive cost of eating in the dining car, passengers frequently provided their own food. On Pullman coaches tables were furnished which fit between the two seats facing each other and which when pushed together at night made up the berth. My mother had made ample provisions for the long trip with tasty sandwich materials, cold chicken, hardboiled eggs, cheese, fruit, lemonade, and other lunch materials. These dainties were augmented with other items bought from vendors who entered the train at the various stops or from foodstands and restaurants near the stations.

Howard Stahl recalled (1978) with fondness this first experience in transcontinental travel. He remembered seeing the snow-capped mountains for miles and miles as the train, crossing the plains, was approaching the Rockies. He also remembered nostalgically how the fried chicken my mother had provided for the lunches had become spoiled toward the end of the trip; "so at Spokane Brother Shetler had us go to a restaurant to enjoy a good meal of fresh salmon steak." Recounting the events at the end of the journey he said further,

> After several days [from Spokane] we arrived at Portland. We then took a train down the Willamette Valley to Hubbard, our destination. To meet us at the station was S. G. Shetler's married daughter, Mrs. John Bachman and husband, with a horse and buggy [the Bachmans were living there at the time]. Due to the number in the group and much luggage, they had arranged for several friends . . . to come to the depot to haul us all out to the J. D. Mishler residence where the Shetlers were to reside while in Oregon.[45]

It was an almost festive occasion, involving a reunion with loved ones and former friends. The new home, formerly occupied by the J. D. Mishlers and vacated after the unexpected death of Mrs. Mishler, was ideally located a mile east of town and about an equal distance from the meetinghouse. In typical housewarming fashion many items of food and home furnishings as well as household items had been provided by members of the congregation.

Shortly after arrival in Oregon the annual meeting of the Pacific Coast Mennonite Conference was held at the Hopewell Church, one of the first major activities in which my father was involved. He preached the conference sermon [keynote address] and was again appointed to several committees. J. D. Mishler and S. G. Shetler were assigned joint bishop oversight of the Hopewell, Creston (Montana) and Nampa and Filer (Idaho) churches. The overflow attendance at the conference, the hospitality of the host church, and the warm spirit of fellowship and spirited singing made deep impressions even on us younger members of the family. The conference secretary, describing the meeting in his minutes, noted that "an excellent spirit prevailed, and there was a unanimous vote on every action taken."

One of the chief roles assigned to my father by conference was to serve on a committee to help arrange a merger between the Mennonite Church and the Amish Mennonite Church of the West. Similar mergers had been effected already in Indiana some years before. A "Conference Merger Committee" had been set up in the western area of the church to initiate proceedings. At the time the Western Amish Mennonite Conference included churches in the states of Kansas, Missouri, Illinois, Iowa, Nebraska, and Oregon. The proposal was to have the Oregon sector of that large conference merge with the Pacific Coast Mennonite Conference.

At the first meeting of the Joint Merger Committee (which represented both the Amish Mennonite Conference and the various Mennonite conferences west of the Mississippi) at the East Fairview Church near Milford, Nebraska, May 26-27, 1920, proposals for the new merger had been adopted, as well as proposals for a new alignment of conference districts west of the Mississippi. The June (1920) conference in Oregon appointed three brethren to cooperate with this new committee. The appointees, J. D. Mishler, J. P. Bontrager, and S. G. Shetler subsequently signed the merger proposals adopted earlier by the other participating conferences.

The merger committee, including this time also the Oregon delegates, held a second meeting at Tremont, Illinois, September 9 and 10. At this meeting S. G. Shetler represented the Pacific Coast Conference and C. R. Gerig and A. P. Troyer, the Amish Mennonite churches of Oregon. The merger was made official the following year at the annual conference at the Fairview Church near Albany, Oregon.

Following the June 1920 conference at Hopewell, life settled back into a regular routine. To help supplement the income received through the church, my father worked at various jobs provided by members of the church. Although he was least of all a mechanic, he worked part time at a nearby garage owned by one of the brethren of the church, Ed Watkins. And although he had previously done very little carpenter work, he found himself doing some interior remodeling for another member of the church! In addition to these jobs there were always plenty of family chores to keep him occupied physically.

During the month of July he conducted revival meetings at Kalispell, Montana. In the fall he was at Los Angeles and Upland, California, and also at the Firdale Church near Albany and at Nampa, Idaho.

The other major undertaking for the 1920-1921 period was my father's part in the establishment of the Pacific Coast Bible School. In June the conference inaugurated this work, placing him on a committee of three to formulate plans. This new school was intended to be the beginning of an established institution on the West Coast similar to Hesston Academy in Kansas. At the beginning it was arranged to have a six-week school at two locations—three weeks at Hubbard (Hopewell) and three at Albany, 60 miles to the south. This plan was to make it possible for more to attend, but as it happened, many persons attended both sessions. My father served as principal; the other instructors were Bishop Fred Gingerich and Moses Hostetler, the latter a well-known lay music teacher from the Zion congregation. The Pacific Coast Bible School operated successfully for a number of years.

In the 1940s Western Mennonite School was established on a more permanent basis with a campus and buildings north of Salem, Oregon. Marcus Lind, son of Bishop N. A. Lind, became its first principal. Fred Gingerich became an ardent supporter of this work along with many other ministers and lay leaders of the conference.

During the years that our family lived in Oregon my father served on many committees and spoke in many congregations—probably in all of the conference congregations. It would be pointless to list all of the numerous assignments. Appointed to write a history of the Pacific Coast Conference, he completed this task some years later after the family had again returned to Pennsylvania. This 100-page book, published by the Mennonite Publishing House, 1931, gives an interesting account of the beginnings of the work in the "West."

Throughout the time spent in Oregon members of the Hopewell congregation and some from other conference churches continued to supply the family with material aid. A very strange and interesting incident took place one time. My father received an unsigned letter saying that he was about to receive a "pounding." The family was a bit apprehensive, since every person has his enemies. The fears were soon allayed, however, when an express package arrived shortly after from a certain Moses Evers of the Albany area, containing a pound of this and a pound of that—rice, beans, prunes, walnuts, crackers, *et cetera!*

An impressive feature of Hopewell Church life was that the social, spiritual, and business life of the Hopewell people seemed to be woven together into one solid fabric in a unique manner. There seemed to be no stilted or artificial distinction between the "sacred" and the "secular." Spiritual conversation was a natural part of daily life as much as talk about jobs and money or social events. There was also always some kind of activity for young and old, frequently both combined. It was not unusual for whole families to spend several days or a week at the coast, which, of course, was not too distant. Our own family, in company with friends—and sometimes on our own—spent several vacation periods at what became a favorite coastal spot, Newport. On one occasion the congregation took an all-day trip down the scenic Columbia River Highway.

The year between June 1920 and June 1921 again passed rapidly and the time arrived to return to Pennsylvania. Only frequent return trips for brief visits or for church assignments in after years helped satisfy the somewhat thwarted desire that many of the family had to make Oregon a permanent home. Incidentally, all of my sisters and their families made Oregon their home for a number of years as I and my family also did. In addition to spending several summers on the West Coast, I resided there for nearly a year during the time I served as co-principal at Western Mennonite School (1951-1952). After my mother's death in 1932, my father had also returned to Oregon on various occasions for various assignments. He was principal of a two-week winter Bible school at the Sheridan Church for two terms in the late thirties.

The Oregon years to this day represent a kind of romantic period in Shetler family history. There existed in the brotherhood such a pervading spirit of friendliness and Christian hospitality that many lifelong friendships and memories emerged from this whole experience.

The War Years (1917-1918)

In 1917, when the United States entered "The World War" on the side of the Allies, a great strain was thrust upon the Mennonite Church because of its pacifist tradition. It became a time of severe testing on a principle for which Anabaptists had stood firmly for nearly 400 years. War was officially declared against Germany and the Central Powers in April, and when the Mennonite General Conference met at the Yellow Creek Meetinghouse near Goshen, Indiana, August 1917, the major concern before the conference was how to deal with the new draft that was involving all of the nation's ablebodied men between the ages of 18 and 45. Of particular concern was the treatment conscientious objectors were receiving in the army camps where they had been placed after induction. There were no exemption privileges for COs or any form of "alternate service," so that the men who were drafted had to take their stand in the army camps. A number of young draftees had been receiving rough treatment at the hands of officers when they refused to wear uniforms and to take part in military drill.

It was a tense period, and it was in a spirit of humility and deep concern that the assembled delegates met at the Yellow Creek Meetinghouse, seeking divine guidance as to what course the church should pursue. After due deliberation, the group decided to contact the proper authorities in Washington. A committee composed of three bishops, S. G. Shetler, Aaron Loucks, and D. D. Miller, was delegated to go to Washington, D.C., directly from the conference grounds. It had been learned that through the efforts of officials of the Franconia Conference of eastern Pennsylvania an interview had been arranged with the secretary of war, Newton D. Baker, through Senator Boise Penrose of Pennsylvania (the Franconia Conference was not a member of the denomination's General Conference). Their scheduled appointment was delayed to allow the three men from Mennonite General Conference to join them. Several Amish leaders also joined the group and the meeting with Baker by the conjoint committee on Saturday morning, September 1, was carried out in a most cordial manner.

The interview with the secretary of war had also been aided by Senator Atlee Pomerene of Ohio, who, as was learned later, had called Baker by phone upon learning of the meeting, assuring him that the Mennonites planning the interview were "well-meaning people." Senator Pomerene had grown up in Holmes County, Ohio, where he had made first-hand acquaintance with these people and he understood their position.

Earlier it appeared that Baker had not been inclined to lend much sympathy to the conscientious objector cause. Douglas MacArthur, who was then a young major, was serving at the time as Baker's military assistant. In an article in *Life* magazine (Jan. 17, 1964), "The Wild Adventures of a Young Officer," General MacArthur gave his impressions of Mr. Baker. He wrote: "I had never met Baker, but I knew him by reputation. I found him to be diminutive in size but large of heart, with a clear brilliant mind."

He did indeed prove himself to be a man "large of heart." My father, who frequently spoke of this interview in later years, always recalled this experience with the kindest of feelings toward

Baker and toward the government which he represented. The secretary of war, who at that time had the final word in matters of camp discipline, assured the group that immediate action would be taken to alleviate the strained situation and end the mistreatment of the Mennonite men. Concerning the enforced wearing of the uniform, Baker remarked, "Because your church has always made dress a tenet of its faith, your boys will not be required to wear the uniform."[46] He gave the General Conference Committee copies of a letter that were to be forwarded to camp officials, guaranteeing proper treatment of COs in the various camps, and exempting them from wearing the uniform. The same privileges, which also covered other phases of camp life and the conscientious objector problem, were later extended to all conscientious objectors of other branches of the Mennonite Church and of the different peace churches.

Immediately after the interview with Baker, the committee back at their hotel, drafted a night letter (telegram) to be sent out to the churches in the various areas. The letter, dated, September 1, 1917, as taken from my father's original copy, ran as follows:

Washington, D.C.,
September 1, 1917

Dear Brother,
    In an interview with the Secretary of War, Baker, who received us very kindly, we received the following information and instructions:

    1. That none of our brethren need serve in any capacity which violates their creed and conscience.
    2. When they are called, they should report at the place designated on their notice.
    3. From the place designated on their notice, they should go with others, who are drafted and called, to the training camp.
    4. Report to the army officers the church to which they belong, and their belief in its creed and principles.
    5. This non-resistant position will place them in detention camps, where they will be properly fed and cared for.
    6. In these camps they will not be uniformed or drilled.
    7. A list of services considered non-combatant will be offered, but they need not accept any in violation of their conscience.
    8. Those who cannot accept any service, either combatant or noncom-

batant, will be assigned to some other service not under the military arm of the government.

9. Our ministers will be privileged to give this information and advice to our brethren in private or in public meetings.

As a committee appointed by General Conference, assembled at the Yellow Creek Church, near Goshen, Ind., Aug. 29, 1917, in consultation with a committee of brethren appointed by the Franconia Conference and a committee of Old Order Amish brethren, we have unanimously agreed to advise the following:

1. Since our interview with the War Department, we advise our brethren to state their position on church, creed, and principles to the army officers at mobilization camps.

2. We again encourage our brethren not to accept any service, either combatant or non-combatant, under the military arm of the government in violation of their conscience and the creed and principles of the church.

While our brethren will not be freed entirely, yet freed from serving under the military arm of the government, we should be very grateful for the consideration that the authorities have shown us.

May our churches everywhere continue to send prayers to the Throne of Grace in behalf of our young brethren in this trying hour and for those in authority so "that we may lead a quiet and peacable life."

> Your brethren,
> *Aaron Loucks*
> *S. G. Shetler*
> *D. D. Miller*
> General Conference Committee[47]

The *Washington Star* reported briefly the event with this note, under the heading, "Conscientious Objectors Advised":

> Conscientious objectors for military service were advised by Secretary Baker yesterday to make no protest until assigned in training camp to some particular duty violating their scruples. The opinion was given to a delegation of Mennonite leaders.[48]

As chairman and spokesman for the committee, my father received many inquiries from persons in the local church area as well as from other parts of the church concerning problems arising out of the camp situation and also on the matter of the purchase of war bonds. A letter in my father's files from a well-known pastor in Indiana and lifelong friend, dated December 1918, making inquiry about discharge procedures (Armistice had been signed in November) is typical of these.[49]

During the war my father made a number of official visits to army camps on the Eastern Seaboard. Benjamin S. Ebersole, a camp resident from Mount Joy, Pennsylvania, recorded in his diary some details of one of these visits, giving also some interesting sidelights on camp life.

Sunday, Sept. 30, 1917 (Camp Meade)
Clear—We were told to clean the room and arrange bunks, etc., very neat and in order, as Secretary of War, Baker, was coming. When he came we were told to stand in a row or semi-circle. He asked us our names and religion. Did not ask many questions. He asked some of the boys more than he did us. He is a very pleasant man. Several officers accompanied him. Among them General Kuhns.

Sunday, December 16, 1917
Clear. Went over our Sunday School lesson, then we listened to a dunkart [sic] minister preaching. When we returned Bro. S. G. Shetler and several people from Hanover were there to see the boys. Bro. Shetler spoke to us in the afternoon from Psalms 119:89. After services he talked with us. We missed our supper in order to be with him as much as possible. In the evening he preached to us again using as his text Genesis 3:9. While Bro. Shetler was preaching the lights went out for a few seconds. Bro. Shetler just kept on preaching.

Enjoyed his visit very much.

In at least two instances my father was able to use Baker's communique with effect when he called it to the attention of camp officials who had forced uniforms on Mennonite inductees. The officers who themselves had received copies of this order prior to his coming promised to have them removed immediately and return to them their civilian clothes. There were three men in camp from our own congregation, Lloy A. Kniss, Ammon Sala, and Harley Hershberger. All three encountered some unpleasant camp experiences.

In the local area my father was looked upon for counsel in regards to the CO position. Many men of both the Mennonite and the Brethren churches, as well as some others, came to him to have their questionnaires filled out for the War Department. On a given evening our living room looked like a doctor's office with men awaiting their turn. In a reply to Bro. Loucks, who had evidently asked him to attend some conference meeting, my father answered in his usual telegraphic style (Oct. 2, 1918): "Your letter received. Would like to be with you. Am in work that I can hardly turn. Went to bed at 1:30 last night. Have filled out over 100 questionnaires." It was during this period that he purchased a typewriter to aid him in this work. It was a small, portable Corona, manufactured by the L. C. Smith Company.

As already suggested, the war years also proved a time of testing for the folks at home, and extra tension on the Shetler family because of my father's visibility on the war issue. The Mennonite and Brethren churches opposed the purchase of U.S. Liberty Bonds, since this was considered inconsistent with our peace position. For this a number of local Mennonites, including my father, were threatened with physical harm. He was informed one evening by phone by a friend that a group of vigilantes was on its way to our house to tar and feather him. I recall as a lad how frightened the family was. His first suggestion was to drive away in the car. (We had just bought a new Dodge.) But my mother, who always seemed to remain more calm in such situations suggested that we stay and pray. Providentially, the group never arrived, although, as we learned later, they had last been seen just two miles from our home.

On top of all this, the Espionage Act which had been passed by Congress in 1917 allowed the government, through its U.S. marshals and designated persons (there was no FBI then), to keep close surveillance on all activities in the United States which had the appearance of aiding the enemy and working against our own government.

As a result of these, officers attended our church services on various occasions to check on what was being said over the pulpit, and to observe the general activities of the church.

During these trying months every car that stopped at our house created some apprehension. On two occasions army officers called to make inquiries. It was a form of harassment. One time this occurred at the nearby school where my father was teaching.

A carful of men stopped and called him out to talk to him and then left. While we were probably told later what the conversation was about, regrettably no record is left of what was said.

On another occasion a car with uniformed men stopped at our home one evening and two men came to the front door. I can still hear my father saying, "This time I'm afraid they're going to take me," thinking they would take him into custody. But as Providence would have it, a guest had come to our home for some business, a James Cassler, of nearby Hollsopple. Cassler was a friend of the family, a former normal school student, and also, unbeknown to us, a U.S. marshal!

He said, "Don't worry, Mr. Shetler, I'll take care of this," and pulling back his coat lapel revealed his badge! He stepped out on the front porch and spoke with the officers. My father learned later that he had given them orders to let "Rev. Shetler" alone, that he was by no means a national enemy.

During those years the Espionage Act was rigidly enforced, however. For some months my father had to report regularly each week to a certain bank official in Johnstown—a government appointee—about the nature of his activities and whereabouts. The purpose was largely to intimidate him. My father, however, was not easily intimidated, although it is true that he, like all Mennonite preachers during this time, carefully avoided making public statements that could be misconstrued.

In Virginia his good friend, Bishop L. J. Heatwole, had written a letter to Rhine Benner, a young minister in West Virginia, advising him on how to counsel young men and on buying war bonds. The authorities intercepted the letter, and for his advice against participating in the war fined Heatwole $1000, and jailed Benner for a time. Nothing of such a consequence occurred to my father, but, nonetheless, the months between April 1917 and November 1918 were months of uneasiness and strain.

Our family will never forget that night in November when the news reached our area that the Armistice had been signed. We were sitting in the living room when suddenly we began to hear the nearby city factory whistles blowing and church bells ringing. We could not imagine at first what it was all about—in those days there were no radios to keep the public informed. We stepped out onto the porch to listen, the medley of bells and whistles continued for a long time. I recall vividly my father saying in a moving voice, "That means the war is over." And indeed it was as we learned the next day. The Armistice had been signed in Europe and peace had once more returned.

The experiences of those years as well as the supper-table conversation about the Christian's relation to the government left lifelong impressions and gave us our first lessons on nonresistance and church-and-state relations.

12
Home and Family Life
(1900-1932)

The house around which most of the family life centered for the entire family had been erected in 1900. As noted before, after having lived the first number of years in Hollsopple, a decision had been made to relocate to be nearer to the Stahl Church. My father and mother were able to secure from John Stahl a three-and-one-half-acre tract of land adjoining the church grounds on which to build. Stahl was the same man who had donated the ground for the church (built 1882) and for whom the church had been named. The Hollsopple residence, which had originally been purchased for $1200, was sold to some close friends, the Eli Gaschos, for the sum of $1350.

The building contractor for the new house in "Soap Hollow" was my father's uncle, Kore Kaufman. The substantial nine-room, two-story frame dwelling was built for the fantastic sum of $700. Wages, of course, for a good carpenter then were only 90 cents a day! Some years later a large porch, extending around the east side of the house, was added to connect the original front and back porches, but by then prices had already gone up to the extent that the porch alone cost $700. Still later, in 1926, two large roof dormers were added to create bedroom space on the attic floor, and this addition by now cost $1000. The chief purpose of this last major improvement was to make it more convenient to accommodate Bible school boarders and guests, both a common part of Shetler life through the years.

The building site for the new home was a gentle, rocky slope, which required considerable landscaping to make it suitable for a home. To accommodate the building to the slope, the front yard was terraced to provide several grades of level terrain for a yard, the remainder being sloped gently. In time the space beneath the rather high front porch was enclosed with lattice work, and foundation planting was added. Other shrubs and flowers were planted to grace the large lawn. There were flower beds and "hot-beds" to raise lettuce and plants for spring planting in the garden. There were also several large grape arbors. A huge mock orange bush added its unique fragrance in springtime and a brilliant firebush added color. Two sizable flowering yucca stalks with their annual display of large white, lilylike blossoms graced the higher of the two front terraces at each end of the porch. In later years a water-lily pool was added in the back yard. Mother was a lover of flowers and shrubs.

The yard was amply provided with concrete walks and steps, a kind of luxury for that day. My father often spoke of the hard work that had gone into building these, a fact we didn't realize as children when we rolled over them with our coaster wagon. Where the walk met the roadway there was a sizable concrete block used as a mounting platform in the horse and buggy days. Imbedded in the front of the block was the customary steel ring to fasten the tie rope.

Other buildings added later to complete the Shetler complex included a hen house neatly finished in siding to match the house, a hog house of similar construction, a small barn, and—after 1917—a garage. Also in the early years a substantial cottage was erected just to the rear of the main dwelling to serve as a "summer house." In the custom of the times it was used for cooking and canning in the hot summer months. In later years this building was converted into a comfortable dwelling to accommodate my mother's father and stepmother. Then, besides all the other buildings, there was a small woodshed and coal house combination, the woodshed also serving as a small shop. And in 1918 a "wash-house" was erected over a newly drilled well. This facility also served as a "butcher-house."

Running water and sanitary conveniences were a part of our family life from the early 1900s. My father had dug by hand an 1100-foot ditch from a spring on the hillside of the adjoining John Stahl farm which lay to the west to provide running water by gravity flow. A huge storage tank, built at Preacher Gid Miller's machine shop at Springs, Pennsylvania, was placed in the attic to ensure an ample supply of water and also to maintain the necessary pressure.

In its heyday the whole layout presented a beautiful sight and drew many comments from visitors. One man of the community, Sam Livingstone, often said, as he stopped to chat on his way to and from town, that if ever the day came when the folks wanted to sell, he wanted to have the first option to buy. While he himself never actually came to own the place, interestingly, years later his daughter Cora and her husband, Charles Ross, did become the owners and occupants of the old homestead. In 1974, after having changed ownership a number of times through the years, the property fittingly became the property of the adjoining Stahl congregation, which now rents out the two houses. It should be noted that the Johnstown Bible School had, for a few years, owned the property and used it for a dormitory.

Looking back over the years, after having built and maintained a home of my own, I can really appreciate the many hours of tedious labor that went into the making of that home. To grade the lawn by the old hand methods, to plant all those trees and shrubs, to build a picket fence around that large yard, all this, besides trying to maintain a heavy schedule of preaching and teaching, and assuming the heavy responsibility of caring for a family of five, seems now to have been an almost impossible task. To complete the picture, through many of these years the family operated a small truck farm and sold produce, eggs, and butter on a regular huckster route in the city.

During the early years after 1900 my parents had also the additional responsibility of operating the community telephone exchange of the Citizen's Telephone Company. The equipment was installed in the front room of our house and my mother and older sisters served as operators. My father was a stockholder in the small company, which eventually sold out to the General Telephone Company of Pennsylvania, a part of the Bell system. After a few years, however, the telephone exchange was moved to a small building erected for the purpose across the road from our home and a special operator was hired for the job. Still later that same building was moved to its present location, a quarter of a mile to the south, where it continued to be used for the same purpose until the local company was dissolved. It is now a dwelling.

With the many family duties, commonly the homes of that time divided the labor so that not all of the duties fell upon father and mother. All of us knew from early childhood the meaning of "chores," which in that period were regarded with almost religious sanction. These chores included for my sisters a share of the regular daily household work, washing the cream separator after the daily milking, and also some outside work in the garden. Every weekend the kerosene lamps had to be cleaned, the wicks trimmed, and the lamp wells replenished. This was never a sought-for job. In 1923, however, this chore came to an end when the Stahl congregation built an electric power line through the community, a kind of "social service" project. All local citizens, regardless of faith, were allowed to connect with the line without any fee.

Although our parents were strictly opposed to attendance at any form of commercialized recreation, there was a variety of fun and activity through these years. They provided many family excursions and other diversions. On our several trips to the West Coast, for example, they would always see to it that we would take the various sight-seeing tours and side trips to parks and zoos and other points of interest. There were also family games for exercise. Amid the heavy work of the summer months, regular days were set apart for excursions to nearby retreats. I recall one summer in particular how that a day a week was set apart for that. How our parents could afford such a luxury in their stewardship of time, seems almost unbelievable now, but the motivation this provided for us children to do our jobs during the rest of the week is quite obvious.

While our family never enjoyed a superabundance of material blessings, we came to own some of the new appliances and household conveniences as they came along. And although my parents were conservative in their Christian commitment, they were at the same time progressive in terms of adopting new methods and products of a technological age. They were not opposed, for example, to my purchasing a radio in 1925, one of the earlier ones in the area. Interestingly, the outside antenna for the little "Crosley Pup," a one-tube set with headphones (now a collector's item) was fastened to a treetop in the adjoining churchyard!

Before the family owned a car, some of our friends who were already car owners took us on trips on various occasions in their "machines." On one such occasion the J. T. Eashes took us to Springs, Pennsylvania, to visit my oldest sister, Luella, who lived there with her family. Another time the Calvin Lehmans took us to Gettysburg for a tour of the famous battlefield. Any auto tour in those days was an event, since radiators heated easily, and there was much chance of mechanical failure. It was always taken for granted, too, even on short trips, that one would have at least one or two flat tires! Many cars were equipped to carry two spares. But even then sometimes one needed to make repairs on the road when a third tire blew out.

One memorable short auto ride took place on a Sunday evening when the minister E. J. Blough picked up the family to take us to the Kaufman Church where he had invited my father to speak. Going up a very steep grade on a short-cut country road, the gasoline failed to reach the carburator because of the car's gravity feed system, and the car stopped. Hanging there precariously on the side of the hill, Blough, equipped for such emergencies, had my father pump air with a tire pump into the gas tank (which was under the front seat), while Blough drove. My father stood on the running board during this procedure while the rest of us walked to the top of the hill.

Between 1917 and 1942 the family owned six cars: a 1918 Dodge touring car bought in 1917; a 1924 four-cylinder Buick sedan purchased in 1926; a 1925 Model T Ford pickup truck bought in 1929; a 1930 Nash business coupe, bought in 1931; a 1933 Model "B" Ford coupe, purchased new that same year; and a 1938 Dodge coupe bought in 1940. The last two were bought after my mother's death in 1932.

The longest cross-country tours were made to Ontario in 1929 and to Archbold, Ohio, to General Conference in 1931. In his lifetime my father traveled thousands of miles by rail but never by ship (excepting on inland waters) or by plane. Commercial air travel was actually not too common even as late as 1942. In 1941 he had made tentative plans to take a trip around the world, but because of failing health these plans were dropped. My father had always desired to visit the India Mennonite Mission, but his dream unfortunately never came true.

Several kinds of experiences, representing the quality of life we enjoyed, stand out in my memory. One of these, already described, was the many family trips and excursions. Another was the Sunday gatherings, once so common. On such occasions the young people of the area, including those of other denominations, would gather at a home for Sunday dinner. At one such gathering in 1923 at our home, 49 people were present, 43 of whom were young people, and representing three denominations. This particular event was written up for the daily paper (*The Johnstown Tribune*), a copy of which was handed to me by William Saylor shortly before his death. After listing the names of those present it noted that the afternoon had been spent in "music and games."[50] Groups of such size would frustrate the average hostess today, but in that era somehow they managed. I recall distinctly how my parents were pleased to have this kind of contact with the young people and to observe how well the young people mixed with the older people present.

Another outstanding experience in family living for us was the daily table conversation, a kind of education for us. Besides the usual chitchat, there was always a wide range of discussion on church happenings and of world news events and issues. My sister Rosella reflected this experience in an article written for the *Herald* (Feb. 1916) titled "Conversation in the Home." In it she noted that "among amusements the best is the good habit of conversation, the talking over of the events of the day, the bright and quick play of wit and fancy, 'the story that brings the laugh, and the speaking of the good and kind and true things which all have in their hearts." She also mentioned singing in the home, which was also a family tradition.

Much is made today of decision-making and democracy in the home. In the Shetler home we were introduced to these processes very early in our lives, though at the same time all of us also learned something of "law and order." An example of decision-making came at the time when I was trying to make up my mind about going to high school. There was no local area high school and those living more than two miles from a high school were exempt from attending any secondary school. For me to go to Johnstown meant a four-and-one-half-mile walk daily, one way, excepting the rides one might be offered. It was in late August 1925 and my parents were at the time attending General Conference at Eureka, Illinois. I consulted with my sister Goldie with whom I was staying during the time they were gone, and she thought it would be all right to go.

This was more than an ordinary decision and involved more than merely the matter of getting to the school. At that time no one from the local church had attended high school. I decided to go. A few days after I had enrolled I received a card from my parents saying, "If you are still thinking of going to high school it will be all right with us." Many important decisions of this sort were left to us children with the assurance that somehow we would honor the highest wishes of our parents. It was this reassuring attitude that helped to give us stability and prepared us for more difficult situations ahead.

My Mother's Role

This biography would not be complete without some appropriate tribute to the woman "behind the man." Whatever success may be attributed to my father—to the glory of God—my mother certainly deserves her share of the recognition. She served as a steadying force in his life, and his wide ministry would never have been possible without her assuming many of the home responsibilities in his absence.

She epitomized for us all the virtues of motherhood. She was concerned, kind, and generous, and had a deep loyalty to her faith and to Christ. The word that seems to describe her best for me was "stately." Of medium height and portly, she carried herself well, so that most people took her to be taller than she was. She had a gentle dignity that set her apart from many of her peers.

Maggie Jane Kaufman was born on April 22, 1876, a direct descendant on her maternal side of Christian Blauch, one of the early pioneer settlers of western Pennsylvania who had migrated from the area east of Berne, Switzerland, in 1767 to the Somerset County area near the present town of Berlin. Interestingly, up to 1963, 90 percent of the Mennonite ministers who had been ordained to serve in the Johnstown area had either been direct descendants of Blauch or, as in my father's case, had married relatives of his descendants. It is also of some sentimental note that Roger Blough, a former president of United States Steel Corporation, was my mother's second cousin, and her great-grandfather (also my father's great-grandfather) on the paternal side, was "rich Isaac Kaufman," said to have been the richest man in Somerset County at the time of his death in 1884.[51]

True to the old adage that a woman's intuition is often better than a man's deliberative judgment my mother seemed to have an uncanny sense of evaluating people—a gift my father came to respect, though not always ungrudgingly. This ability made her more selective in her choice of close personal friends. My father, on the other hand, was more impetuous and emotional and hence too often ready to admit people into his confidence whom he had not known too well. She was also a discerning critic of his teaching and preaching—sometimes a bit too severe it seemed to us who stood by.

A woman of unimpeachable character, she disdained gossip preferring to withhold judgment about others until she knew the facts. And although she had never acquired more than a grade school education she was an avid learner and a sharp grammarian. She frequently corrected our usage, including her teacher-husband. In one Mother's Day sermon some years ago I referred to this and said that my mother never *done* her work—she always *did* it!

She and my father helped us, too, to overcome our use of Pennsylvania German idioms and "Dutchified" English. In our daily conversation we sometimes used expressions such as "it wonders me," and "make out the light." Pennsylvania Dutch, incidentally, was our language around the house. "Wooden oaths" and slang were strictly forbidden.

Among my mother's various gifts was her artistic skill, which was demonstrated in her original quilt patterns and in her free-hand painting and designs on such household items as magazine racks or wastebaskets. One of her achievements in needlecraft was the designing and embroidering of the coverings and curtains of a miniature replica of the Old Testament Tabernacle which had been constructed by one of the Johnstown Bible School instructors. She also loved to make elaborate signatures with chalk or pencil in her good Spencerian penmanship.

Typical of the reputation of Pennsylvania Dutch cooks, my mother excelled in the culinary arts, always tantalizing her family's tastebuds with her new creations. She excelled in trying to get us children to taste "just once" whatever was set before us, even if it didn't appeal to us. Salads were one of her specialties, although my father could never be tempted with these. His chief food delights were dairy products, particularly sour cream, buttermilk and cheese. A connoisseur at packing lunches, she made every picnic or school lunch an experience. Peanut butter sandwiches, enhanced by homemade salad dressing and a lettuce leaf, seemed to carry her trademark. The peanut butter was Mosemann's, manufactured and sold commercially by Bishop John E. Mosemann of Lancaster, who was a close friend of the family. Not only were we avid users of the product, but for years we sold it in the community. At that time it was packaged in 5- and 10-pound pails, which when emptied made excellent lunch pails. I can still see the lunch shelf at our country school lined with many shiny, bronze-colored Mosemann peanut-butter buckets!

My mother's domestic expertise also was shown in her housekeeping. Scrupulously clean, our family grew up with a kind of perfectionist revulsion of dirt and untidiness which sometimes worked against us when we visited homes where the standards seemed to be somewhat lower.

Mother also made a worthy contribution to the church in a number of ways. She served for years as a song leader and also conducted choral groups. She was able to read music so well that frequently she was called upon to lead a song that she herself had never sung before. She did not have perfect "pitch" but approached this and would never use a pitch pipe. A lover of music, she would end the day sitting in her familiar rocker singing through the hymnbook or some new songbook she had just purchased. She had built up a small library of these. She also directed choruses in the nearby winter Bible school where she served as matron for a number of years. While she never considered herself a public speaker, she did conduct children's meetings publicly and was quite successful in these. As suggested earlier, she loved to entertain young people in the home and many of these frequently came to her for counsel.

She loved humor and enjoyed playing jokes on others, but withal was serious-minded and deeply concerned for the spiritual welfare of the church. Although many felt she was quite gifted she herself lamented that she had not done more. On her deathbed she requested that the words of Jesus to the woman who anointed his feet with oil be used for her funeral text—"She hath done what she could."

The year 1932 definitely marked the end of an epoch for our family and home. That year I, her youngest child, was married and although she was still able to attend the wedding at the nearby meetinghouse, less than two weeks later (June 14) she passed away. Many people attended her funeral. J. Irvin Lehman of Chambersburg, Pennsylvania, preached the funeral sermon.

A fitting tribute to my mother was given by a friend of the family and a member of another faith—Maude (Yoder) Williamson in 1973:

> Maggie Shetler, as affectionately known to hundreds, was a stately, gracious woman of many talents. Her daughter, Goldie, and I have been close friends from the age of six, and due to this friendship I spent much time in their home.
>
> Maggie had great ingenuity and knack to improvise so many original and beautiful things in her home. I've always been very appreciative for the opportunity to spend so much time with her. So many valuable ways of cooking and homemaking I have done "her way" all these years.
>
> Just this autumn, as many friends and passersby stopped for cuttings from the plants in my yard, I told them to get them early. I quoted Maggie: "As an old friend of mine [Maggie] always said, Take them into the house early before the cold winds of September blow over them."
>
> She was very good in spelling. Often even S. G. could call on her for verification of the spelling of a word.
>
> No matter how many unexpected guests arrived and filled that long dining room table, she was always equal to the occasion. By supper time on Sunday afternoons the crowd would often get quite large on that large, lovely porch. Quickly Maggie would come bustling to the kitchen, and say, "Girls, we'll just fix plates." Many times there would be at least twenty, but everyone would be served on the porch with a plate of refreshments. I think this was a simple version of the elegant buffet serving of today.
>
> After all this would be done, there would be a quick grooming and everyone took off across the yard and the [adjoining] church yard for the evening services. More likely than not, she would lead the singing [that evening] in her clear, lovely voice.
>
> On her cemetery stone are the words: "She hath done what she could." She did so much for so many. I cared for her deeply and the memories grow richer with the passing years.

13
The Decade of the Twenties
(1921-1932)

After the busy and somewhat turbulent period of the "war and Oregon years" S. G. was back at his old profession teaching in the one-room Miller School a mile from home. It seems strange now, looking back, that the man who had had the opportunity to head a church school in Virginia and who had served as a high school principal in Oregon, not to mention the other posts of responsibility he had held in the church, should return to a simple teaching position in a one-room country school. But whatever his role, my father's sense of the "task" never diminished. He was certainly not one to sit around and pout because he was not at the time occupying some top position.

It was during this period that the three youngest members of the family grew to maturity and established homes of their own, which changed the pattern of home life considerably. In my bedroom hung a picture that my mother had gotten with a purchase of Cloverine salve, showing a small pup crated for shipment and the mother standing close by the box. Beneath the picture were the words, "The Last of the Litter." Not until *my* last child got married and left home did I fully understand the feeling my mother must have had when she had that picture framed and placed in my room.

The very fact that these were crucial years for us younger children growing up made it the best arrangement for him to be home during most of the time in this period. One of the chief outlets for his teaching gifts above the elementary level was the Johnstown Bible School which he had helped found in 1922, and in which he served as principal for many years. This was a six-week school held each winter during January and February at the nearby Stahl meetinghouse. For more than 25 years it served a notable role as a conference-sponsored school, offering training for scores of young people and preachers from a wide area, including those from out-of-state churches. In the period of the 1920s many young people of the local area did not have the opportunity of attending high school, and for these this was the only training above the elementary level they ever received. More will be said later of the Johnstown Bible School and other Bible schools in which my father served in the last two decades of his life.

In addition to these teaching responsibilities, he also conducted revival meetings and Sunday School Teachers' Training classes in area churches, and served as a weekend speaker and evangelist in other parts of the church. One summer (1929) he served as interim pastor of a small church at Selkirk, Ontario. This, with his various local and conference committee assignments, helped make up a busy schedule for him. And, as noted previously, during all this time he was a truck farmer!

My father's life was not without its mistakes. In writing a biography there is a temptation to bypass these and attempt to surround the subject of the story with a halo. On the other hand, I see no point in highlighting these mistakes either. In the early part of the twenties a shadow fell over his life which caused him much anguish of soul and created some misunderstandings. At such times there are always those who, instead of helping to lift a man, take it as an opportunity to gloat over his mistakes. It was at this low point of his life that his lifelong friend, Bishop L. J. Heatwole of Virginia, wrote him a beautiful letter of encouragement in the classic eloquence so characteristic of that man's pen. The letter, dated June 28, 1922, ran as follows:

The letter heading above leads you to know who is the author of this letter, and may I, with your generous consent and most gracious good will be permitted to communicate to you the few thoughts set forth below?

My motive for so doing has been prompted through a feeling of charity that does not "behave itself unseemly"; and to exercise myself with the degree of friendliness and patience that "suffereth long and is kind."

I have gone through the records of the Mennonite General Conference, and see from its earliest beginnings and its later work and activities within the past twenty years, or more, that you have been called to fill many places of trust and responsibility, and that your voice has often been heard on its council floors.

The degree of confidence and trust this great body of believers has placed in you and your good name have been amply proven in the position you have held on its various committees—even to that of being intrusted with the responsible position of serving as Moderator at the time of its Eleventh biennial session of August of 1919 in Virginia.

And again, as I glance down the vista of 18 years—when making your first evangelistic tour to the congregations in Virginia, there rises before me the vision of a most vigorous and strenuous life—dedicated to God and the Church—a life through whose instrumentality God has won unto Himself many of our people who are now devoted and loyal Members.

With the memory of the past still before me, I am led to refuse and continue to refuse that anything come before me that might mar or bedim, to eclipse or obstruct the vision I have heretofore had of a benevolent and most fruitful life that has personally afforded me so much inspiration—and that has lent such glad hope and good cheer to the receding years of my own life.

Since I have been so much associated with you in the activities of the Church through all the passing years, I have thought that at this particular time it might be opportune, and in Gospel order, for me to send you this message of testimony and greeting.

It was through the encouragement and healing of this sort that S. G. Shetler's service to the church was spared and subsequently continued after a one-year period of inactivity in the ministry.

The following list of appointments beyond those already mentioned indicates his program of activities from the mid-twenties on:

Revival meetings, Breslau, Ontario, 1925
Bible Conference, Pinto, Maryland, 1925, 1926
Delegate to General Conference, 1925
Sunday School Conference, Marion Church, Chambersburg, Pennsylvania, 1926
Weekend Conference, Cedar Grove Church, Greencastle, Pennsylvania (with J. L. Stauffer)
Dedication Sermon, new Pinto, Maryland, church, 1926
Message at General Conference, 1927
Conference Sermon, Southwestern Pennsylvania Conference, 1929
Special Services, Waterloo, Ontario, 1929
Weekend Meeting, Martinsburg, Pennsylvania, 1929
Revival Services, Middlebury, Indiana, 1930
Revival Services, Latchar and Snyder Churches, Ontario, 1930

During this decade two of my father's closest friends and colleagues in the ministry, both well-known throughout the denomination, passed away, both rather suddenly. The first, Bishop Abram Metzler, father of A. J. Metzler, in 1924, the other, Bishop N. E. Miller, 1930. He was asked to speak at Metzler's funeral, along with J. A. Ressler, J. N. Durr, C. A. Graybill, L. A. Blough, and E. J. Blough. He preached Brother Miller's funeral on the text, "The Unanswered Why?"

On October 17, 1926, my father preached another funeral sermon for a Jacob Shank of Dayton, Virginia, who had made acquaintance with him during revival meetings in that area in the early 1900s and who requested that he should preach his funeral. Shank's last business transaction, in fact, had been to write a check to cover my father's traveling expenses to Virginia. A Harrisonburg attorney present at the day of the funeral was so impressed with the message that he requested a copy of it. On this same trip my father was asked to address the students and faculty at Eastern Mennonite School in a morning assembly and also at an evening service that same day.

Two other events of rather unusual interest took place in 1926. One of these was the Sunday School Conference at Chambersburg. This was probably the only time in my father's entire ministry that his own father accompanied him to an out-of-district meeting. My mother and I also were with him. I recall quite well the trip in the newly purchased 1924 four-cylinder Buick, which was for that time almost a luxury car. But although it had on the cover of the spare tire mounted on the rear of the car the words, "Power to Start and Power to Stop" (it had "four-wheel" brakes!), it didn't, however, seem to have much power to go as we climbed the several ridges of the Alleghenies on our way eastward on the Lincoln Highway (Route 30).

The second unusual event was the farewell meeting for six missionaries to India, held at the Stahl Church on the evening of September 26. The missionaries were: J. N. and Elsie Kaufman, Lloy and Elizabeth Kniss, and George and Ida Beare. Kaufman was my mother's brother, and Lloy, her first cousin. Kniss, who had grown up in the congregation, was in a very real sense my father's Timothy. He had in fact named him, and as a youth Lloy had attended his summer normal to prepare for teaching. He had also been ordained at the Stahl Church as a co-minister and had traveled with our family to Oregon. Now he was being sent out as a missionary.

It was a highly emotional moment for my father and that evening, as host pastor and leader of the meeting, he was in his full glory. Then, to climax the event, while the meeting was in progress, in walked Bishop J. N. Durr, who had held the first revival meetings at the Stahl Church 36 years before (1890). At those meetings my father and mother and Lloy Kniss' mother and Ella Weaver, the mother of Mrs. Kniss, had accepted Christ! Fittingly, Durr was asked to come to the platform to make some remarks. Visitors from many places were present that night. Some of the out-of-town guests were Bishop Aaron Loucks from Scottdale and A. J. Metzler and C. A. Graybill from Martinsburg.

Reporting the meeting for the *Gospel Herald,* my father wrote:

> One cannot express the feeling and spirit of the meeting. Public school pupils, Sunday School scholars, members of the congregation, members of other denominations, neighbors, relatives, and friends all seemed to blend into this one wish: "God bless you in your mission for the lost!" After some remarks by the writer, James Saylor [bishop of the area churches] led in a benedictory prayer.

Additional references should be made at this point to my father's public school teaching. This remained an active part of his life up to the last decade before his retirement. During the course of his teaching years he had taught all of his family at one time or another, as well as several of his grandchildren. Also his three oldest daughters had attended his local normal school.

In 1928 Pennsylvania state law made it mandatory for teachers to have two years of state normal in order to secure certification. Those who had been trained under the old local normal school system and who had acquired teaching certificates from the county superintendent, were permitted to continue teaching after having their normal school credits validated by the state. They also needed to take additional college level courses. Some credit was also allowed for teaching experience.

During this transition period my father was busy filling out the required forms for his former students (and now colleagues) to help them get recognition for the schooling they had obtained under him. Because of the new law, he decided to drop his own certification procedures and simply retire from teaching. He was then 57. However, several of his colleagues and members of the school board persuaded him to pursue the certification process and stay in the profession. Somewhat hesitantly he finally filled out forms and along with letters of recommendation filed them with the state. He was agreeably surprised some weeks later to receive from the State Department of Public Instruction a permanent standard certificate, a much higher rating than he had expected. This certificate was in essence the equivalent of a college degree and made him eligible to teach in any elementary or secondary school in the state. Listed on his certificate was a wide range of subjects—English, German, Latin, history, geography, civics, algebra, geometry, botany, and astronomy. Such a spread of subjects few present-day teachers, if any, could possibly hope to be accredited to teach. However, much as he was pleased with his certificate, he never had the opportunity to use it in any secondary school. He still continued teaching in the local elementary school for four more years.

14
"Retirement"
(1933-1942)

After the passing of my mother in June 1932, my father began to make some major readjustments in his life routine. With many invitations coming in from various parts of the church for revival meetings, weekend conferences, and Bible schools, and with domestic responsibilities no longer requiring him to remain at home, he decided to end his public school teaching career in favor of full-time church work. After due notification he resigned, effective at the end of the calendar year, 1932.

In addition to his service at the local Johnstown Bible School which was always held the first part of the year, he began in January 1933 what might be called a new career. He conducted two-week winter Bible schools for adults and summer Bible schools for children, both being types of Christian education which were just beginning to come into prominence in the Mennonite Church. He also assumed a more active pastoral role, and, as suggested, held revival meetings and weekend conferences—maintaining a schedule reminiscent of his earlier years. From 1933 until the last month before his death he followed a crowded routine that would make many younger men cringe. The few times that he was ill during the last five years of his life, when he had to cancel appointments, were hard on his spirits. He had never been a man to take extended vacations, nor did he seek a life of ease in retirement. But there was also a practical side to all of this. He received no pensions, was the recipient of no Social Security benefits, had no returns from investments, and received no pastoral support.

After the six-week term of Johnstown Bible School in January and February he launched into a series of revial meetings that took him into eight states. From March to December (1933) he held meetings in these congregations: Pike, Harrisonburg, Virginia; Tressler, Greenwood, Delaware; Bowne, Clarksville, Michigan; Clinton Brick, Goshen, Indiana; Emma, Topeka, Indiana; Pleasant View, Schellsburg, Pennsylvania; Pleasant View, Chambersburg, Pennsylvania; Pond Bank, Chambersburg, Pennsylvania; Filer, Idaho; Nampa, Idaho; Mountain View, Creston, Montana; Beech, Canton, Ohio; and Shore, Shipshewana, Indiana.

A typical schedule for an eight-month period just two years prior to his death included three weekend conferences (usually Saturday night and three services on Sunday); seven revival meetings of a week or ten days; three two-week winter Bible schools; and one summer Bible school. From November 8 to the following June 22, he was in the following places to serve in these capacities just mentioned: Midland, Michigan; Breslau, Ontario; Hay Church, Ontario; Shipshewana, Indiana; Archbold, Ohio; Columbia, Pennsylvania; Wakarusa, Indiana; Wichita, Kansas; Wooster, Ohio; Onego, West Virginia; South Boston, Virginia; Middlebury, Indiana; and Walnut Creek, Ohio. During this same period he preached twelve times in his home church, and he was also principal of both the summer and winter Bible schools at the home church.

In addition to the above activities, he also filled numerous conference posts. In 1940, for example, in the annual district conference session, when he was 69, he was elected conference representative on the important General Conference Committee on Arrangements (planning committee); reelected summer Bible school director; and reelected for a three-year term on the ministerial committee. At the time he was also chairman of the advisory board of the ladies' sewing circle of the conference; a member of an *ad hoc* committee on rearranging district meetings; a member of an *ad hoc* committee to rearrange the conference cycle (of the annual meeting); a member of the Johnstown Bible School Board; and a member of the constitution committee for the Young People's Institute Committee of the conference.

At the same annual meeting he also served in a number of activities of that session. He was a member of the nominating committee, conducted a devotional service, discussed a topic at the mission board meeting and also a topic at the Sunday school conference, both of which preceded the conference sessions proper. At the Sunday School Conference he served also as a leader of one of the discussion groups on "The Relation of the Home to the Church." His section, incidentally, was for teachers of the intermediate grades (13-16 years)! The wide scope of responsibilities and span of the age-groups he was called upon to serve showed his remarkable versatility and his ability to bridge generations.

One must realize that there were many other capable persons in the conference at this time. It was simply a case of a man's gift making room for him and of his being used by God in a remarkable way to the end of a very busy and interesting life. He was never one to boast, however, either privately or publicly of the many positions he had held or of the number of appointments he filled. I never knew, for example, that he had been moderator of General Conference until I read about it in the church literature years after his death.

The last full calendar year that he lived (1941) he held revival meetings in the following churches: Salem, Ohio; Salem, Indiana; Wichita, Kansas; Mt. Hermon, Virginia; Liberty, Iowa; Hay (Amish Mennonite), Ontario; Zurich, Ontario; Turkey Run, Ohio; Maple Grove (Lawrence County), Pennsylvania; and Pleasant View, Ohio. Most of these were small churches, but there was altogether a total of 68 converts. He visited approximately 318 homes.

Summer Bible Schools

As indicated, the period of the thirties marked the beginning of summer Bible schools in the Mennonite Church, although a few had already been held in the decade before. Known as vacation Bible schools in most denominations, these schools, like the Sunday school, became an institution in the life of the church.

It was rather significant that my father became involved in these, as with the winter Bible schools, chiefly in the closing decade of his life. Still more significant, much as he had been one of the outstanding leaders in the Bible conference movement at the beginning of the century, he now became one of the chief promoters of both the winter and summer Bible school movements in this era.[52]

As principal of a summer Bible school S. G. was in full stride and all of his early zeal seemed to return. Not many people in their sixties could successfully handle the younger groups, particularly in large numbers. "Law and order" was his first rule, but he maintained this in a way that the pupils actually enjoyed it, excepting, perhaps, for an occasional obstreperous youngster who would listen to no one. In addition to serving as principal, he would also serve as the teacher of either the high school or adult class. Visitors to these schools and those who came to the closing night programs would marvel at the ease with which he could handle as many as four hundred youngsters. A big feature of the Bible school was the group singing, which he directed. He would have the children stand, sit, sing loudly or softly, all at a given signal or gesture. Hearing several hundred children sing with gusto was a great experience for any observer, though some objected to the way he would ask them to sing so loudly at times.

The summer Bible school provided an opportunity for many young people to serve as teachers. He had recruited some of these from various states and they went with him from school to school to serve in the different areas of the church and without pay. This was a kind of early "voluntary service" program, now an integral part of Mennonite Church life.

Through these schools S. G. made literally thousands of

friends, many of whom still remember him very distinctly and with a certain nostalgia. The influence went far beyond the immediate church fellowship of the respective areas, since the schools were frequently community enterprises with many denominations participating. By conviction, however, he used only Mennonite personnel to operate them. In many cases Mennonites seemed to have the first summer Bible schools in their respective areas. Townsfolk would talk about the Mennonite school with pride for months and even years afterward. Pinto, Maryland; Pigeon, Michigan; and Coatesville, Pennsylvania, are examples of this movement.

Winter Bible Schools

As with the Bible conference movement, S. G. Shetler's name came to be associated in a large way with winter Bible schools. Shortly after the turn of the century (1904) he had become principal of the "short term" at Goshen College, and in 1916 served as an instructor in the winter term of what was to become Eastern Mennonite School. In 1921 he became principal of the Pacific Coast Bible School and in 1922 he helped found the Johnstown Bible School. From 1920 to 1940 he was responsible for starting or leading twelve different schools in the Mennonite Church. In a peak year (1938-39) he was principal of eight of these.[53]

The first of these Bible schools, known variously as "winter Bible school," "short Bible term," "special Bible term," had been held at Elkhart Institute (later Goshen College) at Elkhart, Indiana, in 1900. Winter Bible schools gradually assumed much of the role that Bible conferences had once filled in the church. Chronologically, of course, the two institutions overlapped for some years. The winter Bible school filled a large place in the life of the church at a time when many young people did not go to high school or college, and they had the commendable feature of serving the church at the grassroots level. Because both youth and older people attended, this brought the generations together. It is doubtful whether youth today are as well trained in the full scope of Bible teaching as they were in that Bible school era. In fact there was perhaps no other period in the history of North American Mennonites when such a large segment of the church had the advantage of concentrated Bible teaching.

By 1939 the total number of students attending Bible school in the Mennonite Church was 2,000.[54] As stated, my father served as principal in eight of these. By this time many were held in congregations as two-week schools, and by staggering the dates for these, he could fit them into his schedule. The schools for that given year with their respective enrollments were: Archbold, Ohio, 217; Bowne, Michigan, 35; Midland, Michigan, 132; Leo, Indiana, 51; Maple Grove, Atglen, Pa., 184; Fairview, Michigan, 30; Sheridan, Oregon, 77; and Shore, Indiana, 100. The total number attending these schools was 826, representing well over a third of the overall total of students attending Bible schools that year.[55]

As the Bible school movement grew the schools became institutionalized. In 1927 my father had developed a course of study at Johnstown Bible School which covered a six-year cycle, similar in essence to a plan formulated for the Ontario Bible School by S. F. Coffman in 1912. The Johnstown plan was later adapted for use in his two-week schools. For the six-week school, for example, the epistles required six years; the Pentateuch, minor prophets, and historical books, 5 years; the poetical books and major prophets, 4 years; church history, 3 years; Bible psychology, 2 years. The following courses were offered annually: Bible doctrines, Bible geography, Christian principles, character study, homiletics, missions, Sunday school methods, young people's meetings, summer Bible school course, English, German, music.[56]

A Christian workers' meeting became an annual event at Johnstown as did also the ministers' week and Sunday school week. Literally hundreds of Christian workers and Sunday school teachers and ministers from various parts of the church profited from these added features. Several extracurricular features such as midweek and evening programs, "literaries," social gatherings, and excursions were also introduced.

The method of conducting these schools was in keeping with S. G.'s usual enthusiasm. Although he was principal of a school he also taught full time. The usual schedule included seven or eight 40-minute periods. To avoid student restlessness, study periods were eliminated as a rule. He also was not one to be encumbered with an administrative staff of any size with secretaries and assistants. This does not mean that he did not believe in a division of labor. Frequently he had students perform the routine tasks that go with any school. Punctual to the nth degree, his Bible schools started promptly each morning with a spirited song period, followed by a pithy devotional period. With clocklike precision the schedule was carried out from the word "go" until 4:00 p.m. His eye missed nothing as he scanned the implementation of the program of activities.

His teaching outlines, like his class discussions, were concise and to the point. He spent many hours and even days in preparation for each school and filled his notebooks with the necessary materials. A review of these shows he used a wide range of source materials. He always integrated the Bible with those classes that did not deal directly with the Bible, such as English or pedagogy. In English class, for example, when he was teaching the use of possessives, he would take Bible examples, such as: Lot's wife (Luke 17:32); conscience' sake (Rom. 13:5); Jesus' breast (John 13:23); and Apostles' feet (Acts 4:35).[57] Instructions on how to write telegrams (something important then) drew in church figures, as, for example, he asked his English class to reduce to ten words the following: "T. K. Hershey telegraphed his wife at Elverson, Pa., that he would stop at Mattawana for an evening service and that he would be home the next morning."

There is no doubt that his Bible school work helped to characterize him as much as any other single type of service, and many remember him just for that.

Young People's Institutes

In this last decade of his life it so happened that he also came to be associated with Young People's Institutes, another new "institution" of the church for a time—now replaced for the most part by youth camps and youth seminars. His association with the institute movement again seems strange in reflection, as my father was then in his late sixties. Two communities where he made a lasting impression on scores of young people, as evidenced from comments one still hears from those who attended and who are now past middle age, were Archbold, Ohio, and Wellman, Iowa. His personal interest in each young person, his spirited conducting of music periods (by no means on a professional level), his interesting classes, and his evening lectures captivated and inspired the young people.

Pastoral and Bishop Roles in the Johnstown Area

With all of my father's away-from-home schedule, it would seem that he could hardly serve also as pastor and bishop, looking after several congregations.[58] Yet if one were to evaluate his entire ministry in terms of the pastoral role, these last ten years stand out as the most active of his life. This activity was all the more amazing because his physical affliction, a serious bronchial disorder, would have kept many a person of his age totally "grounded."

As a pastor he took a personal interest in each member through systematic home visitation and detailed membership files with interesting notations. He would, for example, check carefully at communion time to see who had or had not participated. He wrote pastoral letters, averaging from 1935 to 1942, 4.5 letters a year. Some of his pastoral letters were sent to the youth of the church. From these letters, often sent from distant points where he was at the time engaged in evangelistic services or Bible school work, one catches the spirit and enthusiasm he maintained for the home church and the concern for building a spiritual church. These letters also provide additional information on his activities during these years.

He wrote the first one of these in 1935 from Creston, Montana, where he was conducting a winter Bible school at the time.

From Coatesville, Pennsylvania, he wrote (August 6, 1936) to the members of the Stahl congregation:

The Summer Bible Schools have been well-attended. Following is the total enrollment of each school: Stahl, 323; Pigeon, Michigan, 273; Pinto, Maryland, 410; Springs, Pennsylvania, 252; Coatesville, Pennsylvania, 318. Eighty-seven teachers have helped in this work. . . . I expect to spend five Sundays in Montana with the daughters [Rosella and Goldie] from October 11th on. I am anxiously looking forward to this time. The railroad company is again granting me a free trip, which I appreciate very much. [He is referring here to passes he received over several years from the Western railroads, because of his many travels in the interest of church activities and for his earlier years of paid travel.] Let us all seek to improve our congregation by devoted service, faithful attendance, consecrated living, and spiritual cooperation.

In another letter sent from home on August 13, 1937, he wrote:

On August 11-15 I expect to work in the Y.P.I. [Young People's Institute] in Iowa and then I shall go to visit my daughters in Montana, and after that go to General Conference. I shall come home the latter part of August. . . . I want to thank you for the cooperation you have given Sanford and me. . . . We are happy to say that all the young people except two communed at our last communion. We hope to see the time when everyone of you, both young and old, will remember the death of Him who did so much for us.

o   o   o

Brother J. S. Neuheuser [from Leo, Indiana] will be with us for revival meetings September 1-12. Think and pray for some young people who should be gathered into the fold. . . . Dear young people, upon your loyalty and effort will depend much of the success of our future congregation.

And again on February 18, 1941, he wrote:

Sanford and I have arranged our work so that one of us will be at home every Sunday [church services were then held only on alternate Sundays]. I will be home ten Sundays out of 13 during the first quarter of the year. With the many calls coming in [for church assignments away from home] it is difficult to always make the proper decisions as to where to work.

In view of no pastoral support at that time his devotion to the home church was all the more commendable, but yet not out of keeping with the kind of service preachers during that period gave to churches which actually—in modern terms—had no strings on them. His total income was received from churches outside his own district, except for occasional revival meetings in the home district or the local winter Bible school.

The last of his pastoral letters was written from Pigeon, Michigan, where he was conducting summer Bible school, shortly before his passing in 1942.

The Stahl Church

Frequent reference has been made to the Stahl congregation in which my father served most of his lifetime, either as deacon, pastor, or bishop. Ordained there in 1897, he became the first resident minister, and with the exception of a few years, served there until his death in 1942. His ministry, incidentally over-lapped my own by ten years, which means that both of us served here, either singly or as a team from 1897 until 1970, or a total of 73 years. In 1970, after my resignation as pastor I continued to serve as bishop for another four years.

It should be noted, however, that during these years there were also other ordained men who served the congregation. This was during the time of the circuit ministry. Ministers who were resident here and who served for varying periods of time, were: S. D. Yoder, W. C. Hershberger, and Lloy A. Kniss. After my father's death in 1942, David C. Alwine was ordained at the Stahl Church to serve a mission church established by the Stahl con-gregation. Later (1969) David Alwine and I served as interim copastors. In 1969 Arthur McPhee became the new pastor, and he in turn was succeeded in 1973 by Curtis Godshall. Resident dea-cons who served during my father's tenure were Loranza Kaufman and John F. Harshberger. After his passing Harold Thomas, Levi Thomas, Melvin Nussbaum, and Marvin Kaufman were ordained, successively, to serve in this office. The last named, a grandson of S. G. Shetler, was later ordained to the ministry and became pastor of the Carpenter Park congregation.

From the time of the organization of the Stahl Cemetery Association my father served as secretary of the board of trustees. He had, in fact, helped to write the charter for the organization, and from its inception had always looked with a certain pride on the orderly way in which its business and administration was carried out, as well as the neat and orderly manner in which the cemetery itself was kept. During this period many rural Mennonite cemeteries were a secondary matter. He served on this independent board until the time of his death.

As a pastor my father always tried to make the church a center of activity and to keep himself involved. Although he never took the position that a pastor had to be *ex officio* member of every committee of the church, he was nevertheless elected to serve on numerous committees. He was a strong supporter of both the Sunday school and the Sunday evening "Young People's Bible Meeting." Seeing the need for improved methods of teaching in the early years he conducted teachers' meetings in his home to take a preview of the weekly lesson. Later he conducted teacher training classes in the district. A note in the *Gospel Witness* in an August 1906 issue stated, for example, that Ed Miller of Springs had been at the Stahl Church on July 28 and that he "also attended teachers' meeting Friday evening at the home of Bro. S. G. Shetler." He took a special interest in seeing young people "get on the floor" in Young People's Bible Meeting to lead their first song or give their first talk, never failing to encourage them after the meeting.

He was strong on the idea of having special weekend meetings, inviting in capable speakers from various parts of the church. This brought into the congregation some of the top speakers and leaders of the denomination, including many foreign missionaries.

Interest in extension work and missions was part of the life of his home congregation, resulting in opening work in two nearby villages that were unchurched—Carpenter Park and Walsall. Reminiscent of his earlier solicitation for the new Hopewell Church in Oregon, he launched an almost one-man solicitation program to secure funds for a new chapel at Walsall. Services at both places had been conducted at first in school buildings. The records show that money for the Walsall building came from various parts of the church. With the help of much local donated labor and donations the project was brought to a successful completion in 1940.

Some years after his death the Carpenter Park school building became the property of the church—after the schools of the area had consolidated—and the building was renovated and enlarged into a beautiful chapel. Both missions in time became organized churches, although Walsall was later closed and the building sold to another denomination.

15
Sunset and Beyond

For many years my father had been afflicted with a chronic bronchial disorder which produced periodic spells of incessant coughing. All kinds of home remedies and aid from medical doctors seemed to be of no avail. In 1941 he underwent a series of medical tests at the Cleveland (Ohio) Medical Clinic, and the physicians there diagnosed his case as "bronchiectasis." Otherwise they found his body to be in excellent condition.

In the spring of 1941 he suffered an attack of pneumonia which left his body in a weakened condition. He appeared to have recovered from this quite satisfactorily, but the continuing heavy schedule of activities began to take its toll.

The family had often urged him to slow down because of his age and particularly his health, but this was hard for him to do. Invitations for meetings kept coming in and he couldn't resist. During one short sickness he was quite disturbed when he couldn't fill some engagements. Musing over his depressed feelings he said that he supposed he had gotten at least a little work done in his years of service. If he couldn't get anything more done he probably shouldn't worry about it. I assured him that this was the case and that if he didn't get better he would definitely have to work on a more restricted schedule.

Another seige of illness in the early part of 1942 added to his problem, but again he made a fair recovery and returned to his work. He decided to accept an earlier invitation to conduct a summer Bible school at the Meadow Mountain congregation near Grantsville in early July. This was located about 70 miles from his home. He was also asked to preach the dedication sermon for the new basement chapel on the afternoon of July 7 prior to the opening of the Bible school. That same morning he had preached at his home church. The text for the dedication sermon, which was preached to a full house, was 1 Kings 9:3: "I have hallowed this house, which thou hast built, to put my name there for ever; and mine eyes and mine heart shall be there perpetually." He also preached on Sunday evening and was asked to preach on Wednesday evening, but that afternoon he became ill. He remained in the home of the host pastor, Roy Kinsinger, where his wife, a registered nurse, waited on him. That same afternoon after Bible school, he with some of the teachers, had visited 13 homes of the community to create interest in the school! The Sunday evening sermon at Meadow Mountain had become his last sermon, and the Bible school, his last school.

When I visited him in the Kinsinger home shortly after this sad episode, as I walked into the upstairs bedroom, he said, "Sanford, this time I am going to listen to you," meaning that he would now take the family's advice to relax his heavy schedule. But his little appointment book found in his personal effects after his passing showed that he had a full program of activities lined up for the coming year.

"Laying down his armor"—a familiar expression of his—was one of the hardest things he was ever called upon to do. While in a certain sense he grew old gracefully, it was not easy for him to lay down his work gracefully. In the later years of his life he resented that some of the younger church leaders were not, as he thought, always very gracious in taking over some of the roles which older men were forced to relinquish. More than once he said, "Just wait, one of these times they will be old too."

Transferred to his own home (he was staying at my sister

Margaret's home during my year's service as director of the Civilian Public Service Camp for Religious Objectors at Sideling Hill, Pennsylvania) he lingered on for a month. In addition to his bronchial condition his heart had weakened, and his body was in a dropsical condition.

During those last days in early August the family had gathered to be near him. Rosella and Goldie had come from their homes in Montana and Luella from Indiana to be at his bedside. This concern he took at first as having a negative effect on him, psychologically, in his fight to recover. To him, recalling a similar gathering ten years earlier when my mother had passed away, it was simply a sign that death was near. But later that same week he became resigned that he would have to move on. He was happy then that he could have all of his family close by.

The various church activities which he had always enjoyed so much and which had become an inseparable part of him were still with him as he lay there. His mind was somewhat detached from his surroundings. He was imagining himself conducting summer Bible school, first at one place and then at another—giving out instructions to teachers and children and directing the work with audible commands.

Needing some reassurance of faith he asked to have a Scripture read. I selected John 10, the story of the Good Shepherd. When I had finished, he said, "Read it again!" Concerned about the future of the church he would be leaving behind he called for his fellow-ministers (Lloy Kniss, who had just returned from India on a furlough and was at the time serving the local congregation, and myself), admonishing us to try to keep the church "pure."

As he became aware that the moment of death was drawing near, he asked, somewhat symbolically, that the electric fan on the dresser be turned off, saying, "I won't need that anymore." As some of the family stood there we watched his heart laboring in its last struggle, beating gradually slower and then finally stop. Only those who have observed death close at hand know the strange feelings that overtake you. As a boy I used to watch the wheels at the nearby feedmill come to a gradual stop at the close of day after the miller had disengaged the gears. There was a final whir-ring of the wheels and pulleys and a slapping of belts, and then— a final turn or two of the huge flywheel as everything ground to a final stop. For him the wheels had now made their last turn, and his soul had gone on to "the Master."

I stood and looked for a long time at that silent form—his hands lying across the bed in a somewhat curved fashion, the face pale and still. Those hands which had so deftly handled the Word of God in the pulpit for so many years now lay rigid and silent in death!

Many thoughts cross the mind at a time like this. Death is al-ways hard to face. It seldom seems real. Your loved one will surely return, will speak again. You try to satisfy your mind. But as we turned away our task had now become clear. We would have to try, at least in part, to take up the work which he had laid down and help perpetuate the heritage that was ours.

Sympathy cards flowed in from many parts of the church. A line on a card from the Dewey Wolfers in Oregon seemed so ap-propriate: "School is out, the teacher has gone home." The teacher and the preacher had indeed gone home, and "the mourners were going about the streets."

My father had often said that when he died the banks would not close and business would go on as usual. In a few years he would probably be forgotten. The banks and stores did not close, but a thousand people took off from their work to attend the me-morial services at the Stahl meetinghouse. In that long procession of viewers on August 14 as the body lay in state were the rich, the poor, business and professional men, workingmen, housewives, and many children. Friends were present from far and near, including representatives of church boards and from two of the church colleges. There were those of his own faith and many out-side his faith.

The sermon was preached by his son in the faith, Lloy A. Kniss, whom he had ordained to the gospel ministry thirty-two years before. Kniss was assisted by two men whom he had come to respect highly, Bishop John L. Horst and Robert Dayton. The latter, another son in the faith, had grown up in another faith but was won to the Mennonite Church as an adult lay leader through a Bible conference at Pinto, Maryland, twelve years earlier. James Saylor, an area bishop, spoke, and brief tributes were given by the following: Bishop Daniel Kauffman, editor of the *Gospel Herald*, the official church publication; Bishop A. J. Metzler, manager of the Mennonite Publishing House; Pastor J. Irvin Lehman, a former colleague at Johnstown Bible School; Bishop Allen Erb, superintendent of the Mennonite Hospital and Sanitarium, La Junta, Colorado; Bishop S. C. Yoder, professor of Bible, Goshen College, Goshen, Indiana; Bishop Roy Otto of the Casselman Valley churches; and Bishop D. I. Stonerook, moderator of the Southwestern Pennsylvania Mennonite Conference. Pallbearers had been chosen from the local ministry: Charles Shetler, Harry Shetler, Irvin Holsopple, John A. Lehman, and bishops Harry C. Blough, and Aldus Wingard.

Music was rendered by a male quartet, composed of draftees then stationed at Sideling Hill Camp. It was a fitting tribute to have men who represented the peace testimony to sing for one who had spent so much time in behalf of conscientious objectors in World War I. The numbers, sung so impressively by Dennis and Paul Miller, sons of Bishop D. D. Miller, of Berlin, Ohio; Abe Willems, D. D.'s future son-in-law; and Warren Myers of Goshen, Indiana, were: "If I Have Wounded Any Soul Today" and "Beyond the Sunset."

Two "field notes" appeared in the August 20 issue of the *Gospel Herald*, written by the editor, Daniel Kauffman, reflecting the impact his passing had on the church. The first one was as follows:

> About a thousand people attended the funeral of Bro. S. G. Shetler at the Stahl Mennonite Church in the Johnstown District on Friday of last week. Among the attendants were nearly all the ministering brethren in Bro. Shetler's home conference district, as well as many people, ministers, and others from other districts. The obituary notice will appear in next week's *Gospel Herald*, D. V.

The obituary, August 28, 1942, listed 28 ministers, 12 bishops, and

9 deacons as having been present at the funeral.

The other note:

> Bro. S. G. Shetler of Hollsopple, Pa., one of our foremost widely known
> evangelists and Bible school teachers, answered the heavenly summons
> and passed to his reward on Tuesday evening of last week. The funeral
> was held last Friday forenoon at Stahl Mennonite Church where he had
> served as minister and bishop for many years. May God comfort the be-
> reaved and raise up others to fill the vacancies in the church left by our
> brother's passing.

His body was laid to rest on the hillside adjoining the churchyard by the side of his companion, Maggie, and near the twins,
Ralph and Rena, and his parents. On his pink Georgia granite
tombstone is inscribed one of his favorite Bible texts, "The sleep
of a laboring man is sweet."

At the close of his last chapter in the *Ministers' Manual*,
published in 1915, he had written these words, under the title
"The Hope of a Glorious Future":

> "I have fought a good fight, I have finished my course, I have kept the
> faith: henceforth there is laid up for me a crown of righteousness, which
> the Lord, the righteous judge, shall give me at that day." Sometimes the
> argument is presented that the reward should never be thought of. This
> does not seem true of Paul. Repeatedly he refers to what is in store for him
> after he lays his armor down. Blessed is the peace of the servant of the
> Lord, who has earnestly contended for the faith, and who continually
> realizes that "to depart and to be with Christ is far better."

S. G. Shetler's name after these thirty-eight years has become
almost a legend in the circles in which he had served. Though the
banks and stores did not close on the day of his death, his name
has not been forgotten by the hundreds of boys and girls—now
men and women—and by the scores of young people and adults
who had sat under his teaching and preaching. They can never
forget his zest as a teacher, his incisive use of Bible texts and illustrations, his humor and his pathos. Though it may seem strange to
some, a compliment given him by his physician, Dr. Keim, a man
of another faith, just shortly before my father's passing, seemed to

please him more than anything anyone outside his own church circles could possibly have said. The doctor said, "You have been a useful citizen." A churchman, my father had been, first and foremost, but the Christian who does his part well in life, while being in the largest sense a citizen of heaven, is also to the highest degree a useful citizen on earth.

Beyond the Sunset

Beyond the sunset, O blissful morning,
When with our Saviour heav'n is begun,
Earth's toiling ended, O glorious dawning;
Beyond the sunset, when day is done.

Beyond the sunset no clouds will gather,
No storms will threaten, no fears annoy,
O day of gladness, O day unending;
Beyond the sunset, eternal joy!

Beyond the sunset, a hand will guide me
To God, the Father, whom I adore,
His glorious presence, His words of welcome
Will be my portion on that fair shore.

Beyond the sunset, O glad reunion,
With our dear loved ones who've gone before;
In that fair homeland we'll know no parting,
Beyond the sunset forevermore.[59]

16
Personal Life and Philosophy

Everyone lives and works by some philosophy (the rules we live by), although it is seldom written down. One might well gather from what has already been written of my father's life what his philosophy was. Yet in closing this story it is not inappropriate to summarize his basic qualities and ideals, adding some other details and incidents that helped to characterize him.

It is not my intention here, nor has it been throughout the book, to present a larger-than-life portrait of him. Instead, I have tried to show him in authentic perspective, while obviously underscoring his contributions and successes.

His Personal Life

One of my father's outstanding qualities was his resilience or bounce in pulling himself out of discouraging experiences and reverses. Anyone who makes some mark in life is also bound to face some opposition, and he seemed to have his share of it, little as it may have been known to the public. My father soon recovered from these discouraging experiences and moved on. In 1915 he wrote in the *Ministers' Manual* that God is the great "equalizer," balancing the good and bad events of life. In later years he used the term "compounder" (or chemist), saying that

God knows how to mix the good and bad ingredients of life in just the right proportion for our individual good.

Basically he was an optimist and felt that one should never overemphasize the negative aspects of life. This spirit was reflected in nearly all of his messages, which he invariably closed on the "bright side" after having first discussed the "dark side." This he applied also to himself. No matter what happened, there was always "a way out." A poem found written on the flyleaf of his Bible after his death characterized his feelings in this regard:

Don't Give Up

God can read each falling tear.
He knows the heart that's needing cheer.
He sees the path that's hard and drear.
Don't give up, for he is near.
August 9, 1935,
Coatesville, Pennsylvania

There was a certain underlying serenity that seemed to mark my father's life and disposition considering his somewhat emotional and impetuous nature. Quick-tempered, he was at the same time ready to forgive and immediately grieve over his hasty conclusions. Full of humor, he was quick to balance whatever there was of the "dark side." He was of moderate speech, chaste, and devoid of unsuitable bywords or slang. His conversation around the home seemed always to be interesting. Vocal and overt as he was and outgoing in public, he was not an outstanding conversationalist when he was to act as host in the home. It was not uncommon for him to slip away to his desk while the rest of the family entertained the guests.

In business affairs he was a man of complete integrity, and though he lived for many years on a very ordinary income, he always met his obligations. His business judgment was recognized to the extent that he was asked to settle a number of estates, and he wrote wills for many people. He took pride in his ability to write wills in such a way that they could not be misconstrued, something he observed that lawyers were not always able to do.

He was never tight with money, but he also despised wastefulness. He enjoyed relating in public the day the last payment had been made on his home—how that my mother had made a special dinner that evening to celebrate the occasion. He could never approve of people going to court to sue for their rights when they felt they had been cheated or misused. One of his oft-quoted stories was that of two men who fought over a triangular plot of ground that lay between their properties that was not even wide enough to provide burial space for either of them!

My father was a good giver and often helped people in need with small donations. In the several years he served as deacon, he had made it his personal duty to see that the needs of a certain poor family were met, even if it meant money out of his own pocket. Some in the congregation thought this family to be unworthy of help. In later years he helped to support some preachers and missionaries who were having what he called "a struggle." He did the same for friends in the community. One of his very favorite verses was 1 John 3:17: "But whoso hath this world's good, and seeth his brother have need, and shutteth up his bowels of compassion from him, how dwelleth the love of God in him?" Tithing became his practice in his later years.

Characterized more perhaps as the man on his feet than the man on his knees, he was nevertheless a man of prayer, his personal prayer life becoming increasingly meaningful as the years went by. Interestingly, his prayer concerns went first toward those who were in spiritual need rather than those who suffered physically, though these were certainly not forgotten. He strongly believed in divine healing according to James 5 and he witnessed through his own ministry some remarkable healings.

It is of interest to note that his last article to the *Gospel Herald* (March 5, 1942) in the feature section dealt with the minister's devotions and personal study. Under the caption, "Our Ministry Under the X-Ray," he wrote among other things:

> Since a very large percent of our ministry are engaged in some secular work, and since there are so many additional religious duties, the minister's real and private devotional hour is frequently crowded out or

shortened. This close touch with the Lord, if neglected, robs the minister of much power. It is worthy of commendation that some ministers regardless of other duties, spend an allotted time in reading and prayer. To neglect this shows in the minister's own life, in his sermons, in his pastoral work, and in his religious work in general.

He spoke also of ministers sometimes wasting time by reading the daily paper or listening to unprofitable things on the radio, and noted that "neglect of study means mental and spiritual decay." He referred to the need of those who are extremely busy to find some time, "even if it is by the midnight light or in the early morning hours." The study hour, he wrote, "is indispensable to any successful minister."

Ideally to him the devotional side of life needed to be complemented by the practical, and he stressed much the need of living an exemplary life in harmony with strong personal convictions based on the Word of God. He disdained the wishy-washy type of individual who was quickly moved from his beliefs.

S. G. Shetler's faith was marked with an unequivocal acceptance of the entire Bible as the inerrant Word of God. He totally repudiated false science and mythological ways of explaining certain portions of the Bible. I recall his denouncing a particular Bible geography book that attempted to explain the Israelites' crossing of the Red Sea on the basis of a natural landslide that had cut off the waters. If the children of Israel crossed on dry land, how then could Pharaoh's army drown on dry land as it attempted to pursue them? He had similar ridicule for the evolutionary theory which was beginning to become more and more popular. Obedience to the Word of God was for him a necessary requisite for every Christian if he was to succeed spiritually. People who took emotional "spurts" in their religious experience or who chased after movements of one sort or another were considered suspect. He admired those who were constant in their experience and who were thoroughly grounded on the Word.

Many persons still recall his unique and concise way of interpreting the Old and New Testaments. His hermeneutics were simple but sound. His outline ran as follows:

Four Rules in Interpreting the Bible

1. Some things are alike in both Old and New—Keep them.
   Exodus 20:12—Ephesians 6:2, 3; Psalm 13:6—Colossians 3:16

2. Some things are not in the Old but in the New—Keep them too.
   Mark 16:15, 16; Acts 2:38; Romans 16:16

3. Some things are in the Old, and dropped in the New—Drop them too.
   Genesis 17:10; Hebrews 9:2; Leviticus 16
4. Some things in the Old are changed in the New—Change them too.
   Leviticus 24:20—Matthew 5:38, 39; Exodus 20:8—John 20:19, 26

He stressed the providence of God. That all things worked together for good (Romans 8:28) was a reassuring motif in his life and he tried to convey this to all those who sought his counsel. When there were stresses (as during the two World Wars), when the labor union issue came to the forefront, or when people were tested in their jobs (such as working on Sunday), he always came through with the unequivocal position that everyone should "take his stand," knowing that God would in some way reward them. To follow the way of Christ and the way of the cross in human relations was his model for Christian living.

On the Home and Parental Discipline

Having visited so many homes in all parts of the church, my father had come to observe firsthand many ways of managing a home. He was a stickler for good discipline and opposed the new permissiveness of modern psychology. The attitude of the home toward the church and its ministers was also paramount in his thinking. He had seen homes where children had been lost to the church largely through a constant spirit of criticism toward the church and church leaders. To him respect for authority at home, church, and citizenship levels was a definite essential. To him the home was the backbone of the church, and when it failed, churches were sure to suffer.

On the matter of stewardship and the simple life he did not believe an expenditure for ornate furnishings and lavish living was proper. His own home, always neat and comfortable, reflected his teachings on the simple life. The same was true of his apparel.

On Church-and-State Relations

One of the very strong principles my father adhered to was his belief in the separation of church and state. He saw the hazards of political involvement and became disenchanted through his observation of corruption in government, such as the Teapot Dome Scandal of the early twenties. He preached against Christians' electioneering in political campaigns and noted that those who were often fervent in this seemed to lack an equal fervor for the work of the church. World War I reinforced his belief that a person's position in a time of testing on the principle of nonresistance would be judged according to his consistent life earlier in reference to the church and political judgment. He often used the illustration of the politician whom he had known who claimed to have performed certain acts as a politician and not necessarily as a Christian. My father asked him what he thought would happen when he died. If he would be judged as a politician, what would happen to the Christian!

On Conference and Church Statesmanship

Having worked for years as a "conference man," my father had a high regard for the place of district conference and for the denominational "General Conference." He felt that one could not operate independently of the church's official bodies and had noted some unhappy consequences where ministers and churches had operated independently. He often spoke of the Jerusalem Conference in Acts 15 and how that group sent out "decrees for to keep." He saw conference as more than a mere fellowship body with no authority. Yet, at the same time, he never approved of any actions that seemed to represent manipulation and politics. To him everything in church administration should be open and "above board," no matter how right a given action was considered to be. He disdained "rubber-stamping," having church bodies simply approve what a few officials had already mapped out. He had seen too much of this in his time. Fairness for him was one of the outstanding ideals, although, to be sure, he did not always escape criticism on this himself. Frequently when he sat through a conference session he would become depressed momentarily because of the "machinery" he had seen in operation. There were those, for example, who he felt had reached top posts without their gifts necessarily making room for them. Or some action had been "railroaded through" with little recognition of the opposition. But he would quickly pull himself out of this slump and get involved in the work of the church—at the grassroots level—where he thought the action really was anyway.

In spite of his somewhat critical attitude at times, and perhaps less than courteous ways of expressing this at times on the conference floor, his was not the role of the hypercritic. His motive was never to tear down but to build. He was much opposed to factionalism and church splits, since he had seen the bitter results of many of these. He was thinking particularly of those which had been the result of personality clashes. One could disagree constructively, he reasoned, without immediately withdrawing and starting a new group. He used to say frequently that if a group of "cranks" started a new church they would soon be "cranking" among themselves.

He grieved the loss, too, of members who disassociated themselves from the Mennonite Church because of their own "worldliness" or for greener fields in other denominations. He had also seen some leave for a supposed deeper spiritual experience, feeling that the Mennonite Church's more formal environment was not large enough to include those who sought an emotional type of experience. He had noticed that some of these invariably dropped some Anabaptist teachings they had once cherished. What was to be gained, he would ask, by taking up one teaching and dropping another? At the same time he was aware that the church was at times too slow in recognizing the gifts and in using those in the work of the church, causing them to leave for the exercise of those gifts.

Through the years my father was much disturbed at those in the church, frequently leaders, who seemed to feel their mission to be to modernize the church in faith or practice. He seemed to be able to sense quickly such efforts. If people were Mennonites, why not be Mennonites? Many conference sessions tended to make him edgy, because he felt there was too much effort expended in trying to innovate and push new programs that did not appear to be for the good of the cause. He was not opposed to change, however, but against a kind of "forced obsolescence." This frequently put him into the position of a dissenter. For many years in his earlier ministry he held correspondence with various ministers concerning vital issues in the church, particularly as they related to the interpretation of the Scriptures. He had a keen sense of discernment and tried to seek scriptural answers.

He was no less opposed, however, to conference resolutions that were expected to be binding but which he felt were not scriptural. He often referred to these as "whip-socket" resolutions, referring to a certain Mennonite body which had passed a rule that members were not permitted to have whip-sockets attached to the dashboard of their buggies, a new accessory developed by buggy makers. These whip-sockets were regarded by some members as a sign of worldliness. In time this particular church divided over this issue and another church was started.

In practice he was in a sense neither a conservative nor a liberal, but he definitely supported the conservative viewpoint. In theological matters he held a very high view of the Scripture. His position on nonconformity has been clearly stated earlier in the book.

It can be said that theologically he was warmly evangelical, but did not care to associate himself with the new Fundamentalism as such. He also had a spirit of concern for every person, preferring to consider his background and apparent motives before passing judgment. To him it was not as important to know where a man *stood* as to know which way he seemed to be *moving*. His teaching on forgiveness and genuine brotherliness was classic, and his illustrations on this were moving. Where brethren in the congregations had fallen out with each other he urged reconciliation at all costs. No one could afford to die with hatred for his brother. Christianity from pulpit to pew was one solid unit with no parts missing.

On Training and the Common Man

With all of his personal academic training in a day when church leaders did not go to college and with his strong emphasis on the teaching program of the church, my father clearly was not opposed to formal training. But he had no room for showy intellectualism nor for speakers who tried to impress their audiences with their knowledge. He always stressed the need for the use of a simple vocabulary in preaching. This is what helped to make him a preacher of the people. He was quite skeptical of seminary training for Mennonite ministers. He had seen some unfortunate results of this in other denominations and always coupled this with the salaried ministry which he felt was fraught with numerous hazards.

S. G. Shetler always remained the friend of the "underdog" and championed the cause of the common person. He was not an ivory-tower preacher trying to map out new strategy from the remote sanctum of the preacher's study. To him the layman was often the forgotten man. In his visiting as an evangelist or weekend speaker, as noted earlier, he would deliberately plan to visit the laypeople in the host congregation and make his home there during the stay, rather than be the guest of the pastor, which was the usual practice. For many people this was often their first visit by a minister. He also loved to serve small churches which, as he had observed, some popular speakers avoided, claiming to have too busy a schedule. He always took his invitations chronologically, whether the call came from a small or a large congregation.

It is not too difficult then to understand why that now after these many years since his passing, he is still remembered by many in the heartland of the Mennonite Church with deep personal affection. In his preaching and in his personal contacts he is remembered with fondness as truly the "preacher of the people."

Notes

Chapter 2

1. "Möllinger, David," *Mennonite Encyclopedia*, Herald Press, Scottdale, Pa., Vol. III, p. 731.

2. Marburg State Archives (Germany) records, and "Gingerich" *Mennonite Encyclopedia, op. cit.*, Vol. I. The first lease had been issued to a "Güngrich" in 1743.

3. Dr. Kampfmeyer, Head City Planner of Frankfurt, Germany, in an interview which I had with him on a train in Germany.

Chapter 3

4. A passport was needed at that time to travel from one province to another. It should be stated, however, that in that period of Mennonite history, it was not altogether unusual to be employed in this way. The Oberholzers who came to America actually operated a brewery in Westmoreland County, Pennsylvania, as also did Benedict Miller, a prominent Amish bishop in Somerset County, Pennsylvania. [Shetler, Sanford G., *Two Centuries of Struggle and Growth*, Herald Press, Scottdale, Pa., (1963) p. 183.]

5. Kaufman, Ammon, in *Weekly Budget*, Sugarcreek, Ohio (Dec. 26, 1935).

Chapter 4

6. From Ammon Kaufman papers, Goshen College Archives, Goshen, Indiana.

7. Shetler, Sanford G., *op. cit.*, p. 30.

Chapter 5

8. Interview with Mrs. Irvin Kaufman, former Nannie Gindelsperger, November 1970.

9. Shetler, S. G., "One Hundred Years of Sunday Schools," *Gospel Herald* (Oct. 7, 1940).

10. Layman, John, letter to the Johnstown *Tribune* (Oct. 25, 1940) describing old-time husking bees of "Fifty Years Ago" (c.f. Shetler, Sanford G., *op. cit.*, p. 31).

11. *Herald of Truth* (Jan. 1, 1891)

By some error the date of this baptism has been reported at various places as having been December 13, 1892. I reported this incorrectly in the sketch of my father's life in the history of the Allegheny Conference. It is reported this way from a sketch of S. G. Shetler in the *Mennonite Encyclopedia*, but we have evidence from four sources that this is not correct. The above report in the *Herald of Truth* is one. Also, in the *Gospel Herald* (Oct. 21, 1926) an article appeared, written by my father, in which he gave a report of a farewell meeting for six India missionaries (J. N. Kaufmans, George Baeres, and Lloy and Elizabeth Kniss). In this impressive meeting, J. N. Durr walked in as a surprise guest and my father noted in recognizing his arrival that it was he who had held services in this same church 36 years before, and that among the six missionaries there was a son and daughter of two people who were "among the converts at that time." The "two people" had been Louisa Blough (mother of Lloy) and Ella Weaver (mother of Elizabeth).

A third documentary source is a note found in the late Ella Weaver Luther's personal effects which gives the names of the eighteen young people and states that "all these were baptized at the same time in the Stahl Church in 1890." She lists the eighteen: Mary Blough, Louisa Blough, David Mishler, Sallie Stahl, Mary Yoder, Josiah Mishler, Susan Weaver, Mary Weaver, L. D. Yoder, Laura Eash, S. G. Shetler, Maggie Kaufman, Elias Blough, Josiah Gindelsperger, Elizabeth Livingstone, William Sala, Alice Stahl, Ella Weaver. The fourth source is my mother's obituary in the Johnstown *Tribune* (June 15, 1932), which states explicitly that she had been baptized in December 1890 by J. N. Durr.

Chapter 7

12. From interviews with individuals who had attended this conference, John A. Thomas, in particular. (*Appendix*, family lists, Springs, and Canada lists)

13. Mennonites of the area were at this time conducting services at Union Chapel with Lutherans, United Brethren, and Progressive Brethren on a rotating schedule.

14. From an interview with Grant Stoltzfus, Eastern Mennonite College, 1973.

15. Refer to testimony in the *Appendix*.

Chapter 8

16. Wenger, John C., *The Mennonite Church of North America*, Herald Press, Scottdale, Pa. (1966).

17. From the files of S. G. Shetler.

18. Taken from testimony appearing in the section "From the Mouths of Many Witnesses."

19. Coffman, J. S., *Outlines and Notes*, Mennonite Publishing Company, Elkhart, Ind. (1898).

20. Coffman, J. S., *ibid*.

21. Wenger (*op. cit.*, p. 193) names S. G. Shetler as one of 17 prominent Bible conference speakers of the Bible conference era. It is not certain how he arrived at his figure since his list does not coincide exactly with the lists compiled here. Other important leaders which he names, some of whom we know served after 1916, are: J. C. Clemens, C. C. Culp, T. M. Erb, John S. Hess, J. B. Smith, A. I. Yoder, and Abner Yoder.

22. The data for the years 1897 to 1906, before there were regularly published lists, was obtained by scanning the news items in the church papers.

23. Coffman, *op. cit.*

24. Coffman, *op. cit.*

25. Coffman, *op. cit.* The booklet included the notes of M. S. Steiner, Daniel Kauff-

man, K. H. Bender, J. S. Coffman, and A. D. Wenger.

26. Lederach, Paul, quoted in Wenger, *op. cit.*, p. 193.

27. This story was related in September 1972 by Elizabeth Showalter of the Zion Church near Broadway, Virginia.

Chapter 9

28. Virginia Mennonite Conference minutes.

29. Referring to a book by Matthewson, *Robber Barons*, written in 1936.

30. Interview with John Alger, 1972.

31. Interviews with John Alger and Lewis Showalter, 1972.

32. Interview on July 16, 1972.

33. *Gospel Witness* (Dec. 18, 1907).

34. This is an interesting figure and is probably correct. The largest single list taken from the November lists of Bible conference announcements included 22. Obviously the total for the year would have been far above this.

35. Miller, Mary, *A Pillar of Cloud*, Mennonite Press, North Newton, Kansas (1959).

36. Card in possession of Lloyd K. Lefever, East Petersburg, Pennsylvania.

37. Interview with Rhine Benner, Harrisonburg, Virginia, 1972.

37a. *Ibid.*

38. It is interesting to note, however, that in later years after the Miller family had moved to Goshen, Indiana, Luella took additional schooling at the college and reentered the teaching profession, teaching 11 years in the public schools of LaGrange County, Indiana. Her seven children, incidentally, had all graduated from the college prior to this.

39. Interview with Elizabeth Showalter, 1972.

40. Interview with Mark Showalter, 1972.

41. Field Notes, *Gospel Herald* (Nov. 6, 1913).

Chapter 10

42. Pellman, Hubert, *Eastern Mennonite College—1917-1967, A History*, Eastern Mennonite College, Harrisonburg, Virginia (1967), pp. 19-32.

Chapter 11

43. Mishler and my father had met each other both in the home area and in Indiana where Mishler had first served before he moved to Oregon. "J. D.," as he was commonly known, had attended a Sunday school conference in the Johnstown District on September 4, 1913. He was the grandfather of the late bishop, Raymond Mishler, Sheridan, Oregon.

44. Kniss had been ordained to the ministry on May 30 at the Stahl congregation and on May 31 the group left for Oregon. His first sermon was preached at a small mission outpost near Albany, Oregon, shortly after his arrival there.

45. Stahl, Howard, in a letter (1971) in which he relates "Memories of Contact and Fellowship with Rev. S. G. Shetler."

46. This statement appears in one of my father's pastoral letters, and I also heard him quote this many times in his messages.

47. This statement has been recorded in several denominational records of the war years.

48. *Washington Star* (Sept. 2, 1917), Reel 5, Vol. 44, opposite page 153 of ACLU Microfilm Records, New York Public Library.

49. It should be noted that the Franconia and Lancaster conferences of Pennsylvania were not under General Conference, although they were also (Old) Mennonite bodies. This accounts for Franconia having taken action on its own. As it turned out, however,

the General Conference Committee became the voice largely for all Mennonite bodies. S. G. Shetler, being moderator-elect, seemed to be the logical spokesman for the committee and the wording of the above communique to the churches definitely reflects his style of writing.

Chapter 12

50. The following guests were listed: Misses Stella Yoder, Fannie Kaufman, Carrie E. Mishler, Lizzie Sala, Carrie Yoder, Anna V. Mishler, Minnie Wingard, Edith Blough, Edna Hostetler, Nora J. Blough, Olive Zimmerman, Mabel Blough, Blanche Layman, Elizabeth Luther, Mary Veil, Irene Miller, Maggie Sala, Lizzie V. Kaufman, Emma Sala, Edith M. Alwine, Freda Wingard, Nora Weaver, Messrs. Erwin Harshberger, David C. Alwine, Henry Kaufman, John E. Wingard, Ralph Yoder, Morton Stayrook, John Lehman, Arlo C. Alwine, Paul B. Kniss, John E. Yoder, Clarence C. Miller, Norman Hostetler, Ernest R. Blough, Herbert S. Blough, Calvin Kaufman, and Ammon Wingard. Also present were Mr. and Mrs. John Kniss, Mrs. Polly Shaffer, Mr. and Mrs. John M. Bachman and their son Karl.

51. According to the records, at the time of his death he was worth $250,000 in landholdings and stocks. Three years before his death he had distributed $100,000 among his children.

Chapter 14

52. This is based again on statistical information gathered from church publications.

53. Clarence Fretz, in *A History of Winter Bible Schools in the Mennonite Church* (1942), lists 34 different church leaders who served either as principal or teacher in the various schools held throughout the denomination. S. G. Shetler is listed as having served in 12 of these, while none of the other 33 men is listed as having served in more than two each. Actually he served in 14. Fretz does not mention his connection with Goshen and the school at Harrisonburg. On the other hand it should be noted that Fretz does not attempt to list all of those who served and we know from other records that a number of instructors served in more than two schools, two of whom were J. Irvin Lehman of Pennsylvania and C. C. Culp of Michigan.

54. Shetler, S. G., "Winter Bible Schools," *Mennonite Yearbook and Directory*, Mennonite Publishing House, Scottdale, Pa. (1941).

55. *Ibid.* "Johnstown Bible School," *Youth's Christian Companion*, XII (Nov. 29, 1931), p. 795.

56. It should be noted that for a few years S. G. Shetler was not connected with the Johnstown Bible School except for the special weeks. The high point of enrollment for that school was reached in 1928 with 86 enrolled. The average enrollment for all the years was 59.

57. Outline of possessives used in Johnstown Bible School (1924-1925).

58. Stahl, Pleasant Grove, Walsall, and Carpenter Park.

Chapter 15

59. Words by Virgil P. Brock; music by Blanche Kerr Brock. Copyright by Rodeheaver Co. Sole selling agent Robbins Music Corporation, 799 Seventh Avenue, New York, N.Y. Used by permission.

Appendices

Appendix 1

In the Mouths of Many Witnesses

Most of the following testimonies were solicited from individuals who were closely associated with my father through the years. Some of these, however, came unsolicited in correspondence and in sympathy cards at the time of his death in 1942. Most of the solicited testimonies were collected in the period from the 1950s to 1973 during which time research for the biography was being done. A few were collected as late as 1980. The testimonies come from ministers, professional men, laymen, former students, family members, housewives, and close associates in the church. If there have been any names omitted whom the reader feels should have been included it was purely unintentional. There were literally hundreds more who would no doubt have responded had they been contacted, as we gather from conversations with individuals all over the church. A number of those whose testimonies appear here are since deceased.

It is with deep appreciation to those who responded that these testimonies are being reproduced here, all for the glory of God. There is no particular significance to the order in which they appear.

As a teenager I considered S. G. Shetler one of my favorite preachers. He was guest speaker at a conference at Surrey, North Dakota, that I attended, then went to my home congregation at Kenmare for a week of revival meetings. During that week he stayed at our home. We considered this a great privilege. He was a delightful guest, an interesting conversationalist, and he treated all, including the youngest, as persons. Adults and children alike looked forward to his "children's meetings." While they were most interesting, they also vividly portrayed biblical truth. His sermons were full of human interest stories, yet packed with quotations from the Word of God.

While the times that I spent in close association with S. G. were limited, I must say that he had a profound influence upon my life. As he served far and wide in the Mennonite Church in evangelistic meetings, Bible conferences, and in other ways he greatly influenced the church as well.

—*Milo Kauffman*, former president of Hesston College, bishop in the South Central Conference (retired)

When I was just a lad, Brother Samuel G. Shetler came to our little rural church (Valley View at Stuarts Draft, Virginia) for a revival service. At such a young age, I was deeply impressed by his enthusiastic preaching and his Bible-centered messages. In a little "fertilizer" note pad which my daddy had given me I wrote down the various Bible references to which Brother Shetler referred. These I looked up again in later days.

Several nights during the series, Brother Shetler spent a good period of time with us children. The church was packed with worshipers, so little backless benches were brought from the two little Sunday school rooms in each front corner of the frame building and arranged between the front bench and the pulpit. There were more than enough of us to fill the little benches, so some needed to sit on the pulpit steps. What a wonderful time we had singing together.

One children's meeting impressed me deeply. While telling the story of the lost sheep in his picturesque manner, Brother Shetler illustrated it with a pastel drawing of the Good Shepherd reaching over the edge of a cliff to rescue the helpless animal.

This scene made a lasting impression upon my spirit.

No doubt the spiritual impressions and teachings which brethren like S. G. Shetler, William Jennings, Oscar Burkholder, and George Brunk sowed within the hearts of the youth of our area a generation ago is today bearing much fruit for the glory of our eternal Lord.

—*Roy D. Kiser*, bishop in the Virginia Conference

I remember my father's first acquaintance with him when he spoke at Hershey's Church near Kinzer. He saw this young fellow sitting on the pulpit bench with the ministers and he wondered what that little fellow would have to say. He was really surprised, and he became acquainted with him and it was the beginning of many appointments in our district.

My first time that I met Brother Shetler was when a group of thirteen young folks went to Johnstown to a Bible conference at the Stahl Church. If I remember correctly the speakers were J. S. Shoemaker, Eli Frey, and your father. This was in the year 1908, and I was the youngest of the group. We visited with Lewis Shetlers because William gave us such a hearty welcome to be there during the conference.

He was at Maple Grove on June 4, 1915, at a weekend conference and spoke on 2 Samuel 19:35. Again at Maple Grove C. Z. Yoder and your father had a weekend conference and he spoke on 2 Samuel 19:34. This was November 28, 1917.

I think we had one of the first Bible schools here in this part of the East, which was held at Coatesville in 1935.

—*John E. Kauffman*, Atglen, Pennsylvania

In 1902, Benjamin W. Weaver was ordained bishop of the Weaverland district. He as a layman in the church lived through the troubles the church encountered through the ministers. He became a great leader in the church with a clear vision guided by the Spirit. The church under him grew rapidly, solidly on the rock, Jesus Christ.

Soon after the new bishop took charge he made great progress in solving old problems in the church and energizing it with life with the faithful support of his home ministry. This was the era when your father Samuel G. Shetler, Daniel Kauffman, and other mighty teachers of the Word came among us and aided the bishop in building up new life in his congregations. I recall the interest with which we absorbed the dynamic teaching of your saintly father. His enthusiasm in teaching the Word was marvelous. His eloquence and zeal moved people to put forth more effort. He was a resourceful and energetic speaker. I am sure he did our ministry and the church much good. His visits to the Lancaster Conference were always refreshing in the Spirit of the Lord.

—*George S. Sauder*, Goodville, Pennsylvania

I had S. G. Shetler as a teacher when I was in Bible school before my marriage. Very often I think of some of the precious truths he presented. He was a *real* teacher in every respect—he caused us to love learning; he mixed just enough humor in, with the serious teaching, to make for good classroom demeanor—we all admired him in many ways.

Your father, Brother D. A. Yoder, and Brother J. Irvin Lehman taught us a good number of years. And I do cherish the memories of those days.

—*Beulah M. Nofziger*, Archbold, Ohio

During the 1920s your father visited Lancaster County quite frequently and I made it a point to go to hear him whenever I had the opportunity to do so because I considered him not only an excellent expositor of the gospel, but also a great orator. As a matter of fact, I have frequently stated that in those days I had heard two great orators—S. G. Shetler and William Jennings Bryan. It had happened that I had heard William Jennings Bryan give his famous lecture on evolution when I was twenty-two years of age—just about the time when I was hearing your father, and so I had an excellent opportunity to compare the two men.

—*Samuel S. Wenger*, attorney, Lancaster, Pennsylvania

S. G. Shetler was a man in whose presence you felt very comfortable. He was pleasant to be about, always jovial and full of fun, but he could also be stern and very solemn when the occasion called for it. He had an aptitude to detect when one tried a new venture to give the help needed at the right time and was not slack in commending that same individual for a job well done. He was a congenial co-worker as some of us learned who worked closely with him in the various Bible schools and in conference work. It was largely through his influence that I was led into many phases of Christian service.

As a teacher and principal in winter Bible schools he was especially good. One never regretted being enrolled in his school. One thing that stood out above all the other good qualities was that he lived what he taught.

May 30, 1897, he wrote in my mother's autograph book:

> When our joys on earth are ended
> And our lives on earth are past,
> May we live in hope of meeting
> In our heavenly home at last.
> This is our hope and prayer.

—*Katie Thomas*, Johnstown area

In the early 1900s the country churches of Elkhart County, Indiana, looked forward with great anticipation to the revival meetings which were held in each congregation by some of the most outstanding and capable evangelists throughout the church.

These meetings were usually held during the winter months, and at that time automobiles were not used in this area, but when it was announced that Brother S. G. Shetler of Pennsylvania would soon be at any one of these churches the farmers made sure that their bobsleds were in good running order and would make them as comfortable as possible to take not only their own families, but also the neighbors to these meetings.

One of these big sleds often brought from ten to fifteen people to church, and the crowds came and filled the house. Often it was necessary to place benches in the aisles, there were no comfortable folding chairs then, but sometimes even standing room was appreciated.

In those days there were no snowplows, though they were often needed, and sometimes it was necessary to detour through the fields in areas where the snow drifts were too deep on the road, but these inconveniences were forgotten as soon as the service began.

There were several interesting and unusual traits about this preacher. It seemed he was in the community only a few days when he knew the names and ages of practically every child in the congregation. Of course this pleased the children, and the extra lessons he gave before the sermon were always enjoyed by the children and adults alike.

He seemed also to be able to turn to any page in the Bible instantly, and could quote many Scripture references in one minute on any subject he was talking about.

In March of 1910 Brother Shetler came to the Olive Church for a two-week series of meetings, intending then to go to Michigan for a similar service. There were a number of converts during those two weeks, then news came that there was scarlet fever in the Michigan congregation and their plans must be canceled, so the meetings at Olive continued another week with wonderful results, for now there were altogether thirty converts, none under sixteen years of age. Among these were nine husband-and-wife couples and there was great rejoicing in the church, and all felt that third week was very profitable indeed.

—*Mrs. Aaron Wise*, Wakarusa, Indiana

It is a privilege to write something about S. G. Shetler who was an outstanding man in the Mennonite Church. Needless to say such a personality made a great and lasting impression on me. I recall listening to S. G. preach as he filled the circuit preaching program of our district churches. He would use illustrations which would portray the message he was presenting. Even the young could grasp the message.

I remember him as a teacher of teacher training classes which were held at different churches in the area during the summer and fall months. I still see him illustrate by drawings and maps the lessons at hand. It seems to me as though I can hear him speak now, so vivid are these impressions.

Winter Bible school was a highlight in S. G.'s life. Each winter for six weeks for many years he organized and taught in the school. During this time many features were added because of his keen vision and intellect to make the Bible school program challenging and inviting. The winter Bible school trained and educated many for Christian service which is a real tribute to S. G.'s efforts and vision.

S. G. also worked hard to establish summer Bible schools at different places in the Allegheny Conference. Nearly all of these are still in operation.

S. G. had a definite and profound influence upon my life as he was instrumental in getting me started in mission Sunday school work. It was at Carpenter Park Sunday school and then years later at Walsall that I received his guidance in directing the Sunday school and particularly at Walsall in the building of a chapel in the early forties.

At one time in my early teens he spoke to me concerning the ministry, giving me encouragement and challenging me to continue in the work of the church. Soon after his death I was called to the office of deacon and three years later into the ministry. I am sure his life had an important influence in shaping my life to responsible work in the church. I shall always cherish the memory of S. G. and his influence upon my life. My life has been the better because he lived and dedicated himself to Christ and the life of the kingdom.

—*Harold E. Thomas*, former pastor Weaver Mennonite Church, public schoolteacher, and speaker on *Gospel Fellowship*—a weekly radio program sponsored by Johnstown area churches.

I remember S. G. Shetler as an effective evangelist who came into our community on a number of occasions, ministering in various congregations. Outstanding among these was a series at Lindale Church, in the Northern District, when many from other congregations also gathered nightly under his ministry. He was present in the community on an earlier occasion when my youngest brother was born. Significantly the new arrival was named Samuel Shetler Shank—after his paternal grandfather and the visiting evangelist.

During the series at Lindale Church, referred to above, a woman was reported to have said to Brother Shetler that his sermons were too short, that she could listen to him all night. His reply was to the effect that if she could live up to what he spoke in a half hour, that would perhaps be sufficient.

I remember Brother Shetler as superb in the use of illustrations. His broad experience had given him a store of incidents which he used effectively in eluci-

dating the truth and in evangelistic appeal.
—*J. Ward Shank*, bishop in the Virginia Conference and editor of *Sword and Trumpet*

We came to know S. G. Shetler as an evangelist and Bible school teacher during the years from 1932 to 1938. Whenever we heard that he was going to be the main speaker, we wanted to go and hear him.

At Central, Archbold, Ohio, Bible school S. G. Shetler, J. Irvin Lehman, and D. A. Yoder really worked hard because each evening for two weeks they also preached evangelistic sermons. God used the three Bible school teachers to bring 118 new converts in 1933 into the Christian fellowship, many in their late teens and early twenties. That last Sunday evening service at Lockport was long remembered because "the ice finally broke." Many young people accepted Christ. Bible school was at Central in the day times, and in the evenings sermons were given at West Clinton, Central, and Lockport. My wife, Rosella (Miller) Nofziger was one of the converts on February 27, 1933, on Saturday night at West Clinton.

D. A. Yoder says that they studied until two o'clock in the morning to prepare their lessons. S. G. Shetler had special prayer for D. A. Yoder because he was sickly and he was concerned for his life. The prayers were answered by extending D. A.'s life many years. (He passed away in 1980.)

Brother S. G. Shetler played a big part in the growth of the Mennonite brotherhood in Fulton County, Ohio.
—*Mr. and Mrs. Glen W. Nofziger*, Archbold, Ohio

My first acquaintance with S. G. Shetler came in 1933 when he held a series of revival meetings in Elkhart, Indiana, where we lived at the time. His ability to relate to children and to keep the interest of the audience impressed me very much. Having sensed the call to the ministry I studied his procedures and sought to evaluate them for future use. Following this various contacts continued as we met in conferences, mission meetings, young people's institutes, and other churchwide services.

Our second form of contacts was related to our interchange of revival meetings. He conducted services where I served as pastor in Canton, Ohio, and I led services at the Stahl and other Johnstown area churches.

Our third form of contacts was as teachers and administrators of winter Bible schools. Here again there were interchanges for special services and consultations.

Brother Shetler was very observant in his ministry and congenial to work with. He provided me as a young minister with helpful counsel and suggestions. He also affirmed me in my work with children and evangelistic preaching as being strongly Bible-based with gospel content. Once he told me that I had more Bible material in my children's lessons than he had been using. While staying in his home during a series of meetings he took my shoes each morning and polished them. He thought a minister should be well groomed and he was willing to serve in such menial tasks. I also recall his readiness to take time for visitation and counseling in the interests of both unsaved and church members. As we spent a number of days together in visitation I was able to learn many techniques that proved valuable to my ministry. I thank the Lord for the privilege of knowing and working with Brother Shetler.
—*J. J. Hostetler*, for years an active committeeman and bishop in the Mennonite Church, former principal of Canton (Ohio) Bible School, now residing in Goshen, Indiana

As a child I thought Brother Shetler was the most eloquent preacher I ever heard. My more mature evaluation did not change a lot. The audience was held in rapt attention from the moment he stepped into the pulpit until the usually sudden last word of his message. Sometimes there was laughing, and at other times crying, but always a keen sense of meeting with God. My second thought is of the intimate friendship between him and my father. He was often included in my father's voluminous correspondence. This was usually straight across, unpolished and unsparing, because S. G. with all his aptness as a teacher, preacher, evangelist, and administrator was yet not without human weakness and faults. My father's close friendship sensed this, and shared in the balancing process.
—*Marcus Lind*, bishop, Bible teacher, and former principal of Western Mennonite School, Salem, Oregon

My first recollection of S. G. Shetler goes back to the year 1906 when I was eleven years old. He came to Springs, Pennsylvania, for a series of evangelistic meetings and during his forceful preaching I became conscious that I would be eternally lost should death overtake me. About midweek I told my parents and that evening I joined the rapidly growing class of converts. His daughter Rosella (about my age), had come with him and she also decided to take her stand for Christ at that time. When the meetings closed the class numbered 50 and I clearly remember how we knelt in a semicircle in the front of the old church to receive baptism.

Several years later when the Southwestern Pennsylvania Conference (now Allegheny) met at the Stahl Church, I with others from Springs went by train to attend. The train stopped at a "whistle stop" called Mishler. There were quite a number in the group, perhaps a dozen or more, including my sister Fannie, and there were not enough conveyances (horse-drawn) for everyone to ride, so it was decided that the 4 or 5 teenage boys would walk.

I do not recall the distance, only that I was desperately hungry and in making that fact known to the others was told to keep my miseries to myself as I was not the only one. In due time we arrived at the Shetler home. There were my brother-in-law D. H. Bender, and my two sisters, Ella and Estie from Scottdale. A wave of homesickness overwhelmed me and I quickly went to the barn lest they see my tears. The call to supper put an end to my homesickness and I thoroughly enjoyed my stay for the duration of the conference.

In 1930 my brother Noah (N. E. Miller), Springs, Pennsylvania, died and Brother Shetler preached the funeral sermon. His theme was "The Unanswered Why," enlarging on the fact that so young a man "in the prime of life" should be taken away. My brother being 50 while I was but 35, I could not then think of him as a young man. Now (1970) I am 75 and 50 does seem young.

Several years after this Brother Shetler came to the Mt. Pleasant Church near Fentress, Virginia, where we live, and conducted a series of evangelistic meetings and it was our privilege to entertain him in our home. All through my life he has been an inspiration to me even since he is gone.
    —*Ira E. Miller* (brother of the late Bishop N. E. Miller), Chesapeake, Virginia

I think back to the time in my life when I sat under the instructions of Brother S. G. Shetler during a six-week term of winter Bible school, held at the Hopewell Church—three weeks at Hubbard, Oregon, and three weeks at the Albany, Oregon, Mennonite Church. I feel that the Lord used him in a special way to instill in my young life the need of consecrating my life entirely to God, to be used of him whenever and wherever he would find a place for such an unworthy person to labor for him. I expressed myself to Brother Shetler as wanting to be used of the Lord in the city of Portland, Oregon, should our people ever start a mission there, providing I would qualify. Little did I think that this would materialize within a couple of short years. I started working in Portland, only one week after a mission was started, and became active in the program there, which was the proving grounds of my life in the vineyard of the Lord.

As a minister and pastor I say, "God, give us more men dedicated to the work of the Lord and the church like our Brother S. G. Shetler."
    —*Joe H. Yoder*, former pastor, Portland, Oregon, and Albuquerque, New Mexico

I had the privilege of knowing S. G. Shetler from the time I was a lad until the time of his death. My high regard for him when but a lad was because of the fact that though he seemed to be such a superior person he made me feel that he was interested in me by noticing me and taking the initiative to speak to me. Even at that early age I listened with rapt attention to his sermons and Bible lessons. Through my late teens I took every opportunity to attend programs where he was scheduled to speak. That was the "Chatauqua" era when a week of entertainment composed of plays, musicals, and lectures, were brought to communities in a large tent. I recall making the observation then that S. G. Shetler could easily have become a popular Chatauqua lecturer if he had chosen this career.

During my early married life I became more and more involved in church-related activities and was given the privilege of associating with him as a Bible teacher at Johnstown Bible School, although I was an untrained layman. Surely consecrated courage must have been required on the part of the one recommending such an appointment. S. G. Shetler not only rallied me to this position but never made me feel inferior during the many years that I served with him in this capacity.

It was during these years that I became intimately acquainted with him and his family, for until the time of the death of his companion, Maggie, I with others boarded in their home during the Bible school terms. We were all one big, happy family. As I observed him spending hours at his desk each evening, preparing for his classes next day, I learned part of the secret of his ability to hold the undivided attention of every pupil in the class until the bell rang.

In later years I continued to be impressed with the enthusiasm he put into the winter Bible schools and summer Bible schools for the youth and children until the Lord called him home. Certainly as one of God's servants he made a tremendous impact on the Mennonite Church during his age.

> —*E. C. Bender*, Harrisonburg, Virginia, former treasurer and committeeman of the Mennonite Board of Missions and Charities, and former president of the Mennonite Publication Board

"For such a time as this," 1920, God raised up S. G. Shetler to start the Johnstown Bible School at the Stahl Mennonite Church near Johnstown. The building itself was a simple edifice located on a hillside where you could slide in as easily as slide out during January and February. The furnishings were old-type country church benches. Lap boards were provided for the attendants. There were the necessary blackboards, maps, and other school facilities. Rustic outside toilets were located a hundred yards from the building. Water supply for washing and drinking was provided in the basement, where kitchen, dining room, and some classrooms were located. Such in brief were the school facilities.

Teachers were competent persons from the churches, near and far. The bulk of the students came from the local churches and nearby communities. These were augmented by attendants from many sections of the church—the far West, Canada, the East and New York, and the South, even Florida. Age was no barrier, and neither was academic attainment. Being able to read and write and possessing a willingness

to learn were sufficient.

But what made the school? What attracted students from all sections of the church? It certainly was not the facilities or the conveniently accessible location! It was the head master, S. G. Shetler. He had been widely known as an evangelist and Bible conference leader. As a brilliant teacher and influential leader, he attracted followers who became strong and enthusiastic supporters of his work—the Johnstown Bible School.

I well recall the day he invited me to teach during the Sunday school week of the six-week term. This week was a high-water mark for attendance and to me also as editor of the *Youth's Christian Companion*. It gave me opportunity to observe and associate closely with a master teacher and a successful promoter of Christian education. As summer Bible school secretary in the Allegheny Conference, he provided the needed leadership and organized new schools in remote and neglected areas. In brief, he was successful in every endeavor of his gifted endowment.

But he was not only a very talented man of God, and extensively used; he was also a good mixer and friend of the common people. Mrs. Yake recalls serving him sweet potatoes in the jacket for a Saturday evening supper. With enthusiastic appreciation he thanked her, observing that in his travels, well-meaning friends often provided too sumptuous meals. And so I remember him, not only as a great man, highly endowed by God, but also as a humble Christian with a deep sense of appreciation, spreading encouragement to all he met.

> —*C. F. Yake*, former editor of *Youth's Christian Companion*, promoter of young people's institutes, and member of the Mennonite Board of Education

My closest acquaintance with Brother S. G. Shetler was in Bible school work. In the fall of 1927 he asked me to come to Johnstown Bible School for additional training and to assist as a teacher. For six terms at Johnstown and also six terms at Archbold, Ohio, he gave me very valuable spiritual and professional guidance. I have much appreciation for the help he was to me.

Brother Shetler would plan a year or more in advance for the next school term.

By much correspondence and many personal contacts he would promote the school and guide it on to success. As a result many young people and adults received from him instruction and inspiration of the highest Christian quality. Students found his Bible schools such a helpful experience that many came for more than one term, some completed the four- or six-year course.

During Bible school weeks Brother and Sister Shetler would lodge Ezra C. Bender and me, with others, in their home. We were received as members of their family with its warm fellowship, information, and counsels. By travel, evangelism, and Bible teaching the Shetlers had a nationwide knowledge of our church. The table talk, the stove-side chats, and study periods were times of sharing. Their natural wit and sympathetic pathos made sharing our problems and victories easy.

—*J. Irvin Lehman*, minister, Bible teacher, Chambersburg, Pennsylvania

I got acquainted with the family when Rev. Shetler came to preach at Weaver and Pleasant Grove Mennonite churches in 1905 and 1906. He would always be at our place for dinner as he was a personal friend of my father, the late Daniel S. Yoder.

When my mother died on May 16, 1906, Rev. Shetler, my father, and we children talked over what to do. We thought we should put the children in a home. But after talking it over, it was Rev. Shetler who finally convinced us it would be better for all to stay together.

I have in my possession my father's Certificate of Ordination, dated May 26, 1907. It is signed by J. N. Durr, officiating bishop, and S. G. Shetler, conference secretary. As you can see, the family ties were very close.

When it came time for me to choose a profession, it was Rev. Shetler who persuaded my father to send me to the Miller Normal School in Soap Hollow. I attended this school for eight weeks each summer in the years 1913 to 1916.

In 1915 Rev. Shetler went to Oregon to teach in the high school. Some of the boys that boarded at Rev. Shetler's home were as follows: U. Grant Weaver, Alfred Hershberger, Lewis Wingard, Clyde Naugle, Ortha Weaver, Waldo Hostetler, Clarence Baker, Bruce Luther, Oscar D. Yoder, and S. Newton Yoder. There were many moments of fun and laughter at the

Shetler home in those years. I can still remember as we walked home for dinner, Rev. Shetler would gather specimens for his botany class. If you wanted to take the "Professional Examination," you had to take two high school subjects, botany and physical geography.

The way for us to get to the Miller Normal School was to take the Windber streetcar from Scalp Level to Mishler's Greenhouse. We had to walk from there through Kelso, to the Shetler residence, carrying our suitcases. We stayed from Monday morning to Friday evening.

One service Rev. Shetler conducted when he had revival meetings was Children's Meeting, which many well remember. Another trait he had was to quote Scriptures and flip open the Bible to the right passage where it was recorded.

When I pass the Shetler residence and the Stahl Mennonite Church it brings many pleasant memories which I cherish so much.

—*S. Newton Yoder*, Windber, Pa.

Great men are not born great but become great through growth. I remember S. G. Shetler as an example of this statement. To me he was an individual who did not permit his native ability to lie dormant, but through convictions and faith, activated by self-reliance and courageous initiative, developed into a leader of his people who influenced his own and succeeding generations.

This leadership was most evident in two related fields, that of religion, particularly with the Mennonite faith, and in the field of religious and secular education.

As a boy of a neighboring congregation and a different faith I had occasional opportunities to hear the Reverend Shetler preach. I was impressed by his dynamic presentations. His fast-moving sermons were a welcome departure from the slow, monotonous drone quite common in the pulpits in those days. His knowledge of the Bible and his instant references to specific texts was unmatched. His sermons were replete with enlightening illustrations and references to practical life situations. This was evidence of his innate teaching ability.

In 1921, as an inadequately prepared young man, I entered the teaching profession. Although employed in different buildings in the district, we became co-workers. This gave me the privilege of becoming acquainted with S. G. as I got to know him. It was quite evident that S. G. was intellectually keen, having been self-taught in some of the more difficult areas.

S. G. was held in high esteem by his fellow teachers. He was resourceful in his presentations in the days when good teaching material was at a premium. He was sympathetically analytical in an effort to discover the individual pupil's needs and in providing for them.

S. G. became quite well known for conducting a local normal school each summer to help teachers prepare for certification. I was not privileged to attend his school since horse-and-buggy travel necessitated my attendance elsewhere.

Personally, the most lasting remembrance I have of S. G. was the warm feeling of self-esteem and confidence which I received from our personal associations. This was especially important to a young novice while working with those who were older and more experienced. In unspoken language S. G. seemed to say, "God gave you talents. Develop them." It is humbly hoped that I did not fail him.

I am certain that others who were fortunate to feel the warmth of his aura likewise have been encouraged to higher values and wider horizons.

—*James W. Spory*, former teacher-administrator, Conemaugh Township School District; member St. David's Lutheran Church, Davidsville, Pa.

I fondly anticipated the children's meetings in the late 1920s and early 1930s. He made every child feel important. He had a way of teaching the adults by way of the children. These meetings were conducted in churches in Franklin County, Pa.

—*Russell J. Baer*, bishop in the Lancaster Conference, Elizabethtown, Pennsylvania

The two winter Bible school terms held in 1937 and 1938 at Sheridan, Oregon, proved to be one of the most unforgettable experiences of my life.

Here I received teaching of the basic principles of the Word of God which has stayed with me. Having been baptized in my early twenties, I was still a babe in Christ and I was hungry for God's Word.

Sitting under the instructions of Brother S. G. Shetler was a joy and privilege. I had never heard the Bible presented in such an interesting and understandable way, using many practical and homey illustrations.

I thank God for the memories I have of Brother Shetler, and the inspiration and encouragement he gave to me helped me to become what I am today.

—*Enos Schrock*, Sheridan, Oregon

The turn of this century marked the full development of the "series" of meetings in the congregations of the Mennonite Church. Following the pioneer work of J. S. Coffman, it became customary for each congregation, with few exceptions, to invite an "evangelist" to preach a series of sermons over a period of two weeks, more or less. This came to be the high point of the congregation's evangelistic effort, a sort of ingathering harvest.

Of the scores of preachers who were used in these meetings, some of the best-known were the following: Oscar Burkholder, P. J. and Andrew Shenk, Noah Metzler, Stoner Krady, Noah Mack, H. A. Diener, Allen H. Erb, Milo Kauffman, Elmer Moyer, J. R. Mumaw, C. F. Derstine, E. W. Kulp, J. B. Martin, J. W. Hess, J. D. Mininger, L. J. Miller, O. N. Johns, E. J. Berkey, A. C. Good, John E. Lapp, D. D. Miller, J. H. Mosemann, Nelson Kauffman, D. G. Lapp, S. E. Allgyer, George R. Brunk II, Howard Hammer, William Jennings, C. Z. Martin, and Roy Koch.

S. G. Shetler was one of the most talented and active of these evangelists. He was an eloquent speaker and a man of deep convictions. His sermons sparkled with humor and illustrations, many from his experience as a schoolteacher, pastor, churchman, and family man. His audiences marveled at his ready use of the Scriptures. His Bible seemed to open itself at the verse or passage he wanted to read. Another of his abilities was his memory of names and faces. People were complimented when he recognized them after a brief acquaintance of previous years.

He was an excellent Bible teacher, serving in the annual Johnstown Bible School, and in many congregational Bible schools.

Shetler helped the Mennonite Church, and especially his own Southwestern Pennsylvania Conference, to be well grounded in the faith and devoted to its program.

—*Paul Erb*, minister, lecturer, former editor of *Gospel Herald*

Last evening a group of nearly 200

gathered to recognize one who had given his life's service to leadership in our church.

In addition to a host of fitting tributes to the varied and significant contributions which he had rendered at home and abroad, this man was asked to give a testimony as to how the Lord had led him into this meaningful ministry.

It was indeed striking to hear his several references to the place S. G. Shetler had played in this. He referred especially to the influence during revival meetings (when he accepted Christ and membership into the Mennonite Church), to a number of Bible conferences, and his attendance at the Johnstown Bible School.

Doubtless this is only one instance of the hundreds of congregations and communities and the many thousands of individuals whose lives were touched and changed by the Lord's use of S. G.'s long and fruitful ministry. Truly "his works do follow him."

We continue to thank God and cherish memories of those days of partnership and fellowship.

—*A. J. Metzler,* retired bishop, evangelist, Bible teacher, committeeman, and former manager of the Mennonite Publishing House, now living at Elkhart, Indiana

It was in the winter of 1903 when as a young man I had the privilege of attending a Bible conference that was being held in the Freeport congregation where Brother Shetler was one of the instructors. As a young Christian it was food for my hungry soul. His "Seven Steps to Heaven" made a tremendous impression on my soul. That night when I could not sleep, I was going up those seven steps.

On another occasion we called him to be our evangelist here at Science Ridge. Sinners confessed their Christ and a great spiritual awakening was felt in the congregation. The last, but by no means the least, was when we called him to conduct our first vacation Bible school (1936). It was our first experience in that kind of thing, and we wanted someone who had had some experience in that adventure. He proved himself to be the master of ceremonies. It was something new for our community, and young people came from most of the denominations including some Catholic and one Negro girl. She is now a social worker in our community.

As I remember our attendance was around 300. We brought them by bus from West Sterling—then our mission outpost—from 50 to 60 each day, and by cars from the community. After that some of the Sterling churches started Bible schools also, but were too much in the pattern of day schools, and the youngsters said that they wanted to go out to the Science Ridge school because out there "they taught the Bible." Sometimes I meet folks who say, "I remember when I went to your Bible school years ago." Who can tell what the answer will be when the accounts will all be in?

—*A. C. Good,* bishop in the Illinois Conference

At a very young age I developed a high regard for S. G. Shetler's dynamic personality and the resulting effective ministry. His personal interest in me as a young man and inviting me to become a student at Johnstown Bible School was a tremendous factor in developing my interest in Bible study and helping rear a family that would walk in truth. The study of the Bible cannot be overemphasized in these last days.

—*Lloyd S. Croyle,* active layman, Johnstown, Pennsylvania

As years pass and time moves us on, memories of the past sometimes are erased. But, the memory I have of Brother Shetler today is most vivid. The personal interest and the influence of his life and ministry mean much. Many of my generation have been touched and influenced and might have chosen different roads had it not been for the Bible schools, object lessons, memorization of Scriptures, and with an alertness and challenge to God's call which were a part of his life. I shall ever be grateful for the opportunity of having lived and served the Lord and church in the times and ministry of Brother Shetler.

—*Aldus J. Wingard,* bishop in the Allegheny Conference

My memories of S. G. Shetler are cherished for many reasons. He was my public school teacher for nearly all of my elementary schooling. I remember him as my pastor from childhood. He served as my Sunday school teacher when I was in the young married class. During the five terms I attended Johnstown Bible School I was enrolled in a number of his courses. And he was our next-door neighbor for seven years. In all of these areas he stands out in my mind as superior to his contemporaries. I sensed his deep concern for me as a developing person. Although he was not a conversationalist he was nevertheless a deeply concerned and influential person with a range of contemporary knowledge and a broad understanding of human nature.

As a public school teacher he was strict in discipline and an excellent teacher. He saw the need of providing education beyond the eighth grade, and accordingly set up a ninth-grade course, which he offered to eighth-grade graduates at a time when there was no high school in our township, and he did this without any remuneration. The courses offered were English, Latin, Algebra, and agriculture.

While we were engaged in mission work among the Mexican people in south Texas he came to visit us. He came there from Kansas by train and stayed with our family for several days observing our work and the vastness of the field as there were at that time few evangelical churches working among the Mexican people. After his return he reported his observations in the *Christian Monitor*. He had a deep interest in the extension of the church which was also our primary interest and concern.

He sensed my call to the ministry and consequently, while we were in mission work among the Mexican migrant workers in northwestern Ohio, he interviewed me as to my willingness to serve in the ministry of the Stahl congregation of which he was bishop, and which was then operating two mission stations—Carpenter Park and Walsall. Several years after his decease the call came and was accepted. The contribution he made to my life is inestimable.

—*David C. Alwine*, retired pastor, Allegheny Mennonite Conference, Johnstown, Pennsylvania

After deep conviction of sin for more than a year, at least, the Lord used Brother S. G. Shetler to lead me to Christ on November 1, 1907. I had promised the Lord if he would spare me I would yield to his wooings in this revival. However, the struggle was so great that I resisted the Holy Spirit until the last evening. Brother Shetler said the invitation was over. Then the congregation sang a farewell song,

"Goodbye," No. 404 in the *Church and Sunday School Hymnal*. It seemed as if Something said to me, "It is now or never." All the stanzas were finished and during the last refrain the Lord gave me the courage to stand, thus giving me the peace I had longed for. I couldn't bear the thought of saying farewell even "with tear-dimmed eye" in an unsaved state. After the dismissal Brother S. G. told me to "study the Word, pray much." He also gave me some Scriptures of assurance.

Brother Shetler's influence continues with me. I find myself often quoting him until this day. Many other stalwarts of the faith in that era also influenced me. Among them were Abram Metzler, Daniel Kauffman, Noah H. Mack, John Horsch, J. A. Ressler, John H. Mosemann, Sr., George R. Brunk I, John W. Weaver, John L. Stauffer, et. al. These brethren were all human, yet the Lord used them in a wonderful way.

One of the problems before conversion was which church should I join following conversion. Early in Brother Shetler's meetings instead of the formal "opening" of the meeting each evening he gave a 15-minute instruction on ordinances and restrictions. After sitting through these clear-cut instructions church affiliation was no longer a problem.

Sixty-three years ago we never expected to see a day like this: modernism, liberalism, apostasy, worldliness, ecumenism, etc. May the Lord raise up brethren among us as he describes in Jeremiah 6:16 who will "ask for the old paths, where is the good way, and walk therein."

—*Jacob E. Martin, Sr.*, deacon in the Southeastern Conference, Harrisonburg, Virginia

My remembrance of Brother Shetler goes back to my childhood, because it was in my early teens that my father moved West. I can remember that he made an appeal to children, sometimes with objects and other times with his stories. Even in his preaching he would say, "Here is a story the children will like." His preaching fascinated me as a young person. It gripped me the way he would hold the attention of an audience. I owe some of the inspiration that led me to conviction for the ministry to Brother Shetler.

My mother remembers that he was always interested in recognizing other people. One incident that illustrates it was when my father went to General Conference in Ohio. He arrived a little late and Brother Shetler had just taken the platform. Being ushered near the front Shetler immediately introduced him as J. N. Durr's son-in-law. After the service many came to my father to meet him because it was an area in Ohio where J. N. Durr had a number of relatives.

—*C. J. Ramer*, Duchess, Alberta, bishop in the Alberta-Saskatchewan Conference

S. G. Shetler holds an admirable place in my memory. I always felt it was an honor to be his friend. My Christian life and ministry have been greatly enhanced by his influence.

My first contact with Brother Shetler was in August of 1930. At this time he served as guest speaker on a weekend Sunday school conference in my home church at Allensville. I served on this program with him!

The following summer S. G., who was secretary of the Southwestern Pennsylvania Sunday School Conference (now Allegheny), assigned me a subject on the annual conference program at Springs, Pennsylvania.

Four years later when he was requesting retirement from the office of secretary, Brother Shetler secured approval for me to serve as his assistant during the two-day session of conference at Masontown. I was elected as his successor and served in this capacity for more than 20 years.

My early activities in the Lord's work were encouraged by one who was interested in the young people of his day. Brother Shetler was always eager to promote youth activities within his congregation and throughout the conference. This led to my ordination and thirty years of ministerial service at Masontown and within the conference.

Because of the unique insight Brother Shetler had in discovering potential talent in young people he was never satisfied until the fruitage of these gifts became reality in the church and community.

—*Paul M. Roth*, now of Harrisonburg, Virginia, pastor at Masontown Mennonite Church for thirty years, and associated with Mennonite Broadcasts, Inc., as Home Bible Study director

I just wonder how many people's lives were changed because of S. G. Shetler and the way he preached. I can remember as a boy I never was too anxious to go to church, but when I knew S. G. was preaching I always wanted to go. I only regret that I don't have one of his sermons recorded. I know it would be valuable.

—*William Shetler*, auctioneer, Davidsville, Pennsylvania

I first remember knowing S. G. Shetler when he was here for Bible school at the Casselman Church. I remember going out in the country (a mountain area) with S. G. in his Ford coupe to look for students. This was when I was about five or six years old. When we would come to an old, broken-down house he would stop and say, "This looks like a likely place where there are children who need to go to Bible school." [Though in an area of rather sparse population] we used to have an enrollment of approximately 100.

S. G. was perhaps the best orator that I have ever heard. Outside of my parents, no other person has ever left as deep and lasting an impression on me (at an early age) as did S. G. He was a man that commanded respect by his presence alone. He was a strict disciplinarian with children but in such a tactful way that we were all interested in what he was saying. He could hold the interest of people from the youngest child to the oldest adult. My sister Evelyn and I always made it a point to be there when he would be at a meeting anywhere in the area.

S. G. was a great master in using illustrations to bring out spiritual truths. I have never met anyone like him.

—*Dale Kinsinger*, presently a member of the Springs Mennonite Church near Grantsville, Maryland[*]

---

[*]It was in the Kinsinger home that my father was cared for a week after his sudden illness at the time he was planning to hold Bible school at the Meadow Mountain Church near Grantsville, Maryland. Bro. Roy Kinsinger was pastor of the church. Mrs. Kinsinger was a nurse. Before he left the Kinsinger home to return to Johnstown, he called Dale and Evelyn into his bedroom to talk to them. One of the things he did was to ask them to be faithful to the Lord. It was a month later that he passed away.—*SGS.*

I have a very clear remembrance of Samuel Shetler. When I was a teenager just out of high school, I had a very difficult problem as to what I should believe. It was not easy for me to reconcile what I had learned in school with what I had been taught at home and in our church. Like many of today's young people, I was all mixed up and confused. I guess I was pretty much of an unbeliever.

One Sunday evening in Lancaster, Brother Shetler preached a very powerful sermon on this subject. I do not remember the text, but I do remember that to him the Bible was *the* final authority. It set me to studying the Bible in earnest to find what things were true. Other teachers have been most helpful, but it was this message that got me started in the right direction.
—*C. Mervin Mellinger*, Willow Street Mennonite Church, Willow Street, Pennsylvania

Throughout his ministry he tried to appeal to young people. His efforts to win their service for the church were well directed. It was pleasing to him to see a young man grasp the work which lay before him and dedicate his life in noble service toward God and man. It was also satisfying to him to watch progress in the development of a young student—how his ability to speak in public was enlarged and how his views broadened.
—By a grandson, *Clyde Miller*—from an unpublished manuscript on the life of S. G. Shetler for a college assignment, Goshen College, Indiana

The memory is very vivid—the impression is clear—the retrospect is refreshing as I travel the trails of my boyhood days to recall people whom I loved most and liked best.

It is a good memory that can enable one to remember good things, and good people, and good things that good people do.

My early entrée to life was the inspiration I received from a good preacher. Not all preachers and teachers of that era were "inspirationally" good. Sometimes a church service seemed like trudging through a "valley of dry bones." Singsong intonations and worn-out clichés and tedious prayers were too often the order of the day. But in spite of all the traditions

and tedium, I conscientiously kept an accurate record of church services I had attended as a boy for years.

When a man like S. G. Shetler came to town it was a banner day for my tired spirit. When Brother Shetler preached, my emotions could go on excursions of smiles and tears, and I found the two were not incompatible. And, furthermore, his preaching took my impressionable mind down the pictorial road of life—where I could see and hear and feel life's greatest purposes and projects. The tone of his voice helped to set the tone of my life. And I sort of reasoned that if such preaching were possible then, perhaps similar to that style might be in vogue in the unknown days to come. Although, at the time, I fancied that perhaps someday I might enjoy the spiritual luxury of merely being the song leader for this flaming evangelist.

S. G. Shetler was a champion of children. He had the power to maneuver their tender thought processes and the more polarized thinking of the listening adult audience, in a children's session; that was an act in itself. For example, he would raise a question about the old adage, "We must always start at the bottom of the ladder." Then he would make a beautiful countercharge: "How about it if you are going down into a well?"

But S. G. Shetler was most significant in his presentation of Scripture. He seemed to breathe the very atmosphere of divine revelation. His ability to quote by memory was breathtaking. And his illustrations to match left the flame burning in the mind and heart of the gentle listener long, long after the average normal event or church event was forgotten. "What have they seen in thine house?" "Go ... and tell John." These are Scriptures I can never forget, which were the cornerstone of sermons I can never forget, from the heart of Brother Shetler.

As recently as a few years back I was transacting some special business in the office of a fine old gentleman, an attorney, in Harrisonburg, Virginia. Somehow mention was made of the funeral service of Elias Brunk at the old Weaver's Church along the Rawley Pike, west of Harrisonburg. I had remembered the occasion and funeral sermon, especially. My attorney friend, Mr. Ott, said, "I can never forget that sermon, one of the greatest funeral sermons I ever heard." He added further that he had written to the speaker of the occasion and has requested his sermon outline. The funeral orator wrote back an apology for not having an outline, but he incorporated the scriptural quotations he had used. Well, may God bless the sacred memory of a man who could preach such a soul-stirring sermon without even an outline. That man was S. G. Shetler.

> —*Richard E. Martin*, former pastor of Pinto Mennonite Church, Maryland, and president of the Shenandoah Manufacturing Company

God, in his wise providence, brings various experiences and individuals into our lives which greatly influence us. Brother S. G. Shetler was "a man sent from God" into my early formative years as an effective summer Bible school superintendent. The warmth and joy which surrounded this "Bible study environment" has never left me.

> —*Willard Mayer*, dean, Rosedale Bible Institute

To me S. G. Shetler was one of the greatest. When I began teaching Sunday school back in 1925 and again when I began teaching summer Bible school at the old "Thirty Eight" schoolhouse near Seanor with Menno Eash as superintendent, I asked S. G. a lot of times for help and he was always ready to give help, notes, and advice. Also at Johnstown Bible School he was always ready to help.

In his dealings at our garage he was one man who did honest business. (So many today do not.) I will always remember him as both an honest and spiritual man and one who was always ready to help.

> —*Mrs. Josiah Blough*, member Blough Mennonite Church, Johnstown, Pennsylvania, now deceased

We remember Brother Shetler as an outstanding evangelist of his time in our church. In March 1933, Brother Shetler held revival meetings at the Pike Church near Harrisonburg, Virginia. We counted it a privilege to have him stay in our home during the entire time.

The first night on the way home from church he asked if we thought that would be the average crowd. We told him that we thought there would be more the next night, and there were more. So on the way

home he asked again, and we assured him there would be still more the next night. By Sunday night every seat was filled and people stood in the aisles. From then on the church was well-filled every night.

The interest in the community was good. People came from different denominations, tears were shed by many. Our neighbors talked of him long after he left. Twelve souls confessed at this meeting and four came later.

Brother Shetler's memory was wonderful. He called the youth and children by name as well as the older folks. This made a great impression on them.

> —*William Brubaker*, minister at the Pike Church, Harrisonburg, Virginia (now deceased), written in conjunction with other members of the Brubaker family

Your father meant much in our lives and was very near to our family. He was the first Mennonite preacher we ever heard. The more we heard his heart-searching messages the more we felt and saw there were things in the Bible we were not keeping and couldn't practice in our denomination. So in one of those long-remembered Thanksgiving meetings we all made the change.

He always had a special interest in Pinto and our family. I will always remember his kindness to me at Johnstown Bible School in lending me money so that it was possible for me to attend.

We know he has done a great work for the Lord and the church.

> —*Edna Collins*, member at Pinto Mennonite Church, from a sympathy letter at the time of S. G. Shetler's passing

Your dad was a thoughtful, sincere teacher, not afraid to teach us hymns along with our other studies. I can yet hear him singing "Come, Thou Almighty King." Many—too many—of our schools today have discarded this along with Bible reading, which is so much needed in these evil days.

> —From a letter from a former pupil at the Hooversville School, 1899—*Mrs. S. B. Jones* (the former Blanche Horner) of Johnstown, Pennsylvania.
>
> Letter dated August 19, 1953. Mrs. Jones passed away in October 1976 at the age of 90.

I first met him when just a little girl in the year 1909. He conducted a week-long Bible conference in the West Union Church near Parnell, Iowa. Even as a child I did so enjoy his ministry and was so intrigued to see how he remembered people's names after the first introduction. While in our home he told us about his family which at that time was composed of four daughters, the same as our family. His messages were always so interesting and worthwhile that we children were always ready to go to church when Brother Shetler was going to conduct the services, especially children's meetings. Then after moving to Kalispell, Montana, in the year 1913 it was again our privilege to have not only him but his family except the eldest daughter (who was then married) in our home for a day or two, at which time his daughter Rosella and I became fast friends and that friendship lasted through the years until 1966 when she was called to her reward. I still remember some of the good illustrations he gave in his ministry, some of which I have passed along to my Sunday school classes in my years of teaching. His preaching was always such that when he finished you wished the time had not passed so rapidly as his messages were always so worthwhile.

—*Ella Slater*, daughter of the late D. D. Kauffman, pastor in Kansas, Iowa, and Kalispell, Montana, churches

Brother S. G. Shetler, as that is the only way I ever knew him, was perhaps one of the most popular and well-liked men of his time. He never failed to draw a good crowd and an interested audience.

He was a very versatile man. There are many people with talents and people with many talents and I always felt that he fitted into the latter category. He could spellbind children as well as adults.

His children's meetings were always tremendous and original, but always with meaning and a good point which was well-illustrated so that one seldom forgot what the lesson was regardless of how it was presented. I have never seen a person who could get children to respond as he could, and as I look back on his children's meetings, I never remember one in which he did not have full control of the situation.

His sermons were, as far as I can remember, always attentively listened to and few indeed were the persons who could go to sleep under the sound of his voice. I have listened to many good and wonderful speakers, but I never knew another man who could take a crowd and have them smiling one time and weeping another as he could. He was a great master at moving audiences and I always felt that he did it to the honor and glory of God.

I also remember him as a person who knew one personally, and as an individual. You didn't just belong to a family, but were an individual of that family and he treated one as a personality all his own.

As I remember him, he was a very widely read man, a very well-educated man but also one who could take a joke as well as play a joke on some one if the opportunity presented itself.

He was a very human type of a person but also a very dedicated God-fearing person who took an interest in people, who loved people for what they were and what they might become by the power and grace of God. I know of no other person whose sermons and children's meetings I remember as well or vividly as I do his.

He was a man small in stature but a giant mentally and in his dedication to God.

—*David V. Kauffman*, MD, Whitefish, Montana

The time was spring, 1941. The place was the Lindale Mennonite Church, Linville, Virginia, the home church of my mother. The occasion was a revival series conducted by Brother S. G. Shetler. As a twelve-year-old lad, I was sitting on the second bench with a friend. Brother Shetler preached with compassion and zeal. The Holy Spirit revealed to me my need of Christ's forgiveness. The burden of conviction grew in weight and intensity. At the invitation, I stood to my feet acknowledging publicly my decision to receive Christ. Suddenly the burden was gone. Then came words of encouragement and the deep assurance that "now I belonged to Jesus."

Thank you, God—for that night, that minister, that decision. Enable me to be that kind of minister, leading others to that kind of decision.

—*John R. Martin*, former pastor, Neffsville Mennonite Church, Neffsville, Pennsylvania, presently on Eastern Mennonite Seminary faculty

I must have as a child gotten started appreciating and idolizing Brother Shetler from my parents, because I never heard them say anything against him, but much in praise. I can't think of a time when I didn't know him. He was the minister who married my parents. He suggested my name to my parents when their first baby was born. He was my pastor all the time I was at home. He also officiated at my marriage.

I remember that before I was of school age I had the conviction that I would be a minister some day. I don't know how much that feeling in me was born because of my parents' attitude toward Brother Shetler, but I believe it possible that God used that way to call me to the ministry. As a very young boy I had the call. As I was growing up, whenever I thought of what I might take up as a vocation, my second thought was always that I will never take up any vocation that will keep me from being a minister, or that will hinder me in preaching. I feel quite confident that this attitude in me was largely from the influence Brother Shetler had on my life.

There was never any occasion when he was preaching or teaching that I "turned him off." What he said always seemed right to me.

All these things I say only to illustrate what kind of man Brother Shetler was and how influential he was with young people. He once taught high school in Hubbard, Oregon. A few months after he started his first term the neighbors around the school began talking about how different the schoolchildren are since the new teacher came. In those days there were no school buses and all the children walked to school from home. The neighbors noticed that the pupils were no more boisterous and noisy but behaved like mature people as they were on their way to school or home.

He was an ideal public school teacher. He was sought after by school boards and superintendents. He taught many years. He also enjoyed this work.

One of the outstanding features of his work in the normal school was his wise, witty, and effective way of maintaining discipline in such a school of forty to sixty young people of the ages of sixteen to twenty. While they attended normal school they curtailed their social activities at night so as to have more time for study. Brother Shetler secured this kind of devotion, not by written rules but by the influence he wielded in various ways, one of which was witty and inoffensive ways of exposing any infractions before the whole school.

Brother Shetler had a good share of temper but it always seemed to be well under control. This is a vital combination in a strong character. He was a very strict disciplinarian, but I believe he always loved the one who needed discipline, but hated the evil deeds of bad conduct. He never spoke an angry word to me, but I could relate a number of faults in me which he effectively rebuked by a wise word of a certain "look." He made much use of praise in helping people when he could praise honestly.

Brother Shetler was always beloved of the young people. He understood them. He appeared to be a bit lenient with them at times, but the total influence on them was for their good. He lived in a period of time when in his area of the church weddings were not held in the church. The young couples would come to his home to be married. For a time he performed nearly all of the weddings in his district.

He was a pioneer in conducting short-term winter Bible schools throughout the church. Many who were then young people are now in the retirement age with commendable careers of Christian service behind them, owing their original inspiration to the good winter Bible schools he conducted.

Brother Shetler was never a profuse letter writer as I knew him. I did however receive a few letters from him which I prized highly. He wrote to me once or twice when he lived in Oregon for a year or two and I lived at Johnstown, Pennsylvania. He wrote me a few letters when I was in camp in World War I as a conscientious objector. He also wrote to me a few times when we served as missionaries to India. He never wrote long letters but they always counted much.

He was always a humble man. He was somewhat inclined to introspection, especially when his critics spoke. He realized that he was responsible to God but he also had deep concern to maintain proper rapport with people because helping others was his field and his main burden. He was inclined to blame himself when others found fault with him, and perhaps sometimes forgot that before God his record was clear by the grace of Christ's forgiveness.

Brother Shetler's life was of course not entirely perfect or without flaws. In one particular misfortune in his life he at once, after realizing the mistake he made, made proper amends with the persons involved and secured forgiveness from God, but there were some other people who were less popular than he who took the opportunity to cause him great grief by using the occasion against him. For several years he suffered much and wept often. I believe this experience ultimately refined his spirit further.

He knew God. He knew his Bible. He was devoted to his church. He loved his family. He left the legacy of a good life record for us all—his own children and his many spiritual children.

—*Lloy A. Kniss*, missionary to India, minister, bishop, as well as a teacher in both public and church schools

I count it a privilege to be one of the children of the late S. G. Shetler. I want to express my deep appreciation for the valuable and lasting impressions his counsels and admonitions have made in my life and in the lives of my children. I am grateful to God for having had a father who made God the center of his life and instilled into his children a love and dedication to serve him.

—*Mrs. Margaret Kaufman*, youngest daughter, Johnstown, Pennsylvania

During the early years of my ministry in the Mennonite Church at Midland, Michigan, Brother S. G. Shetler on various occasions served us as evangelist and Bible teacher in two-week winter Bible schools.

Having known many ministers throughout the church at large, I consider Brother S. G. a very outstanding gifted servant of God in Bible ministry, church leadership, and personal worker. He knew how to make contact with people of all ages.

I have "precious memories" of your father.

—*Floyd F. Bontrager*, bishop in the Indiana-Michigan Conference, Clare, Michigan

Brother S. G. or Sam Shetler, as most people called him when I was a youth, was my ideal as a preacher and teacher.

I remember his children's lessons although I don't remember ever being in his class as a boy, but as a young person I had an interest in the way he would present the truth so that not only did the children get the lesson, but the older folks as well.

In his preaching he presented the gospel, not only facts, but with feeling so that people responded not only with public confession, but by deciding in their hearts to live according to the Word that he presented in a meaningful way.

Having received a call to be a minister at a young age, I always held him as my ideal.

He had memorized the Scripture and he seldom made a point unless he had Scripture to prove it.

I remember many of his texts and his apt illustrations and they continue to challenge me as I endeavor to preach the Word. From one who was challenged and blessed by his life.

—*Harry Y. Shetler*, minister, evangelist, and Bible teacher, Davidsville, Pa., Allegheny Mennonite Conference

My first acquaintance with Brother S. G. Shetler was when he held revival meetings at the Sand Hill (later Clarence Center, New York) Mennonite Church in which I grew up. His interesting and forceful preaching challenged me to publicly confess Christ as Savior and to dedicate myself fully to the Lord's service.

Several years later I attended one term at Johnstown Bible School and learned to appreciate him as a teacher and leader of youth. His lively illustrations helped to cement important facts in my mind. Although I had memorized the books of the Bible at the age of five, the book of Hosea was just one of the names of the Minor Prophets until I sat in Brother Shetler's class in "Hosea." I have never forgotten the fascination aroused for the teachings in that class. It stimulated me to study the Word more. I also appreciated the unique way he had of introducing new words to us, often with humor but not detracting from the importance of the information.

I little dreamed then that ten years later I would move into this community and live among the scenes mentioned in this biography. As I live and work here, these scenes help remind me of the commitments I made as a young person under his ministry.

—*Ellen B. Kauffman*, former teacher at Johnstown Christian School and editorial assistant of *Guidelines for Today*

I learned to know S. G. Shetler first as an evangelist in the home community. He put his whole life into the work at hand. He was especially remembered for his ability in getting acquainted with the people of the church where he was working. In a repeat engagement he could recall the names of most of the people whom he had met in a previous meeting. He put all that he had into the work at hand.

Brother Shetler and I worked together in four sections of the church in winter Bible schools. We began to work together at the Central Church, Archbold, Ohio, then we were at Leo, Indiana; Bowne Church, Clarkesville, Michigan; and Shore Church, Shipshewana, Indiana. The schools were of two weeks' duration.

In the various places he was principal of the school and arranged the program. At our first school in Archbold each of the teachers preached a revival message every evening. There were 132 converts—only several that had ever made a profession and all were 16 or more years old. We did the same at Leo once. As principal he was considerate in the assignments he gave to the rest of us. One time he assigned me Bible English. My answer, "No." He said that he was principal! My answer again, "I came to teach Bible." Graciously he arranged the program to meet my request. At all the places we worked he was considerate of his teachers.

His personality was such that he usually attracted most pupils to his class. This was not because he tried to get students to his classes. He seemed to appeal to youth. He was the oldest of the teachers, had more experience, and therefore more living illustrations. He made singing a prominent part of the program. He usually had songs fitting the day's program.

—*D. A. Yoder,* late bishop, Indiana-Michigan Conference, and president of the Mennonite Board of Education

As a boy less than ten years old, S. G. Shetler left a deep impression on me through a sermon he preached at Sycamore Grove Church at Garden City, Missouri, on the Christian home and the relation of parents and children. In my later experience with him, serving together as instructors at the Johnstown Bible School in 1940, as well as working together in Young Peoples' Institute at Kalona, Iowa, Brother Shetler challenged me with his ability to

lead his audiences to laugh and to cry with him. He led his students to see the importance of biblical Word study. As an instructor at J.B.S. I did not fail to sit in as many of his classes as I could find time for. He challenged me early in my ministry to know the Word of God well, and to teach it in a meaningful way. He inspired me as a young man to love and to respect the church. For these things I shall always be grateful.

—*Nelson E. Kauffman,* bishop, past president of the Mennonite Board of Education, evangelist, and conference speaker

For many years past I had known of your father. I think it was the time of my father's first visit to Somerset County that he became acquainted with your father, then a young man. On his return home he told us of a Samuel Shetler, whose birthday was near that of my elder brother, William, who was born on January 13, 1871. The coincidence of the age of my brother, and having my name, associated him with our family and always gave me a personal interest in your father.

In later years, after his ordination, and after my being called to serve the Lord in the ministry, there was a special affinity and interest common to us. On many occasions we labored together and enjoyed each other's fellowship. He filled a unique place in the work of the Lord and had a special work to perform in the church. As a teacher and one who was particularly fitted to impart and implant knowledge into the minds and hearts of the youth of the church, he was blessed of the Lord in leading many to the Lord and establishing them in the way of salvation. For this we praise the Lord.

May your father's children all remain true to the faith which he lived and in which he served Christ—the life and standards which he established for you and by which you were guided. Let the blessings of the righteous be passed on to many generations.

—The late Bishop *S. F. Coffman* (son of J. S. Coffman) of Vineland, Ontario, active churchman, editor of Bible study department of the *Christian Monitor,* and longtime teacher at Kitchener Bible School. From a letter written to the Shetler family after the passing of S. G. in 1942.

We, the faculty of Eastern Mennonite School, feel deeply the passing of our brother and fellow teacher. Few names are more familiar than his in our denomination. Few have spoken as fearlessly as he, and perhaps none has so much as he brought into the pulpit the effective technique of the classroom. He contributed much to the impetus that brought about churchwide evangelism. His life, rounded out by years, closed rich and full in an exceptionally active service in the Lord.

—Part of a letter of condolence sent the Shetler family in August 1942. It was signed by the late *M. T. Brackbill* as secretary of the faculty of EMS

When Brother S. G. came as an evangelist to Lancaster County, especially in 1907, at the Brick Church, there were fifty confessions by people aged 10 to 71—Mary White to John Chryst, the Big Spring tollgate keeper. One was a drinking man who with his wife came because S. G. was so gentle and kind. S. G. asked the ministry whether he was an offense to any, since he was involved in the early evangelistic endeavors in the conference (not yet two years old). Some feared such marvelous success would affect the future adversely. He could sway audiences, with the congregation in tears one minute and joyful the next! The meetings are still remembered by those of the older of this congregation and area.

—*Ira Landis*, minister and historian, Lancaster Conference, Lancaster County, Pennsylvania

As a young man I was privileged to have S. G. for a Bible school instructor several years. He influenced me more than any one minister to live the Christian life with determination. He would bring guilt and conviction to me in such a way that I wanted to clear myself with God and live a holy life.

—*Emanuel J. Hochstetler*, bishop in the Indiana-Michigan Conference

In 1936 S. G. Shetler helped us plan for a winter Bible school, which was held for two weeks. He planned the program and he taught eight subjects each day. We are partially following his program to this day. His son Sanford has taught in our winter Bible school for six years.

Each year we sing the song which he introduced:

"To Canaan's land I'm on my way,
Where the soul of man never dies."

I praise the Lord for his life and the testimony in the years that I had known him as a young man.

—*Reuben G. Stoltzfus*, minister, Millwood Mennonite Church, Parkesburg, Pennsylvania

Remembering my grandfather is always a nostalgic trek back through time to the days of my childhood. His intensity and drive to accomplish his God-ordained mission to teach both in schools and from the pulpit has been an inspiration to everyone that knew him.

I do not remember him as a grandfather that played "hide-and-seek" or bounced me on his knee but he did let me run along behind the old horse and harrow, while he worked the fields. Sometimes he let me hold the reins. Pleasant days and pleasant memories.

As a pupil in his schoolroom in my boyhood years, I will never forget his special way of sparking our interest and attention. There were demonstrations, experiments, and drawings, all coupled with simple, easy explanations that even the dullest of us could understand. He was no easy teacher. Our studies were important and he was totally intolerant toward anything less than our very best effort. He sensed the learning ability of each child, and pushed us to the limits of that ability. I believe that every pupil leaving that little red schoolhouse of long ago had a real feeling of scholastic achievement and a greater degree of self-confidence.

I did not see him often during my teen years. As an evangelist he was traveling almost continuously. On several occasions I had the opportunity to attend his series of meetings and will always remember the dynamic power of his sermons. The force of his spirit, the total dedication to God's mandate, the absolute belief in a literal translation of the Bible, and his worried concern for lost souls gave these services a quality of sincerity in oratory that I have never heard equaled. His ability to control an audience was phenomenal. Sometimes emotional, sometimes smiling, sometimes profound in silence, always persuading, his messages were made clear.

I wish he could have lived longer; he was

important in my life; he was my grandfather.
—*Karl Bachman*, Kalispell, Montana

Mother Stauffer (Mrs. J. L.) remembers that General Conference was held in the old tabernacle in Assembly Park (as it was then called) and Brother S. G. Shetler was the moderator. The conference members (or delegates) were on the platform back of him. If someone (back of him) would call for the floor, he would recognize them by name without looking back; he recognized each one by voice.

The church in those days needed help for the younger Christians by way of instruction in the Bible and in the things of the Christian life. They did not know the Bible as we do today, and they were hungry for the things of the Word. He made a real study of the doctrines of the Bible, and made them clear. He spoke plainly, and was so clear in his discussions. The young people understood what he was trying to say.

Brother Shetler's wife's name was Maggie. Shortly after Sanford's marriage, his mother passed away. Then Sanford's wife did the cooking and he said, "Her cooking is just like Maggie's." He gave her this compliment.

At Spring City, Pennsylvania, he held their first Bible conference. John L. Stauffer and his wife, Lydia Kolb Stauffer, had just been married about two or three weeks previously. In the church community, one church had closed and another was going to close (they said in the community), so the people called on Brother Shetler to have a Bible conference. And the people were so hungry for something like a Bible conference. From the Franconia District they came. To get there in time for the evening services, the farmers would milk their cows early in the afternoon, about three or four o'clock. People also came from Lancaster to the conference meetings, and there was scarcely room to keep them. There were no motels in those days. Some of the families who lived on farms took as many as 30 people overnight. People slept on the floor, on chaff bags, and the like. There were not so many families at Spring City, so we all helped. It was quite an initiation for a young bride. Mrs. Stauffer said, "But I had my older sister with me and she helped me. We lived close to the church, we did not have so many people

overnight; we would feed many of them. Every meal we would have I don't know how many people. We bought prunes and apricots by the box (the big box), large cakes of cheese, and big boxes of crackers."

Brother Shetler was a teacher, and in the church he taught and preached like a teacher; he made everything clear. He spoke in direct language and there was no hesitancy; the words seemed always ready for whatever he had to say.
—Ruth Stauffer Hostetter made these notes from a conversation between Mrs. John L. Stauffer and Mrs. Jacob A. Shenk in 1971.

Being a grandson of S. G. Shetler is special to me. He was my grandfather first, but also a friend, counselor, spiritual leader, and character builder.

He was my schoolteacher for the first few years of my schooling. How can anyone who attended the Miller School under his tutelage forget his teachings on morals, good music, and the values of working, striving, and searching?

When I graduated from high school in 1936, the country was still deep in the depression. Grandpa said flatly that I should have a new suit for graduation. My parents did not have the money for a suit nor did I, so grandpa told me to pick out a suit from the Sears Roebuck catalog, and he would order it for me. Needless to say, that was a special suit.

Back in the early thirties, summer vacation Bible school attendance was lagging in many communities. This was true of our community of Springs (Pa.), so grandpa was asked to become principal one summer, perhaps 1933 or 1934. He came to the community early and took my brother Samuel and me to Salisbury and West Salisbury where we contacted scores of children. There were many children who said they would like to attend, but had no transportation. Not to be stopped by such a small matter, grandpa went to the Otto Brick works and got them to furnish a truck to transport these children daily. Summer Bible school that year was a success!

Perhaps the one thing I remember above all else is how he related to all age-groups, and especially children and young people. His children's meetings were appreciated by all ages, and his object lessons were never forgotten.
—*Allen Miller*, Wadsworth, Ohio

Appendix 2

Churches in Which S. G. Shetler Served

The following list of churches in which S. G. Shetler served in his 45 years in the ministry is by no means complete. There are many other areas and churches where it is known that he served, particularly in the Lancaster and Franconia conferences, and those going over this list may feel sleighted if their particular congregation has been omitted. I have gone only by the churches listed in his records and in the *Gospel Herald* field notes. The list does, however, provide a fair idea of how far his ministry reached. In the last years of his life new churches were opened in such areas as Florida, Wisconsin, Arizona, Georgia, North Carolina, and had he lived longer it is altogether probable that he would have served in some of these areas too. It should be stated further that he preached in many other churches of other denominations. Only a few of these are listed here.

An "r" after the name of a church indicates revival meetings, a "c," Bible conference. Other symbols used are as follows: SBS—summer Bible school; WBS, winter Bible school; YPI, Young People's Institute. Where no symbol appears this either indicates simply an appointment, but more frequently revival meetings or a weekend (or longer) Bible conference. Again, only one year is listed after some churches, but in many cases he was there on other occasions. Also, no dates are given for the home district churches, which are underscored. He spoke in these literally dozens of times. A plus (+) sign after a given congregation means that he spoke here other times through the years as recalled by the writer, although no records are available for all these appearances.

265

It should be noted that he also spoke many times in many schools, teachers' institutes, in Old Folks' Homes, etc., and in funeral services of various denominations, and in funeral homes.

CALIFORNIA (3)
Los Angeles, 1920r, 1921
Porterville, 1915r
Upland, 1920r

COLORADO (5)
Holbrook, 1938
La Junta, 1938r
La Junta Sanitarium, 1938
La Junta Radio Station KOKO, 1938 (only radio sermon ever preached)
Limon, 1938r

DELAWARE (1)
Tressler (Owens Station), 1933r, 1934r

IDAHO (2)
Filer, 1914r, 1921, 1933r
Nampa, 1914r, 1920r, 1933r

ILLINOIS (13)
East Bend, 1917
Flanagan, 1908
Freeport, 1902r
Harmony, 1907c, 1908r
Hopedale, 1909r
Metamora, 1907r, 1908r, 1935r
Morrison, 1917r
Pleasant Grove, 1907c, 1909r, 1917r
Pleasant Hill, 1939r
Roanoke, 1908r
Science Ridge, 1909r, 1917r
Sterling, 1937 SBS, 1938 SBS
Tiskilwa, 1907c

INDIANA (17)
Clinton Amish ?
Clinton Brick, 1906r, 1933r
Emma, 1902r, 1933r
Elkhart, 1933r
Forks, 1901r, 1906r°, 1930r, 1940r, 1941 SBS
Goshen College, 1904r

_____
° First privilege to commune with Amish brethren.

Holdeman, 1909r, 1934r
Howard-Miami, 1907r, 1936 SBS, 1937 SBS, 1938 SBS
Leo, 1935r, WBS, 1936 WBS, 1937 WBS, 1938 WBS, 1939 WBS, 1941r
Maple Grove, 1901
Olive, 1910r, 1934r
Nappanee, 1907c, 1909
Nappanee A.M. ?
Salem, 1906c, 1941r
Shipshewana Methodist Episcopal Church, 1901
Shore, 1901r, 1902r, 1906, 1919r, 1933r, 1938 WBS, 1939 WBS, 1940 WBS, 1941 WBS
Yellow Creek, 1912rc

IOWA (9)
Cedar Creek, 1908r, 1935r
Dayton, 1910
East Union, 1910r, 1936r, YPI, 1937 YPI, 1938 YPI, 1939 YPI, 1940 YPI
Liberty, 1910r, 1941r
   (only 7 members left from 1910)
Lower Deer Creek
Manson, 1908c, 1935r, 1938 SBS
South English, 1913, 1941r
Sugar Creek, 1936r
West Union, 1910r

KANSAS (7)
Calvary, 1937r
Greensburg
Hesston College, 1909, 1939 Ministers' Week
McPherson
Protection
Wichita, 1941r
Yoder, 1940 YPI

MARYLAND (13)
Casselman (Grantsville), 1898, 1937rSBS
Clearspring, 1901
Glade, 1908r, 1932r
Maugansville, 1901r
Meadow Mountain, 1942

Miller, 1901
Oak Grove, 1902r
Paradise, 1901
Pinto, 1925r, 1926r, 1937 SBS, 1938 SBS
Reiffs, 1901r
Ringold, 1901r
Rowe, 1926
Stauffer, 1901r, 1908r

MICHIGAN (6)
Bowne (Clarkesville), 1912r, 1933r, WBS,
    1934 WBS, 1935 WBS, 1936 WBS, 1937
    WBS
Chief, 1909c
Fairview, 1909r, 1908c, 1936 WBS, 1937
    WBS, 1938 WBS, 1939 WBS
Manistee, 1909
Midland, 1934r, 1935 WBS, 1936 WBS,
    1937 WBS, 1938 WBS, 1939 WBS,
    1940
Pigeon, 1935r, 1937 SBS, 1938 WBS, 1939
    SBS, 1940 SBS

MINNESOTA (1)
Alpha, 1908r

MISSOURI (7)
Bethel, 1904r
Cherry Box, 1904r
Garden City, 1904r
Hannibal, 1940
Mt. Zion, 1904r
Palmyra, 1904r
Sycamore Grove, 1904r

MONTANA (4)
Coalridge, 1935
Hinsdale, 1935
Mountain View (Kalispell), 1913, 1914r,
    1920r, 1931, 1933, 1935 WBS, 1936
    WBS, 1937 (2), 1939, 1940, 1941
Red Top (Bloomfield), 1935r

NEW YORK (3)
Alden, 1939, 1940
Lowville
Sand Hill (Clarence Center), 1936r, 1937

NORTH DAKOTA (4)
Casselton, 1940
Fairview (Minot) 1914r, 1937, 1940

Spring Valley, 1914r
Lakeview (Wolford), 1940

OHIO (39)
Aurora
Beech, 1933r
Berlin, 1936
Bethel (Medina Co.), 1904r, 1905r, 1906
Bethel (West Liberty), 1904r, 1907r
Bremen, 1941r
Canton, 1906, 1908r, 1911, 1940r
Charm Schoolhouse, 1901
Eagle Grove, 1908
East Lewistown, 1902r
Farmerstown, 1935r, 1937r
Fulton County Churches, 1907c, 1912r,
    1934 WBS, 1935 WBS, 1936 WBS, 1937
    WBS, 1938 WBS, 1939 WBS, 1940
    WBS
Guilford, 1905r
Hancock, 1901r, 1906c
Leetonia, 1902, 1911c, 1917r
Laurens A. M.
Longenecker, 1904r, 1934r
Martins, 1904, 1932r
Martin's Creek, 1934r, 1936r
Medway (Clark Co.), 1936r
Midway, 1902, 1903r
Millersburg, 1937r, 1937r
North Clinton, 1901, 1912r
    (formerly Clinton Amish Mennonite)
North Lima, 1902r, 1914r, 1940r
Oak Grove (Wayne Co.)
Oak Grove (West Liberty), 1906, 1908r
Pike (Elida), 1902rc
Plainview, 1916r
Pleasant View, 1907c, 1941r
Salem (Elida), 1902r
Salem (Wayne Co.), 1906, 1941r
Sharon, May, 1942 (Last revival)
Sonnenberg, 1904 (German)
Sugarcreek, 1901, 1912c, 1937r
Turkey Run, 1941r
Walnut Creek, 1901, 1911, 1934r, 1937r,
    1941 SBS
West Liberty, 1907r, 1908
Woodville School House, 1902r, 1903r
Zion (Allen Co.) 1901

OREGON (9)
Albany, 1914r, 1920

Airlie, 1915r
Bethel, 1914r, 1917, 1921
Fairview, 1908r, 1914r
Firdale, 1920r
Hopewell, 1913-1915, 1914r, 1920-1921, 1937, 1938r, 1941r
Porter Schoolhouse (Canby), 1941r
Sheridan, 1937 WBS, 1938 WBS
Zion

PENNSYLVANIA (98)
Home District Churches
Stahl, Home Church +
Blough, 1903r, 1936r +
Carpenter Park +
Hyasota +
Johnstown +
Kaufman, 1938r +
Kaufman Amish, 1905
Miller Amish, 1898
Pleasant Grove, 1901r, 1926r +
Shaffer Schoolhouse +
Thomas, 1900r, 1906r, 1926r (?) +
Union Church (Westmont) +
Walsall +
Weaver, 1898r, 1902r, 1907r, 1909c, 1936r +

. . . .

Allensville, 1898, 1903r, 1906, 1917, 1940
Altoona, 1910r
Bally, 1938
Barrville, 1905r
Belleville (Maple Grove), 1898, 1901
Bethel United Brethren (Hollsopple), 1897, 1898
Blooming Glen, 1911c
Britton Run, 1934r
Byerland, 1898
Cedar Grove, 1926
Chestnut Ridge School House (Clearfield Co.), 1906
Churchtown
Coatesville, 1938 SBS, r, 1940 SBS
Columbia, 1928, 1939, 1940, 1941
Conestoga
Coventry, 1898
Delaware, 1902
Diller, 1904
Dohner, 1925
Elizabethtown, 1912

Fairview School House (Juniata Co.), 1902
Florin Methodist Church, 1898
Goods, 1898
Franconia Conference Churches, 1908c, 1911
Groffdale, 1898, 1902, 1910, (2000th sermon)
Hanover, 1904
Holsopple Reformed, 1898
Kinzer, 1898
Lampeter Music Hall, 1902
Lancaster City, 1898, 1902, 1908, 1912
Lancaster Co. Churches, 1907, 1910
Landisville, 1898
Lauver, 1902
Logania (Perry Co.), 1902
Lost Creek, 1902, 1907r, 1916r
Lovet United Brethren, 1898
Martinsburg, 1898r (first revival), 1902, 1929r, 1937r
Maple Grove (Lawrence Co.), 1911r, 1917r, 1932r, 1940, 1914r
Maple Grove (Chester Co.), 1935 WBS, 1936 WBS, 1937 WBS, 1938 WBS, 1939 WBS, 1940 WBS, 1941 WBS, 1942 WBS
Marion, 1907, 1908, 1928
Masontown, 1907c, 1917r, 1937r
Masonville, 1898, 1902
Mattawana, 1940r
Meadville, 1940
Mechanicsburg, 1898
Mechanicsville, 1898
Mellingers
Mexico, 1902
Millersville, 1902
Millwood + (Millwood & Maple Grove District) (see Maple Grove, Chester Co.)
Mount Joy, 1912
Mullen Schoolhouse (Schellsburg), 1902r, +
Mummasburg, 1908 +
Newville, 1904r
Old Road, 1898
Paradise, 1898
Pleasant Grove (Blair Co.), 1902r, 1937r
Pleasant View (Schellsburg, Bedford Co.), 1912, 1933r +
Pleasant View (Franklin Co.), 1933r
Providence (Montgomery Co.), 1898
Pond Bank, 1926, 1933r
Port Treverton, 1907r

Red Well (Lancaster Co.), 1902
River Church (Mifflin Co.), 1906
Roaring Springs, 1902
Rockland (Millcreek), 1937
Rockton, 1897, 1901, 1904r, 1905r, 1906c, 1917, 1933 (?)
Rockville, 1936r, 1938r, SBS
Rohrerstown, 1898
Roxbury Methodist Episcopal (Johnstown), 1897
Scottdale, 1901r, 1902 +
Scottdale YMCA, 1901
Slate Hill, 1898, 1904r, 1937c +
Springs (formerly Folk), 1899c, 1902c, 1906r, 1908r +
Souderton
Stone, 1898, 1902
Strasburg (Franklin Co.), 1909r
Strasburg (Lancaster Co.), 1898
Stumptown, 1898, 1902
Susquehanna (Snyder Co.), 1907r
Tire Hill Church of the Brethren, 1902
Vincent, 1898
   (first sermon outside home conference district)
Weaverland, 1898
Willow Street, 1908, 1910

TEXAS (2)
Normanna, 1938
Tuleta

VIRGINIA (17)
Augusta County Churches, 1910r
Bank, 1906r
Brenneman, 1906, 1913r
Criders, 1940r
Deep Creek, 1940r
Ebenezer
Eastern Mennonite School
   (now E. M. College), 1917c, 1926, 1928, 1929
Hildebrand, 1910r, 1937r
Lindale, 1906r, 1913r, 1935r, 1940r
Morning View, 1935r
Mt. Hermon, 1941r
Pike, 1933r
South Boston, 1941r
Springdale, 1910r, 1941 (?)
Warwick River, 1906c
Weaver, 1906r, 1926
Zion, 1906r

WEST VIRGINIA (2)
Onego, 1933r, 1941r
Riverside, 1938r

CANADA

ALBERTA (6)
Clearwater, 1914r
Duchess
Mayton, 1914r
Mount View, 1914r
Salem (Tofield), 1914r
West Zion, 1914r

ONTARIO (20)
°Almira, 1911r
°Altona, 1911r
Breslau, 1908r, 1925r, 1940r
Cedar Grove, 1911r
East Zorra, 1939r
Hagey, 1938r

Hay A. M., 1940, 1941r
Kitchener (formerly Berlin), 1906r, 1908r
Latschar, 1930r
Preston, 1938r
Selkirk, 1929 (served as interim pastor)
Snyder, 1930r
Strasburg, 1908r
Vineland, 1906c
Waterloo, 1909r
Wanner, 1929r
Weber, 1908r
Weidman, 1911r
Zurich, 1909r, 1941r
Ontario Churches, 1911r

SASKATCHEWAN (1)
Sharon, 1914r

_____
° As recorded by S. G. Shetler.

Churches Served Most Frequently
Outside Home Area

12—Fulton County Churches, Ohio, 1 Bible conference, 8 winter Bible schools, several revivals

12—Mountain View, Kalispell, Montana, 3 revivals, 2 winter Bible schools, 7 other°

9—Shore, Lagrange, Indiana, 5 revivals, 4 winter Bible schools

8—Maple Grove (Chester County, Pa.), winter Bible school, 8 terms— 1935-1942

7—Midland, Michigan, 1 revival, 5 winter Bible schools, 1 other

7—East Union, Iowa, 2 revivals, 5 Young People's Institutes

7—Rockton, Pennsylvania, 2 revivals, 1 Bible conference, other

6—Bowne, Clarksville, Michigan, 2 revivals, 4 winter Bible schools

6—Fairview, Michigan, 2 revivals, 4 winter Bible schools

6—Howard-Miami, Kokomo, Indiana, 3 revivals, 3 Bible schools

5—Leo, Indiana, 5 winter Bible schools

5—Pigeon, Michigan, 1 revival, 4 summer Bible schools

5—Walnut Creek, Ohio, 2 revivals, 1 summer Bible school, 2 other

4+—Allensville, Pennsylvania

4—Lancaster City, Pennsylvania

4—Lindale, Virginia, 4 revivals

4—Maple Grove (Lawrence Co.), Pennsylvania, 4 revivals from 1911 to 1941

4+—Springs, Pennsylvania

° Two of his daughters lived in this area.

Appendix 3

Sermon Outlines

The following are somewhat representative of the types of outlines that S. G. Shetler used for his sermons. They were, as will be observed, short, concise, and to the point, although to anyone but the speaker himself it might be difficult to know what the "point" was in many cases. However, with his vast background of experience each point and subpoint sparkled with ideas and applications. At the bottom of most outlines he listed specific illustrations that he might use in his sermon, depending on the occasion.

The average minister would feel uncomfortable to appear in the pulpit with no more to go on than these outlines suggest. It would be unfair, however, to say that he did not also have longer, detailed outlines which he used for specific occasions. This applies particularly to messages on such topics as the Sunday school, or on Bible teachings on specific subjects and book studies. In the same little notebook from which these particular outlines were taken, somewhat at random, there appeared, for example, a very well-outlined set of notes on the history of the Mennonite Church. While it would be unfair to say that S. G. was not scholarly, his typical sermon represented practical points suited to the average person in the pew.

"Where Art Thou?"
Gen. 3:9

   I. Every man is someplace
      1. Acts 16:28
      2. Eternity, Jn. 14:3; Lk. 16:23
  II. Many men are where they ought not to be, 1 Sam. 28:7, 8
 III. Many men are where others do not want them to be, Lk. 16:28; 1 Pet. 3:9; Lk. 17:23
 IV. Many men are where they did not expect to be, 1 Sam. 30:5
  V. Many men are where they do not want to be

Lessons from the Early Church
Text—Acts 8:

1. Scattered vv. 1, 4
2. Persecuted, vv. 1, 3, Destruction
3. United, v. 6
4. Praying, v. 15
5. Courageous, vv. 5, 4
6. Extension, vv. 1, 4, 25
7. Witnessing, v.
8. Nonracial, v. 27
9. Growing, v. 12
10. Obedient, vv. 12, 6
11. Forgiving, v. 22
12. Weeping, v. 2
13. Powerful, v. 7
14. Rejoicing, v. 8
15. Fasting, 13:2, 3

Mother's Day Message
Text—Ps. 113:9

1. Providing mother, Prov. 31:23
2. Appealing mother, 2 Kings 4:1
3. A yearning mother, 1 Kings 3:16-27
4. Weeping mother, Jn. 20:11-16
5. Rejoicing mother, Jn. 16:21
6. Praying mother, Acts 12:12
7. Giving-up mother, Gen. 21:14-21
8. Loving mother, Is. 49:15
9. Teaching mother, Prov. 31:1
10. Faith mother, 2 Tim. 1:5
11. Heavyhearted mother, Prov. 10:1
12. Caring mother, 2 Kings 4:19
13. Sick mother, Lk. 4:38
14. A departed mother

Illustrations:

Sayings: "Mother passed on. Fresh wounds." "26 years ago father."
"Today I stood beside my mother's grave. I turned away with
a heavy heart."
"Tomorrow she will be laid to rest. Grief and sadness hang
over other homes tonight, too."

Young home—Jas. confessed.
Brother stole.
La Junta mother wept—boys
Mrs. Stuter—Rockville

Marriage
Elverson, Pa.

  I. Heaven and earth linked together, Text, Prov. 18:22
 II. An eternal principle, Gen. 2:18; Mt. 19:6; Rev. 21:9
III. Purpose
    1. Propagation, Gen. 1:28; 9:1
    2. Purity of the race, 1 Cor. 7:2
    3. Mutual help, Gen. 2:19, 20
    4. Joy, Is. 62:5; Prov. 5:18
IV. Considerations
    1. Gospel rule, 1 Cor. 9:5; Gen. 6:2-3
    2. Health, Dr. Hostetler
    3. Location, Ruth, Orpah
    4. Capable of enduring love, Col. 3:19; Tit. 2:4
    5. Selfish or unselfish
    6. Age, Prov. 5:18; Mal. 2:14
    7. Degrees of affinity
    8. "In the Lord," 1 Cor. 7:39
    9. Dress, Prov. 7:10, Zeph. 1:8; 1 Tim. 2:9-10
    10. Civil rules, Rom. 13:1
    11. Economist or spendthrift, Is. 55:2
    12. Gadabout or homebuilder, Tit. 2:5
    13. Housekeeper and provider, Ps. 113:9; Tit. 2:5; 1 Tim. 5:8
  V. The happy home
    1. Sharing joys and sorrows
    2. Kidron—infantile paralysis

Faith
Text-Heb. 11:1

  I. Defined, Heb. 11:1
 II. Command, Mk. 11:22
III. Kinds,
    1. Great, Mt. 15:28, Lk. 7:9
    2. Little, Lk. 12:28

IV. Saved by, Eph. 2:8; Lk. 7:9
 V. Full of faith, Acts 6:5
    1. Stephen, Acts 6:5
    2. Barnabas, Acts 11:24
VI. Erred
    1. Elymas, Acts 13:8
    2. Hymenaeus and Philetus, 2 Tim. 2:18
VII. Departed
    1. Latter days, 1 Tim. 4:1

Jesus, Our Friend
Text, Prov. 18:24

1. Evidences of his friendship
    (a) Gave his life, Jn. 15:13
    (b) Fed the hungry, Mt. 14:15
    (c) Forgave enemies, Lk. 23:34
        Rhine Benner, war
    (d) Healed the sick
    (e) Comforted, Jn. 20:15
2. Intimacy of the friendship, Jn. 15:15
3. Whose friend
    Sinner's also, Mt. 11:19; 9:13
4. Broken friendships, Jas. 4:4; Jn. 15:14

Religion at a Cost
Text, 2 Sam. 24:24

 I. Examples of cost
    (a) Stephen, Acts 7:60
    (b) The lion test, Heb. 11:33
    (c) Torturing, Heb. 11:35
    (d) Sawn asunder, Heb. 11:37
    (e) Destitution, Heb. 11:37
II. What would it cost you?
    (a) Your will, Lk. 22:42
    (b) Worldly pleasures
    (c) Men esteem, Lk. 16:15
    (d) A crucifixion, Gal. 6:14
    (e) Self-denial, Mt. 16:24
Illus. God—Christ
    G. Lefever

The Great Commission
Mt. 28:19, 20

 I. Place—Galilee, v. 16
II. Authority, v. 18; Col. 2:9

 III. Two great classes
   1. Worshipers
   2. Doubters, Jn. 20:19-29
 IV. The Gospel Mission Quartet
    "Go, teach, baptize, teach"
   1. "Go," "Therefore"
    a. Call, separation, ordination
    b. Present-day liberty
   2. Teach, Christ—crucified
    a. The field—all nations
     Nations right at our door
   3. Baptize—difference in mode. Lack of baptism
   4. Teach—observe all things
  V. Necessary conditions to carry out the Great Commission
   a. A strong home base
   b. Surrendered workers
   c. Exemplified prayer
   d. Moral and financial support
Illus. Girl—cancer—"my God"
    Aimee Semple McPherson Dutton
    Jewess—Columbia Mission
    S. B. School—Pond Bank
    Expenses 5¢ per pupil per day, some 1¢

Young Married People
Text, Tit. 2:4; Prov. 5:18

  I. Love in fruition, Col. 3:18, 19. Watch the first 5 years
  II. Blessings of motherhood and housekeeping. Ps. 113:9; 1 Tim. 5:14; Tit. 2:5
 III. Home, a dwelling place, 1 Pet. 3:7
 IV. Relation to fellow couples
  V. Relation to immediate relatives, Gen. 1:28, 29; Gen. 26:35; 27:46
 VI. Relation to church
Illus. 1. Evelyn (Kendall) Howell application for divorce in 6 days
   2. R. Alwine—neighbors
   3. R. & John—supper—town

God's Specials
Book of Jonah

  I. Four specials
   1. Wind, 1:4; 4:8
   2. Fish, 1:17
   3. Gourd, 4:6
   4. Worm, 4:7
  II. God prepared—not man
 III. Small but accomplished a great end. Compare with all creation

IV. Fate of 120,000 children
    a. Responsible ones—cattle
    b. Our fate unseen
V. Served a purpose
    a. Fish—life—salvation
    b. Wind—prayer—"his god," v. 5
    "call upon thy God," v. 6
    c. Gourd—shadow, Ps. 17:8
    d. Worm—sapping life of the church
VI. Temporary specials
    Results for eternity
VII. Seen and unseen
    a. Seen—fish and gourd
    b. Unseen—wind and worm
    c. Results seen
VIII. In nature—results natural and spiritual
    a. Lives saved
    b. People repented
IX. Specials divided to bring satisfaction and grief
    a. Gourd
    b. Wind
X. Several work together to accomplish the same end—worm, wind
XI. May be of quick termination—two days
XII. Change a man's attitude—Jonah changed
XIII. Far reaching results
XIV. Are we learning our lessons from our specials?
XV. The unveiled future
    Illustrations—seemingly unpleasant
    Corp. at Rockton
    Candidate for Co. supt.—death of children
    Revolutionary War—disease of feet
    Man at Longenecker Church—"there is a God"
    Metzler's barn—Martinsburg
      Pleasant specials
    L.S.T.—windows and doors
    Calls from some unexpected place
    Sanford's certificate
    Cambria Fuel S. H. S. S. mission

Appendix 4

Names of Converts in Class of March 4, 1906, Springs, Pa.

1. James I. Miller
2. Norbert Miller
3. Clarence King
4. Elmer Stevanus
5. Sherman Stevanus
6. Earl Blauch
7. Ira Miller
8. Olen Bender
9. Arthur Beachy
10. Victor Beachy
11. William Kimmel
12. George W. Cutrell
13. Harry Miller
14. Lawrence Keim
15. Asa Durst
16. John Stevanus
17. Irwin Tressler
18. Ira Stevanus
19. John Tressler
20. William B. Tressler
21. Harry Maust
22. Lloyd Otto
23. Alice Keim
24. Mary Keim
25. Mary Cutrell
26. Susie Maust
27. Elva Gelnett
28. Twila Gelnett
29. Fannie Wagner
30. Maggie Gnagey
31. Savannah Gnagey
32. Carrie Kimmel
33. Harry Livengood
34. Elmer Gnagey
35. Harvey Handwork
36. Roy Folk
37. Daniel Tressler
38. Joseph Johnson
39. Cleve Alphin
40. William Johnson
41. Barbara Handwork
42. Bertha Handwork
43. Bertha Sluschlag
44. Annie Blauch
45. Estie Lee
46. Esta Kemp
47. Amanda Wisseman
48. Mrs. Joseph Johnson
49. Rosella Shetler
50. Effie King

Appendix 5

Names of Converts in Class of "100" (1908) at Berlin (Kitchener), Ontario

1. Clara Snider
2. Boyd Cressman
3. John Schiedel
4. Solomon Gehman
5. Lizzie Swartz
6. Hannah Clemmens
7. Vera Brubaker
8. Earl Snider
9. Addison Woolner
10. Ada Brubaker
11. Sidney Shantz
12. Hannah Snider
13. Stella Witmer
14. Joseph Shantz
15. Jacob Kolb
16. Edna Bowman
17. Urias Weber
18. Ian Snider
19. Melvin Baer
20. Edgar Snider
21. Benjamin Frey
22. Angus Martin
23. Elam Woolner
24. Elma Rieck
25. Marietta Rudy, Bapt.
26. Walter Hofstetler
27. Mrs. Minnie Stevens
28. Frederick Stevens
29. Bertie Shantz, Bapt.
30. Edna Brubaker, Bapt.
31. Mrs. Leander Snider
32. Louis Hoffels
33. Allen Cressman
34. Lorna Ernst
35. Leander Snider
36. Mary Krampien
37. Barbara Shirk
38. Orrville Clemmer
39. Edwin Eby
40. Josiah Eby
41. Elsie Eby
42. Grace Cressman
43. Alice Bowman
44. Mrs. Bernice Hartle
45. Nora Woolner
46. Orvin Eby
47. Seleda Bowman
48. Ida Woolner
49. Clara Chapman
50. Manda Binder
51. Abram Otterbein
52. Norman Hartle
53. Stella Hallman
54. Almeda Schmidt
55. Harvey Smith
56. Ira Bushert
57. Ivan Bushert
58. Lincoln Snider
59. Allen Schiedel
60. Jeconiah Frey
61. Lanson Schiedel
62. Lucy Hallman
63. Jacob Randall
64. Hannah Schiedel
65. Mrs. Isaac Clemmer
66. Elmeda Becker
67. Simon Weber
68. Menno Snider
69. Simon Weber
70. Amos Randall
71. John Cressman
72. Lizzie Cressman

73. Florence Cressman
74. Laura Shantz
75. Rosa Binder
76. Salinda Becker
77. Nettie Gimbel
78. David Gimbel
79. Edwin Woolner
80. Daniel Kunkle
81. Lloyd Wolf

82. Elvina Cressman
83. Clifford Cressman
84. Stella Baer
85. Rufus Weaver
86. Lloyd Snider
87. Menno Shantz
88. Herbert Wismer
89. Mrs. Ida Smith
90. Gordon Sweitzer
91. Elias Snider

92. Mrs. Elisa Snider
93. Beulah Stauffer
94. Jacob Cressman
95. Irene Woolner
96. Harvey Snider
97. Vernon Cressman
98. Norman Prangue
99. Lillie Witmer
100. Linda Binder

Waterloo

1. Alfred Shantz
2. Edna Shantz
3. Mary Erb
4. Anson Erb

5. Lanson Nahrgan
6. Mabel Weaver
7. Emma Bauman
8. Ada Eby

1909

1. Ida Bechtel
2. Lorne Shantz
3. Gordon Clemmer
4. Hilda Weaver
5. Nora Weaver
6. Lewis Weaver
7. Naomi Weaver
8. Clara Cressman
9. Omer Snider
10. Harold Boehmer
11. Martha Rudy

12. Simeon Snider
13. Mrs. Simeon Snider
14. Jacob Rudy
15. Lizzie Gallagher
16. Lizzie Ziegler
17. Jonathan Ernst
18. Clayton Snider
19. Isaiah Thoman
20. Alton Cressman
21. Beulah Snider
22. Willard Witmer

23. Edwin Snider
24. Vera Brubaker
25. Moses Shantz
26. Clifford Horst
27. Leander Bowman
28. Noah Ernst
29. Fannie Bowman
30. Norman Clemmens
31. Mahlon Clemmens
32. Walter Hofstetter

Appendix 6

Marriages Performed by S. G. Shetler

Husband	Wife	Date	State
1. Edwin Griffith	Mollie Blough	Oct. 23, 1897	Pa.
2. John D. Naugle	Sadie Blough	Jan. 4, 1898	Pa.
3. Jonathan T. Eash	Mary Yoder	Oct. 2, 1898	Pa.
4. Sem Kaufman	Ada Helsel	Mar. 15, 1899	Pa.
5. Hiram Weaver	Lizzie Lohr	Apr. 6, 1899	Pa.
6. Elmer J. Blough	Emma J. Speicher	May 5, 1899	Pa.
7. Amos Ream	Edith J. Roudabush	June 27, 1899	Pa.
8. Thomas Walter McAchren	Lydia Miller	Aug. 22, 1899	Pa.
9. Justus H. Helsel	Jennie E. Cassler	Sept. 5, 1899	Pa.
10. William Weaver	Eva C. Livingston	Sept. 27, 1899	Pa.
11. Calvin Layman	Catharine Lohr	Nov. 15, 1899	Pa.
12. Noah A. Eash	Mary A. Lehman	Jan. 12, 1900	Pa.
13. Amos W. Harshberger	Sue Eash	Mar. 8, 1900	Pa.
14. John M. Ream	Anna G. Foust	June 4, 1900	Pa.
15. Josiah J. Livingston	Amelia Yoder	Aug. 22, 1900	Pa.
16. John F. Harshberger	Jessie M. Kaufman	Aug. 6, 1901	Pa.
17. Samuel K. Yoder	Emma J. Kaufman	Jan. 6, 1902	Pa.
18. Chauncey J. Lehman	Mary E. Myers	Apr. 5, 1902	Pa.
19. Ammon Blough	Rebecca Lohr	Apr. 10, 1902	Pa.
20. Ammon Wingard	Hettie E. Kauffman	Apr. 12, 1902	Pa.
21. Jacob L. Shetler	Katie C. Harshberger	Sept. 18, 1902	Pa.
22. George E. Thomas	Lydia L. Livingstone	Feb. 10, 1903	Pa.

23. Elmer J. Varnes	Mary D. Yoder	Feb. 15, 1903	Pa.
24. Edwin E. Holsopple	Fannie G. Weaver	Apr. 27, 1903	Pa.
25. George Wingard	Catherine Knavel	Aug. 4, 1903	Pa.
26. John Albert Thomas	Mary Berkey	Sept. 8, 1903	Pa.
27. J. T. Yoder	Eliza Jane Berkey	Oct. 2, 1903	Pa.
28. Loransa Kaufman	Annie L. Swank	Dec. 20, 1904	Pa.
29. David L. Custer	Hettie Eash	Mar. 1, 1905	Pa.
30. Josiah Miller	Fannie Hershberger	Sept. 19, 1905	Pa.
31. John A. Hummel	Alice Wingard	Dec. 19, 1905	Pa.
32. Ralph D. Shaffer	Elsie Weaver	May 1, 1907	Pa.
33. John Ezra Blough	Minnie M. Thomas	June 14, 1907	Pa.
34. Ephraim A. Thomas	Katie A. Berkey	Nov. 19, 1908	Pa.
35. Wm. C. Hershberger	Mary C. Blough	May 24, 1909	Pa.
36. Alvin Blough	Anna Eash	Sept. 30, 1910	Pa.
37. Reuben K. Yoder	Mary M. Zook	July 18, 1911	Pa.
38. Arville Roudabush	Leah Livingstone	Feb. 7, 1912	Pa.
39. Harry E. Miller	Luella M. Shetler	Dec. 19, 1912	Pa.
40. Maurice S. Lehman	Carrie J. Baumgardner	Feb. 14, 1913	Pa.
41. Edward Beisel	Sue Knavel	Mar. 17, 1913	Pa.
42. Ross Weaver	Mayme Horne	June 17, 1913	Pa.
43. Simeon P. Martin	Ruby M. Andrews	Mar. 20, 1915	Ore.
44. John F. Harshberger	Amanda Shetler	Aug. 24, 1915	Pa.
45. John M. Bachman	Rosella M. Shetler	June 8, 1916	Pa.
46. Daniel M. Metzler	Freda Pearl Weaver	Dec. 24, 1917	Pa.
47. Joseph A. Kauffman	Mary Daniels	Feb. 1, 1918	Pa.
48. Stephen Blough	Effie Sala	Aug. 16, 1918	Pa.
49. Edgar Thomas	Bertha Hershberger	Aug. 27, 1918	Pa.
50. Harry Cloyd Blough	Freda Emma Berkey	Sept. 11, 1918	Pa.
51. Ammon Sala	Emma Mishler	Feb. 3, 1918	Pa.
52. Harley Hershberger	Margaret V. Kaufman	Apr. 17, 1919	Pa.
53. Clarence L. Shaffer	Gladys Viola Thomas	Nov. 8, 1919	Pa.
54. Uriah Blough	Maggie Thomas	March 9, 1920	Pa.
55. Webster Thomas	Ella Blough	May 26, 1920	Pa.
56. Ralph Kissel	Agnes M. Livingston	June 5, 1920	Pa.
57. Jonas E. Kaufman	Frances B. Lapp	June 8, 1921	Ore.
58. Oscar N. Mishler	Carrie B. Stahl	Nov. 1, 1921	Pa.
59. Howard Stahl	Mabel T. Weaver	March 29, 1923	Pa.
60. Harry S. Byers	Anna L. Kaufman	May 2, 1923	Pa.
61. Elmer F. Thomas	Elda E. Livingston	May 24, 1924	Pa.
62. Lloy A. Kniss	Edna Elizabeth Luther	June 25, 1924	Pa.
63. Calvin E. Kaufman	Margaret A. Shetler	May 28, 1925	Pa.
64. John Sala	Goldie M. Shetler	July 29, 1925	Pa.
65. Erwin L. Harshberger	Trella Eash	Nov. 25, 1925	Pa.
66. Ezra A. Shank	Blanche M. Layman	June 8, 1926	Pa.
67. Ralph C. Croyle	Linnie L. Yoder	June 26, 1926	Pa.
68. Levi S. Thomas	Maggie Sala	July 3, 1926	Pa.

69. Roy C. McDaniel	Emma Sala	Dec. 4, 1926	Pa.
70. Morton R. Stayrook	Ruth E. Miller	Feb. 12, 1927	Pa.
71. John T. Lehman	Linnie Eash	May 4, 1927	Pa.
72. U. Grant Weaver	Edith Mae Blough	June 6, 1928	Pa.
73. Frank Eash	Margaret E. Peterson	June 12, 1928	Pa.
74. Paul B. Kniss	Lizzie V. Kaufman	July 18, 1928	Pa.
75. Henry Kaufman	Marian S. Jacobs	Aug. 22, 1928	Pa.
76. Carl A. Koser	Emma G. Weaver	Oct. 2, 1928	Pa.
77. Kermit C. Yoder	Florence K. Croyle	Oct. 26, 1928	Pa.
78. Harry Y. Shetler	Stella M. Thomas	March 28, 1929	Pa.
79. Clarence C. Miller	Fannie R. Croyle	May 28, 1929	Pa.
80. Walter Moyer	Magaret Fletcher	Feb. 6, 1930	Pa.
81. Arlo C. Alwine	Carrie I. Miller	July 17, 1930	Pa.
82. Freeman J. Thomas	Fannie K. Kaufman	Sept. 25, 1930	Pa.
83. Andrew G. Kauffman	Mabel A. Maust	Apr. 23, 1931	Pa.
84. Jacob Clair Beisel	Mildred P. Knavel	May 29, 1931	Pa.
85. J. Frank Brilhart	Annie V. Harshberger	Nov. 20, 1931	Pa.
86. Sanford G. Shetler	Florence H. Young	June 5, 1932	Pa.
87. Edward L. Yoder	Ethel A. Thomas	Oct. 6, 1932	Pa.
88. Ernest W. Kauffman	Leora M. Alwine	Nov. 23, 1932	Pa.
89. Edward Amistadi	Josephine Fronzoli	June 12, 1933	Pa.
90. William Sala	Mary C. Livingston	Apr. 26, 1934	Pa.
91. Robert R. Shaffer	Beula M. Lehman	June 9, 1934	Pa.
92. Kenneth W. Lehman	Pearl E. Eash	Feb. 14, 1935	Pa.
93. Orvin F. Blough	Mary N. Blough	Sept. 5, 1935	Pa.
94. Elmer Jacob Eash	Dorothy I. Blough	Sept. 18, 1935	Pa.
95. John A. Oswald	Ida L. Lehnart	May 29, 1938(?)	Pa.
96. Minter M. Miller	Catherine E. Blum	Sept. 17, 1938	Pa.
97. Julius W. Schultz	Elsie Schrock	Nov. 16, 1938	Ore.
98. Perry E. Shank	Frances Emmert	Nov. 2(?) 1938	Ore.
99. Slater Carl Gindlesperger	Velma S. E. Kaltenbaugh	June 16, 1941	Pa.
100. Walter B. Weaver	V. Ethel Wingard	June 17, 1941	Pa.
101. Albert Stull	Lucille Beck	July 5, 1941	Ohio
102. Melvin Nevin Nussbaum	Edna M. Thomas	Dec. 1941	Pa.

—He performed the marriage ceremony for all of his children

Appendix 7

Waldeck Churches

The following is given for the historical value it may have. From the old Christian Schöttler records it is learned that young Christian was sent at one time on some kind of mission, perhaps to notify the various Mennonites serving on farms as tenants in the various areas of Waldeck and southward of a coming communion service. The list of villages and towns runs as follows:

1. Wohra, Kreis Marburg
2. Beissheine, Kreis Fritzlar-Hamberg
3. Kirskshausen, Kreis Bergstrasse
4. Wolkersdorf, Kreis Frankenberg
5. Schrecksbach, Kreis Ziegenhain
6. Siegelbach
7. Bittemühl
8. Ober-Urff, Kreis Fritzlar-Hamberg
9. Tutenroth
10. Reinhardshausen, Kreis Waldeck
11. Attenburg, Kreis Nelsungen
12. Zwesten, Kreis Fritzlar-Hamberg
13. Strick
14. Moischeid, Kreis Ziegenhain
15. Hilserhof
16. Merzhausen, Kreis Ziegenhain
17. Mittelhof
18. Cappel, Kreis Fritzlar-Hamberg n. Zeigenhain or Domäne Kappel at Mengeringhausen

Bibliography

Books

Gingerich, Melvin, *Mennonite Attire Through Four Centuries*, Herald Publishing Co. (1970)

Miller, Mary, *A Pillar of Cloud*, A History of Hesston College 1909-1959, Mennonite Press, North Newton, Kan. (1959)

Pellman, Hubert R., *Eastern Mennonite College, 1917-1967*, A History, Eastern Mennonite College, Harrisonburg, Va. (1967)

Shetler, Sanford G., *Two Centuries of Struggle and Growth*, 1763-1963, A History of Allegheny Mennonite Conference, Allegheny Mennonite Conference, distributed by Herald Press (1963)

Shetler, S. G., *History of the Pacific Coast Mennonite Conference* (1923)

Shetler, S. G., and Shetler, Sanford G., *117 Object Lessons*, Herald Press, Scottdale, Pa. (1940)

Shoemaker, J. S., Weaver, J. W., Shetler, S. G., *Christian Workers' Manual* (1915)

Stoltzfus, Grant, *Mennonites of the Ohio and Eastern Conference*, Herald Press, Scottdale, Pa. (1969)

Umble, John Sylvanus, *Goshen College, 1894-1954*, Goshen College, Goshen, Ind. (1955).

Articles, Booklets, and Miscellaneous Sources

Annual County School Reports, Somerset County, Pennsylvania, 1887-1932, Somerset Archives, Courthouse, Somerset, Pa.

Coffman, J. S., *Outlines and Notes*, (1898)

Fretz, Clarence, "A History of Winter Bible Schools in the Mennonite Church," *Mennonite Quarterly Review* (April and July 1942)

Gingerich, Melvin, "Gingerich Family History," duplicated sheets for a family reunion (1935)

Gingerich, Melvin, "Mengeringhausen," *Mennonite Historical Bulletin,* Vol. XXXII, No. 3 (July 1971)

Gospel Herald, Gospel Witness, Herald of Truth, official church organs of the Mennonite Church from 1864 to 1942, in the Mennonite Historical Library, Eastern Mennonite College, Harrisonburg, Va.

Heatwole, L. J., Letters, Archives, Eastern Mennonite College, Harrisonburg, Va.

Interviews with friends, associates, and former students, including the following: John Alger (1972), Rhine Benner (1972), Alvin G. Faust (1971), Milton Hoffman (1970), Joseph Johns (1971), Irvin Kaufman (1971), Jacob E. Martin, Sr. (1970), Raymond Mishler (1970), Elizabeth Showalter (1972), Mark Showalter (1972), Grant Stoltzfus (1973)

Johnstown *Tribune-Democrat,* Obituaries (Aug. 9, 1942) and in *Gospel Herald* (Aug. 15, 1942)

Kaufman, James Norman, "My Autobiography," *Mennonite Historical Bulletin,* XVIII, No. 1 (Jan. 1967)

Kaufman, Ruth, *75th Anniversary Booklet,* Stahl Mennonite Church, (1957)

Kniss, Lloy A., "Samuel Grant Shetler," *Mennonite Yearbook and Directory,* Mennonite Publishing House, Scottdale, Pa. (1943)

Miller, Clyde, "The Life of S. G. Shetler," a college term paper, Goshen College, Goshen, Ind. (1935). This included a report on some interviews which he had had with S. G. Shetler, his grandfather, and Luella M. Miller, his mother.

Records of the Building Finance Committee of the Hopewell (Ore.) Church (1915, 1916) (Charles Bond, Canby, Ore.)

Schöttler, Christian, personal documents: Letter of recommendation, naturalization paper, passport.

Shetler, S. G., "A Backward Look for Forty-eight Years," *Southwestern Pennsylvania Mission News,* Vol. III, No. 5 (May 1939)

——————"Johnstown Bible School," *Bulletin of the Mennonite Board of Education,* Fourth Quarter, (1931) 1-4

——————"Johnstown Bible School," *Youth's Christian Companion,* Vol. XII (Nov. 29, 1931)

——————"Life of Bishop Moses Miller," *Gospel Herald* (c. 1940)

——————"Life of Daniel Rose," in *Overcoming Handicaps,* Mennonite Publishing House, Scottdale, Pa. (1926)

——————"One Hundred Years of Sunday Schools," *Gospel Herald* (Oct. 17, 1940)

——————Personal Records: Bible school outlines; correspondence; pastoral letters (1935-1942); records of sermons (1897-1899; 1901-1903); sermon notes (1897-1942)

——————"Winter Bible Schools," *Mennonite Yearbook and Directory* (1941)

_____Various Articles in *Gospel Herald*

Stauffer, Ezra, *History of the Alberta-Saskatchewan Mennonite Conference* (1960)

Testimonies of many former friends and pupils, correspondence with numerous individuals.

Washington Star (Sept. 2, 1917), Reel 5, Vol. 44, ACLU Microfilm Records, New York Public Library, New York City

Sanford G. Shetler, like his father, has spent most of his life as a teacher and a Mennonite minister, serving extensively as an evangelist and Bible conference speaker.

In addition to teaching 12 years in the public schools, he was principal of Johnstown Mennonite School (an elementary-secondary Christian school), and has taught at Eastern Mennonite College and Rosedale Bible Institute. He has taught first-graders in elementary school as well as college seniors—and every grade between.

Born in Somerset County, Pennsylvania, near Johnstown, Sanford was the youngest of a family of seven.

He received his junior college diploma from Eastern Mennonite College, a BA in education from the University of Pittsburgh, and the MEd degree from Cornell University.

Ordained to the ministry in 1932, he has pastored several congregations in the Johnstown area (the longest at Stahl Mennonite Church). He first served there as assistant pastor for ten years with his father. Sanford was ordained bishop in 1952 and currently is overseer of four Johnstown area churches of the Allegheny Mennonite Conference.

He is editor of *Guidelines for Today* (1966-   ), a bimonthly magazine "for the promotion and defense of historical Christianity."

Sanford and the late Florence (Young) Shetler are the parents of Stanwyn, Leonard, Maretta (Mrs. Allen Hostetler), Anita (Mrs. Wayne Shoenthal), and Carol (Mrs. John Lazer). He has eleven grandchildren and one greatgrandchild. His present wife is the former Dorothy Yoder. They are members of the Stahl Mennonite Church.

S. G. SHETLER FAMILY TREE

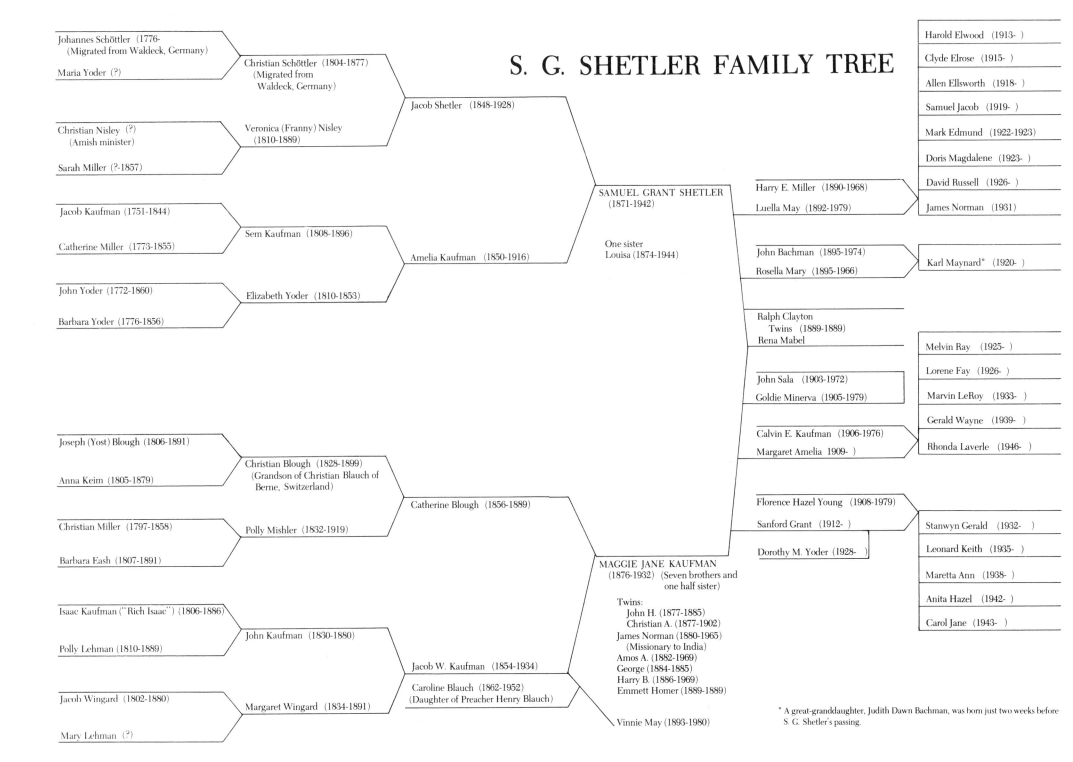

Johannes Schöttler (1776- (Migrated from Waldeck, Germany)

Maria Yoder (?)

Christian Schöttler (1804-1877) (Migrated from Waldeck, Germany)

Christian Nisley (?) (Amish minister)

Sarah Miller (?-1857)

Veronica (Franny) Nisley (1810-1889)

Jacob Shetler (1848-1928)

Jacob Kaufman (1751-1844)

Catherine Miller (1773-1855)

Sem Kaufman (1808-1896)

John Yoder (1772-1860)

Barbara Yoder (1776-1856)

Elizabeth Yoder (1810-1853)

Amelia Kaufman (1850-1916)

SAMUEL GRANT SHETLER (1871-1942)

One sister
Louisa (1874-1944)

Harry E. Miller (1890-1968)

Luella May (1892-1979)

Harold Elwood (1913-)

Clyde Elrose (1915-)

Allen Ellsworth (1918-)

Samuel Jacob (1919-)

Mark Edmund (1922-1923)

Doris Magdalene (1923-)

David Russell (1926-)

James Norman (1931)

John Bachman (1895-1974)

Rosella Mary (1895-1966)

Karl Maynard° (1920-)

Ralph Clayton
Twins (1889-1889)
Rena Mabel

John Sala (1903-1972)

Goldie Minerva (1905-1979)

Melvin Ray (1925-)

Lorene Fay (1926-)

Marvin LeRoy (1933-)

Gerald Wayne (1939-)

Calvin E. Kaufman (1906-1976)

Margaret Amelia 1909-)

Rhonda Laverle (1946-)

Joseph (Yost) Blough (1806-1891)

Anna Keim (1805-1879)

Christian Blough (1828-1899) (Grandson of Christian Blauch of Berne, Switzerland)

Christian Miller (1797-1858)

Barbara Eash (1807-1891)

Polly Mishler (1832-1919)

Catherine Blough (1856-1889)

Florence Hazel Young (1908-1979)

Sanford Grant (1912-)

Dorothy M. Yoder (1928-)

Stanwyn Gerald (1932-)

Leonard Keith (1935-)

Maretta Ann (1938-)

Anita Hazel (1942-)

Carol Jane (1943-)

MAGGIE JANE KAUFMAN (1876-1932) (Seven brothers and one half sister)

Twins:
John H. (1877-1885)
Christian A. (1877-1902)
James Norman (1880-1965) (Missionary to India)
Amos A. (1882-1969)
George (1884-1885)
Harry B. (1886-1969)
Emmett Homer (1889-1889)

Vinnie May (1893-1980)

Isaac Kaufman ("Rich Isaac") (1806-1886)

Polly Lehman (1810-1889)

John Kaufman (1830-1880)

Jacob Wingard (1802-1880)

Mary Lehman (?)

Margaret Wingard (1834-1891)

Jacob W. Kaufman (1854-1934)

Caroline Blauch (1862-1952) (Daughter of Preacher Henry Blauch)

° A great-granddaughter, Judith Dawn Bachman, was born just two weeks before
S. G. Shetler's passing.